Steve McQueen

Also by Marc Eliot

Steve McQueen

A BIOGRAPHY

Marc Eliot

CROWN
ARCHETYPE
NEW YORK

Library of Congress Cataloging-in-Publication Data
Eliot, Marc.
Steve McQueen : a biography / by Marc Eliot.—1st ed.
Includes filmography.
Includes bibliographical references and index.
1. McQueen, Steve, 1930–1980.   2. Motion picture actors and actresses—
United States—Biography.   I. Title.
PN22287.M547E45 2011
791.4302'8092—dc22
[B]   2011002262

ISBN 978-0-307-45321-1
eISBN 978-0-307-45323-5

Printed in the United States of America

Book design by Lauren Dong
Jacket design by Laura Duffy
Jacket photographs: Front and spine: © *1978 William Claxton/mptvimages.com;*
back, fourth down: *Courtesy of David Foster; all others from the Rebel Road Archive*
Author photograph: Courtesy of Marc Eliot

All photos are from the Rebel Road Archive unless otherwise credited.
Frontispiece: © Bettmann/CORBIS

10 9 8 7 6 5 4 3 2 1

First Edition

For bee bee and little Sweetie Pie

Contents

All life is just a progression toward, and then a recession from, one phrase—I love you.

—F. Scott Fitzgerald, "The Offshore Pirate"

Introduction

TERRENCE STEVEN MCQUEEN WAS THE PRODUCT OF A one-night stand that stretched into a year and six months of misery between Terrence William McQueen, a handsome, philandering stunt pilot for a traveling circus, and Jullian Crawford, a teenage alcoholic prostitute. Terrence William left Jullian and Steven for good six months after the boy was born. Unable to cope with single motherhood, Jullian soon abandoned Steven. As casually as she changed clothes (or took them off), Jullian passed him off to her uncle, the wealthy but emotionally distant Claude Thomson.

These early traumatic events helped shape the fragile, needy psyche that for the rest of Steve McQueen's life would bubble just beneath the deceptively smooth surface of his very good-looking exterior. Physically beautiful but emotionally insecure, this shy and withdrawn little boy would grow up to become an international movie superstar. He would be loved by millions from afar, but unable to handle intimate commitment and often lash out at those women who tried to love him in real life.

His emotional insecurity left him extremely sensitive and wary, a combination that would aid him enormously in his early days as an actor, and lead to his powerful attraction to and essential distrust of females—a pattern that began in childhood with his mother and continued into adult life with the three women he made his wives. Marriage to Steve meant swimming in a pool of emotional turmoil. The promise of commitment tempted him, but the fear of abandonment compelled him to run away. He was a lover and a fighter whose emotions were always stoked to the peak of their heat.

Film directors favor those actors who can take their considerable inner turmoil and use it to infuse the characters they play in the movies with a heightened and compelling sense of drama. It is what is called talent in Hollywood, and those who have it, despite the high personal price they pay, are highly coveted.

Steve McQueen had it. His special, unique talent was his ability to balance his inner heat (his emotional rage, his distrust of older authority figures, and his defiance of them) and his cautious, careful, catlike wariness that so beautifully translated to the screen as the ultimate in cool. Although much of what he managed to accomplish in film was the result of his ability to trust his instincts, his emotional balancing act gained him the reputation as one of the best practitioners of the then in-vogue acting style of moody, brooding strength that was the by-product of the so-called Stanislavsky Method. He had studied the Method while a struggling actor in his early New York days, and it gave him a disciplined approach to acting. McQueen's raw intensity—his talent—was always there; he was, in life, an emotional time bomb who ticked with metronomic precision—tick, the need to hold in all the rage; tock, the need to let it all out—on-screen or off. This was what gave his characters their power, and despite all the acting classes, keeping the beat was the only real method he ever used and the only one he ever needed.

In 1958, after struggling as a stage and live TV actor, McQueen hit it big in the filmed TV series *Wanted: Dead or Alive*, his gateway to Hollywood and the twenty-eight feature films he would make in his lifetime. His resume is admittedly brief, with barely enough credits to admit him into the pantheon. His output is not only qualitatively minimalist but quantitatively minimal when compared with the 217 one-hour episodes and more than seventy features made by his contemporary Clint Eastwood (who is still going strong). People tend to forget that Eastwood and McQueen were born the same year—1930—and that their TV and film careers began approximately the same time (*Wanted: Dead or Alive* in 1958, Eastwood's *Rawhide* in 1959).

Interestingly, neither McQueen nor Eastwood ever appeared especially comfortable in cinematic scenarios of romance (although both were very much players in real life). Eastwood, with his poncho, cigarillo, and regal loneness, was able to externally fetishize his ability not just to exist but to thrive on-screen without women, while McQueen seemed too emotionally inhibited, his eyes too haunted, too downcast, to be a truly romantic leading man. Auteurist critic and historian Andrew Sarris pointed out after McQueen's death that he was "that rarity of rarities, a Method Action Hero."

The Method played a key difference between McQueen's approach to acting and to his career and Eastwood's (who is a purely instinctive actor). The Method did to McQueen what it did to a lot of aspiring actors in the mid-to-late 1950s: it held up Marlon Brando as an ultimately unattainable icon to try to emulate. It confused and intimidated novice actors such as McQueen, who didn't fully understand the essence of the Method—that it was intended to personalize performances and liberate emotions within the context of a reality already existing in the actor. In McQueen it led to fake impressions rather than true expressions of pain and personalization, and all the posturing that went with that falsity. (To many of McQueen's teachers, good imitation Brando was better than no Brando at all.) For the rest of his career, McQueen would be saddled with the burden of trying to prove he was an "actor." It led to Method-gone-mad disasters such as *An Enemy of the People* (George Schaefer, 1978) and narcissistic Method-gone-motorized failures such as Lee H. Katzin's *Le Mans* (1971), the latter a dispirited failure that left McQueen's spirit broken and his life, career, and finances in shambles.

Eastwood, on the other hand, from the earliest days of his career, couldn't have cared less about any method but the one that worked for him—looking good in front of a camera and trusting his director enough to know how to make him look good on-screen. His detached professionalism exemplified the angry "old Hollywood" joke that proliferated at the height of Brando-mania. A director tells an actor to cross the set, and the actor asks what his motivation is. "Because I told you to do it!" replies the director. Eastwood not only did it but learned from it, and laid out a plan for himself that would take him from acting to producing, to directing, to acting in films he produced and directed, to forming Malpaso, a production company that operated like a mini-studio and became his Hollywood powerhouse. Ultimately, Eastwood was a businessman who used films to make money, and he was good at doing both. He rarely challenged his own image, and he played essentially the same easy (for him) character over and over again, honing and perfecting it to broaden his films' appeal to the everlasting delight of his enormous fan base.

When Eastwood hit upon the character of Dirty Harry, a rebel detective with virtually no insight or visible sensitivity—a living manifestation of his Magnum .45 who enjoys blowing away bad guys (a contemporary version of the Man with No Name)—he churned it into a mini-franchise, and made a fortune doing so. And he never broke a sweat over how to "act" the character. "Acting" to Eastwood was, in truth, almost beside the point. Eastwood is known for first takes and making it to the golf course in time to play a full thirty-six. If Harry Callahan's eyes are vacant, it's because Eastwood didn't feel the need to provide them with anything beyond his famous squint.

McQueen, too, created his own company, Solar Productions, but was fatally hampered by the residue of his Method-induced integrity that insisted he make personal films to show off his acting abilities even if those films broadly distorted his persona to the point of unrecognizability (*The Reivers* and *An Enemy of the People*, to name two). Steve wanted to make a movie about auto racing, and built and operated Solar for the sole purpose of raising the money to make it the way he wanted, even as more commercial opportunities either passed him by or were let go by him.

When McQueen made *Bullitt*, three years before *Dirty Harry*, it was the closest he would ever come to melding his turbulent personality with his on-screen persona, and the film was a huge success. However, McQueen felt the character of Frank Bullitt was too intense, too aloof, too internal, too Method for him to take it any further, and he turned away from what would have been a franchise that might have rivaled the success of *Dirty Harry*. He also feared he would become trapped within the same single-character gerbil cage his TV series *Wanted: Dead or Alive* had put him in, and that his reputation as a real actor would suffer as his reputation as a real action star grew. To McQueen, *Bullitt* was about acting, not money.

To Eastwood, *Dirty Harry* was about money, not acting. With an eye toward a franchise, Eastwood saw *Dirty Harry* as a step into his future, a new beginning. And while Eastwood would happily turn *Dirty Harry* into an icon that would spark a social debate about violence in film and create for himself a lucrative franchise, McQueen never again made a movie that even remotely resembled *Bullitt*. Nonetheless, it remains his most original, complex, and memorable character and movie. Moreover, *Dirty Harry* was clearly derivative of *Bullitt*, the true original that has no easy or obvious cinematic antecedents. Clint Eastwood loves the game and knows how to play it. Steve McQueen hated the game.

There are two other reasons McQueen's body of work does not have the kind of staying power Eastwood's does. First, from an auteurist perspective, while McQueen worked with a number of competent directors, including Robert Wise, John Sturges, Don Siegel, Sam Peckinpah, and Peter Yates, several of them more than once, his career suffered from almost never having worked with one whose personal vision was strong enough to push McQueen's acting beyond the limits of his formidable star power. McQueen's directors were simply not as forceful or charismatic behind the camera as he was in front of it. They couldn't challenge, push, and stretch him; they didn't know how to convert the tension between McQueen's internal fires and external flourishes into memorable cinematic characters (as, early on, Sergio Leone had managed to do with Eastwood, creating his first franchise character, the Man with No Name).

Without that type of directorial vision and guidance, over time McQueen's intensity, inner turmoil, poor choice of scripts, and reliance on directors he knew he could control reduced him to the level of a two-dimensional actor, leaving his audiences to look for newer heroes. Ironically, the power he had accumulated through his best mainstream films allowed him to eventually run his career off the rails. One can only wonder what type of performance visionary auteurists such as John Ford or Howard Hawks or Francis Ford Coppola or even Sergio Leone could have delivered through Steve McQueen.

Another factor is early death. That is why James Dean will forever be celebrated as a rebel without a cause while fewer and fewer audiences actually see the three features that made him a forceful and driven actor very much with a cause. After McQueen's comparatively early passing, his image quickly ossified into that of the tough, good-looking, blue-eyed, two-fisted kid, the afterburn lasting in the mind's eye of his fans far longer than the recollection of his actual performances. He is remembered today mostly for his boyish cuteness and physical grace in *The Magnificent Seven;* his all-American baseball-glove-and-motorcycle rebel POW in *The Great Escape;* his blue-eyed poker prowess in *The Cincinnati Kid;* his laser-intense car-crazy lawman in *Bullitt;* his psychotic, wife-beating ex-con in *The Getaway;* his obsessive prisoner in

Papillon; and his heroic fireman in *The Towering Inferno.* Of these magnificent seven, not one casts him as a traditional Hollywood romantic lover boy, despite the fact that he was considered one of the major sex symbols of his day; audiences tend to remember his action films more than the early black-and-white romance-novels 1963's *Love with the Proper Stranger* and 1965's *Baby the Rain Must Fall* (both films directed by Robert Mulligan and produced by Alan Pakula). In the end, traditional action embalmed McQueen's memory more than offbeat romance could keep it alive.

Early death also robs movie stars of their deeper legacy when the circumstances of their passing take on far more (often ghoulish) importance than any of the films they made. Who remembers the details of any actual movies starring Rudolph Valentino? Or Jean Harlow? Or even Marilyn Monroe? They are the victims of their disturbingly early deaths rather than victors of their tragically forgotten films. Had Clint Eastwood died at fifty, the same age Steve McQueen was when he died, Eastwood never would have matured into the actor and director he did in his middle-to-late period. His career would have ended with a couple of spaghetti westerns and a few offbeat *policiers;* if he was to be remembered at all, it would be as the Man with No Name or Dirty Harry, rather than the deeper, more complex, talented, and unnerving director of such later classics as *Unforgiven, Million Dollar Baby, Flags of Our Fathers, Letters from Iwo Jima, The Changeling, Gran Torino, Invictus,* and others. It is both tragic and tantalizing that McQueen did not live long enough to direct, and direct himself, although he came tantalizingly close to getting there. Late in his career, McQueen wanted to take over the direction of his final film, *The Hunter,* but because of a tangle of union regulations, he couldn't do it, and he never got another chance.

Nonetheless, Steve McQueen remains one of our most perfect cinema gods. His unforgettable physical beauty, his soft-spoken manner, his tough but tender roughness, and his aching vulnerability were part Dean, part Brando, part Eastwood, part Paul Newman, but all McQueen. We see his screen legacy today in actors such as the sensitive and beautiful James Franco, the all-American good-bad boy Brad Pitt, the charming but elusive George Clooney, and the dagger-blue-eyed, icicle-veined Daniel Craig. All of them owe more than a little to McQueen's style, manner, and attitude, but none can duplicate his unique blend of romantic aloofness and charismatic chill.

In every movie he made—the great ones, as well as the misfires—his star-studded appeal could not be disguised. Perhaps Steve McQueen's greatest talent was to be able to convince audiences that he was who he really wasn't, even as he tried to prove to himself he wasn't who he really was.

PART ONE

Beautiful Wanderer

I left home at the age of fifteen because there really was no home. . . . I have had no education. I came from a world of brute force.

—STEVE MCQUEEN

TERRENCE STEVEN MCQUEEN WAS BORN MARCH 24, 1930, or thereabouts, in Beech Grove, Indiana, a suburban community in Marion County.[1] His middle name was a joke given to him by the father he never knew. "Steven" was the senior McQueen's favorite bookie and the name Steven preferred, Terrence being a bit too soft for him. Terrence William McQueen, Bill or Red to his friends, was a onetime navy biplane flier turned circus stuntman who had no idea what fatherhood was beyond the losing bet on a careless roll with a blond-haired, blue-eyed flapper he called Julia, whose real name was Jullian. He impregnated her the first night they met. He married her out of an uncharacteristic burst of honor, and an honest stab at normalcy that lasted all of six months. By then, the unusually handsome McQueen had packed his travel bags and left Jullian behind to take care of herself and the baby.

Later that same year, unable to cope with single motherhood, Jullian took the infant back to her hometown of Slater, Indiana, in Saline County, where her parents, Victor and Lillian Crawford,

---

[1] Although the county records claim March 21 as his actual birthday, his mother insisted it was really March 24. Steve always celebrated on the twenty-first.

lived. They agreed to help her as long as they were allowed to give the boy a strict Catholic upbringing.

After only a few months of being back with her family, Jullian grew tired of church, prayer, and chastity and returned to Green Grove with young Steven. She still hoped to find a rich man to marry her and provide a comfortable life. But after three more years of struggling to keep herself and Steven warm and fed, she returned to the family farm—this time just long enough to drop off the boy before leaving again to resume chasing her own dreams.

Abandoned now by both parents, Steven was again pushed aside when Victor's business failed and he was forced to move with his wife and grandchild to live on Lillian's brother's farm in Missouri, about six hours away by train.

Claude Thomson took them in but did not make them feel especially welcome or comfortable. He had no use for his sister or Victor, her miserable failure of a husband, and blamed his failure on Victor's laziness rather than the Great Depression. He agreed to help them out only because he felt sorry for the cute little towhead. The boy was the only one, Claude believed, who was not responsible for his own misfortunes, and Claude wanted to redeem him by loving him as if he were his own. The boy's mother was never spoken of on Claude's farm.

Claude, unmarried and childless, owned 320 acres of prime Missouri farmland dotted with thousands of head of free-roaming cattle and endless fields of corn. He also owned an intimidating reputation as a womanizer and possibly even a killer. Rumors ran rampant throughout the county that he had murdered a man over a woman, but no one was ever able to prove such a story about this wealthy and devout Catholic farmer. His presence was imposing, his bankbook fat, his political influence powerful. In a world where money talked nicely and influence talked tough, Claude had plentiful amounts of both.

But he always had a soft spot for Steven. Not that he spoiled him in any way or gave him a free ride. From the time Steven could walk and talk, Uncle Claude expected him to pull his load, and every day woke him before dawn to begin his daily chores of milking cows and working in the cornfields.[2] It was hard work for the boy, but for the first time in his life, he felt he really belonged somewhere and to someone.

When Steven tried to shirk his duties, such as cutting wood, which for a boy of his small size was difficult, he was punished, but never complained. He believed he deserved whatever he got, if not for being not strong enough, then for his lack of determination. "When I'd get lazy and duck my chores, Claude would warm my backside with a hickory switch. I learned a simple fact—you work for what you get."

Claude wasn't a total martinet. He gave young Steven his own room and a bright, shiny red tricycle, which Steven became so good at riding he challenged other boys to races and never failed to clean them out of their gumdrops. And Claude always gave the boy enough money for a weekly trip to the Saturday matinee at the local movie theater. Steven loved the movies, especially the cowboys-and-Indians westerns, with their six-guns that blazed firepower every two seconds and shot the bad guys, who fell off horses with all the fury and balance of Russian ballet stars. These films instilled in Steven a lifelong love of films and guns: "When I was eight, Uncle Claude would let me use the family rifle to shoot game in the woods . . . to his dyin' day Uncle Claude remained convinced I was a miracle marksman with a rifle."

The school he attended was four miles away from the farmhouse and he had to walk it every day, regardless of the weather, but it wasn't the walk he hated, it was the school. His teachers soon decided the sullen little boy who never paid attention to anyone or

---

[2] He was technically Grand-uncle Claude, but Steven always referred to him simply as Uncle Claude.

anything was what was called in those days a "slow learner." Years later it was determined that as a child Steven was probably slightly dyslexic, not helped by an untreated hearing problem in his right ear that left him partly deaf for the rest of his life. The boy would remember most about his school days that "I was a dreamer, like on cloud Nine."

He was a dreamer back at the farmhouse as well. Young Steven would often drift away in thought, and when Uncle Claude inquired what he was thinking about, Steven always replied by asking where his mother was. Uncle Claude would say nothing, just pat the boy on his head and move along.

Jullian was, in fact, busy marrying and unmarrying a series of men. The final count remains uncertain. One day, when Steven was nine, his mother suddenly showed up at the farm and politely informed Claude that she was taking her son back. Claude put up no resistance. He took the boy aside for a few minutes and gave him the gold watch that he kept in his vest pocket, told him to always remember his uncle Claude, and sent him away with his mother.

Jullian took Steven, whose nine-year-old lean physique, curly blond hair, and blue eyes perfectly matched hers, to Los Angeles, where she and her latest husband were living. Soon enough, Steven's new stepfather, Berri, hated having the kid around, wanted him gone, and out of frustration and anger beat him whenever he got the chance. Steven was more than happy to accommodate him, and often spent days and nights away from the house, sleeping in back alleys when there was no place else available. Film documentarian Rob Katz describes this period of time as the "black hole" of McQueen's lonely and violent youth.

Within months he had joined one of the tough L.A. teenage gangs that regularly prowled the neighborhood, breaking into shops after dark. And the streets had something else for Steven. When he was thirteen, a young neighborhood girl took him to heaven for the first time. He referred to this event years later in several interviews but never gave any details except that she was the first of many street girls who would dote over him and give him whatever he wanted because of his warm smile, blond hair, and blue eyes.

Unable to deal with her son's increasingly rebellious behavior and her husband's resentment of the boy's presence, a desperate Jullian called Uncle Claude and pleaded with him to take Steven back. She didn't have to cajole; he was more than eager to have him. During their phone conversation Jullian was surprised to learn that Uncle Claude, now pushing seventy, had recently married his young housekeeper, Eva Mae, age thirty-three. Upon Steven's return to Missouri, Eva Mae efficiently stripped the teenage boy naked and bathed him head to toe. There was no place like home!

One day a traveling circus came through town and Steven went by himself to see it. There he met a fast-talking carny who convinced him he would see the world if he joined the traveling show. Steven never even returned home to pack his few belongings or to say goodbye to Uncle Claude and Eva Mae. Taking only his uncle's gold watch that he was never without, the fifteen-year-old hitched a ride with the circus and rode with them out of Missouri and into his future.

Uncle Claude, meanwhile, searched desperately for the boy, unaware that he had run away and fearing something terrible had happened to him. After several days, he gave up and went back to the farm. If Steven was found alive, Uncle Claude vowed, he would never forgive him. If Steven was found dead, Uncle Claude would never forgive himself.

LIFE IN the circus proved more sawdust than stardust for Steven when he discovered the constant traveling was taking him nowhere fast. He wanted out of the life but could not go home again to face Uncle Claude. He took once more to living on the streets, hitchhiking from town to town and riding the freight trains with the hobos until eventually he found himself back in Los Angeles, where he reluctantly showed up at Jullian and Berri's apartment. His mother was happy to see him but withheld her affection out of fear of setting off Berri, who greeted the boy with an indifference that bordered on anger.

The street kids' greeting was not much warmer than that. They were always suspicious of members who came and went unless that revolving door had bars on it. To make his bones and "win back the other kids' respect he meant to become the baddest ass of them all . . . if the gang leader decreed that ten hubcaps were to be stolen today by each gang member, Steve would bring back twenty."

Besides stealing, the gangs frequently rumbled, fighting other gangs for cock-of-the-walk rights. Occasionally a police roundup would bring them to court. The first time Steven came before the local judge, he threatened to put the boy away for a long stretch if he ever saw his face again.

Jullian took him home, and Berri laid down a much tougher sentence. He beat Steven mercilessly and finished him off by throwing him down a flight of stairs. When the boy was finally able to stand up, bruised and bloody, with Berri hovering over him, he stared into his stepfather's face and said, "You lay your stinkin' hands on me again, and I swear I'll kill ya."

Soon enough, Steven was caught with a bunch of other boys trying to steal hubcaps, and Jullian tearfully signed the court order committing him to reform school. It was that or prison.

The California Junior Boys Republic at Chino was founded in 1907 by Margaret Fowler, a wealthy widow who devoted her life to social improvement and helping troubled youths straighten their lives out. Boys Republic was and still is located on 211 acres in the southwestern corner of San Bernardino County, a farm community that, besides the institution, also housed two state prisons, one for men and one for women. Boys Republic, one of the more progressive reform schools for juvenile delinquents that appeared during the last years of the Industrial Revolution, was filled to capacity in the Depression and again during World War II, times when many boys who got in trouble were either fatherless, gang members, or runaways. Steven was all three. On February 6, 1945, five weeks before his fifteenth birthday, Steven McQueen became number 3188.

The institution ran on a trust system operated by the boys themselves, supervised by adults. Steven twice escaped from the unfenced grounds, but was quickly apprehended and returned. The other boys did not appreciate having their privileges taken away because of one bad apple, and although paddling was the preferred discipline by the authorities, the boys had their own way of treating tough kids like Steven. "The place had a board of governors made up of boys. They tried me and condemned me. They gave me the silent treatment and all that jazz." And they kicked his ass. More than once, Steven was subjected to physical abuse. And on days when the "good" boys were rewarded with trips to the movies, Steven was held back by those who didn't go and was forced to run the athletic track, over and over again. And when he still didn't break, they made him dig ditches all day.

He didn't care what they did to him because he was already planning another breakout, a great escape that would leave the others in his dust. That is, until he first became aware of Mr. Pantier, one of the school's superintendents, who disdained physical punishment in favor of talking things out. He believed that all boys were redeemable, including Steven. Mr. Pantier talked to him without talking down to him, and spent long evenings trying to convince the boy he was worth more than the kind of life he was headed for.

Pantier's kind words of encouragement touched something in Steven, and his transformation was swift. He became a model of good behavior and soon enough was elected to the same self-governing boys' council he had been punished by. That victory meant a lot to him.

WHILE STEVEN was inside, Jullian had undergone some changes of her own, beginning with the untimely but not entirely unwelcome death of Berri, from a heart attack, even as Jullian was preparing to divorce him and move by herself to New York City to find a new and better life. After she buried Berri, she visited Steven one last time and told him that when he got out he should look her up. However, despite her determination to do better this time, she quickly slipped back into the familiar world of drinking, smoking, and "entertaining" men.

In April 1946, having finished his full fourteen-month term at Boys Republic, sixteen-year-old Steven left for New York to be with his mother. What he didn't know was that one night while at a bar Jullian had met an old friend from Los Angeles by the name of Victor Lukens. They had quickly become lovers, and Lukens wasted no time moving into her tiny Greenwich Village two-room cold-water flat.

I'm from the Actors Studio but as far as any set method is concerned, I don't believe there is one. . . . And I certainly admire Mr. Brando, but I wouldn't want to be like him.

— STEVE MCQUEEN

FROM THE MOMENT STEVEN ARRIVED IN NEW YORK CITY, nothing felt right. As soon as he got off the bus at Port Authority Bus Terminal, he spotted Jullian waiting for him. That was good. He went to kiss her on the cheek and smelled alcohol. That was bad. She took him down to the Village and showed him the separate place she'd rented for him, a small alcove in a three-room apartment. That was very bad.

The problem, she explained to him as she helped him unpack his few things, was that she was involved with a new man who was an old friend, and didn't want to screw it up by bringing her grown son into their small apartment. It wasn't what Steven had bargained for. He didn't want to share his mother with anybody else again and he wasn't going to live with a guy he would have beaten up for fun back home, but he didn't want to live alone either.

So there it was, new city, old story. He roamed the streets dressed like a West Coast hick, right down to his high-top shoes, denim jacket, and jeans with high cuffs. With nowhere else to go, Steven parked himself at the nearest bar and was soon engaged in conversation with a couple of drunk tough guys. Their names were Tinker and Ford. They were a little older but reminded him of his friends back at the institution. They told him they were in the merchant marine and talked of the romantic adventure of sailing the world, which struck Steven as not all that bad a way of life. They bought him a drink and told him they could get him signed on, even though he was legally underage. Steven was interested. They made a call, and a little while later someone came by with fake papers and told him where to sign up.[1]

Early the next morning, Steven found himself on the SS *Alpha*. When it left New York, the ship headed to the West Indies to pick up a cargo of molasses. At first, Steven was excited about his new life as a sailor, but the romance of it quickly turned into a nightmare. Being the new hand, he was assigned the dirtiest of jobs—swabbing the deck, cleaning the heads, garbage detail. He hated all of it, and on top of that the ship itself was a rotted hulk. It caught fire at sea and had to stop for repairs in the Dominican Republic. It was there that Steven jumped ship and disappeared into the tropical night. "Taking orders still bugged me. I decided to become a beachcomber and live the free life."

He resurfaced as a towel boy at the most notorious bordello in the country, where blond-haired, blue-eyed boys were in short supply. The working girls, especially, couldn't get enough of him. Now this was a job he *really* enjoyed, especially when nobody seemed to mind if he helped himself to the merchandise whenever he wanted. All the girls loved him.[2]

But after eight weeks he'd had enough even of that and was ready to return to the States. In Port Arthur, Texas, he quickly found work on an oil rig before he quit that job to sell "golden" pen points in a small traveling carnival, a two-ring set-it-up-and-break-it-down affair. Whenever a customer bought a pen point, he also received

---

[1] Tinker and Ford were likely paid recruiters.

[2] Various sources claim that Steve starred in a series of porno films there. None have been reliably authenticated.

a free pen-and-pencil set. "The whole thing was worth, at most, twenty-three cents, and we got a dollar for it. My pockets rejoiced but my stomach couldn't take it and soon I said, 'Stevie boy, it's time to shove.'"

He left the show in Ottawa and found work there briefly with a lumber company as a "hijacker," climbing tall trees and sawing off the upper branches. From there he drifted back down to the Carolinas, where he met a well-bred southern girl whose family was from Myrtle Beach. Her name was Sue Ann and she was young, sweet, and willing. Steven blissfully spent his seventeenth birthday in the comfort of Sue Ann's arms. He wanted to stay with her forever, he said, but one day not long after, he upped and enlisted in the United States Marines. Private First Class McQueen, Second Division of the Fleet Marine Force, was initially stationed at Camp Pendleton, forty-eight miles north of San Diego, California.

In the aftermath of World War II, when most of the wartime recruits had opted for civilian life, only the hard-core vets who had seen it all were left. These marines were tough, hard, strong, and mean and didn't take shit from anyone, especially pretty-boy enlistees they considered still wet behind the ears.

Assigned to boot camp on notorious Parris Island, Steven got off the train, bent over to pick up his bag and was greeted with a drill sergeant's bullet-studded swagger stick across his ass. When he complained, he was marked a troublemaker and assigned to sand decks with a brick in his so-called spare time. He did it until his hands bled. He also had to march through swamps and sleep on a bed covered with twelve loaded guns.

Things were rough for him until someone noticed that Private McQueen looked like he might be a scrapper and slapped a pair of gloves on him. He was assigned to fight the ugliest and biggest marine in the camp. Not surprisingly, it was a one-sided bout. Steve went down ten times and got up nine before giving in (the other guy eventually wound up in Leavenworth Prison because of his penchant for punching out officers). For Steven, the loss was a victory: he had proved his toughness and marked himself a true marine. After that, things got a little better for him.

On his first weekend pass, he met up with Sue Ann and turned it into a two-week vacation in bed, until he was arrested by the MPs for going AWOL and thrown into the brig for forty-one days (twenty-one for going AWOL, twenty for resisting arrest). He was assigned to the engine room of one of the fleet's ships to scrub and repair the asbestos-laden pipes. Upon his release, he was assigned to duty in the tank division, where he learned how to fix their engines.

He was then assigned to duty in the Arctic, barely eighteen, where he saved the lives of five other marines during military exercises when he pulled them from a boat that was about to sink into the icy water. For that he was put into the honor guard assigned to protect President Harry Truman, and when his three-year enlistment was up, he was given an honorable discharge for his heroics. That day he headed straight for Myrtle Beach and Sue Ann.[3]

When he met Sue Ann's family, they took an immediate liking to Steven, especially her father, who'd made his fortune in industry and wanted Steven to marry his daughter. In return he promised he would set up Steven financially for life. Steven thought it over and realized it wasn't what he wanted, and took off in the night without saying goodbye to anyone.

He never saw Sue Ann again.

HE STOPPED off for a while in Washington, D.C., where he got by as a taxi driver and mechanic, on his way to his final destination, Greenwich Village.

---

[3] According to Neile McQueen Toffel, McQueen's first wife, the discharge came exactly three weeks before the outbreak of the Korean War, in which his entire former outfit was wiped out in combat. Toffel, *My Husband, My Friend,* p. 12.

When he got there, he was shocked to discover that Jullian had moved back to San Francisco. He decided to stay on in the Village and found a new small flat to sublet. The rent was $19 a month, and the toilet and shower were shared by everyone on the floor.

Greenwich Village was a section of southern Manhattan that had once been an Indian tobacco field until the Dutch turned it into cow pastures. It wasn't until the British arrived that it became a livable hamlet. Soon its cheap housing and tranquil setting attracted writers, actors, and musicians. By the mid-twentieth century Cole Porter, Martha Graham, Howard Clurman, Eugene O'Neill, James Baldwin, Lillian Hellman, Dashiell Hammett, e. e. cummings, Allen Ginsberg, Edna St. Vincent Millay, and scores of others had all called the Village their home. Coffeehouses, nightspots for jazz and folk music and "readings," and theaters could be found on almost every street. One of them, the Provincetown Playhouse, became O'Neill's favored stage, and actors came in droves to try to be a part of the downtown artistic community.

At the same time, the G.I. Bill made it possible for the scores of World War II veterans who lived in or near the city to take advantage of educational facilities they otherwise would not have been able to gain access to. Dozens of acting schools materialized in the Village and Midtown, with no shortage of young, good-looking men signing up to study in the hopes of making it big in theater, film, and especially television, which was in its golden age of live broadcasts of comedy and drama, most of it coming out of Manhattan, and constantly in need of new faces.

It was into this creative hub that Steven settled, slipping easily into the boho mix of beatniks and cabdrivers, mechanics and musicians, and a seemingly endless supply of young and beautiful (and easy) wannabe actresses. After a couple of months of eking out a living doing mechanical jobs and occasionally posing for the racy covers of detective magazines, always with his shirt open and a woman in a slip in a nearby bed, Steven eventually turned to shoplifting to help make ends meet. "I was so broke I'd go into New York drug stores, pick up an alarm clock or something and walk up to the cashier and say, 'Gimme a refund on this, please' . . . talk about 'beat.' I was it."

He worked as a part-time dishwasher, drove a post office truck every night from 6:30 p.m. until 2:30 a.m., and even tried his hand as a professional boxer, using what little training he had picked up in the marines, until he was knocked out in the third round of his first fight, for which he earned a grand total of $65. He also thought about enrolling in classes to learn how to lay tile. The only problem was, the school he wanted to go to was in Spain— a big move and one he was willing to make, as soon as he saved enough money for the fare over.

A young actress he was seeing on and off who lived in the same building suggested he try acting. She said he should come and sit in on one of her classes at the Neighborhood Playhouse, a downtown school for actors and actresses run by Sanford Meisner. As he remembered it, she looked at him and said, "Say, why don't you come down to the Neighborhood Playhouse with me? They're having auditions, and you look like you might have some talent stashed away in you."

Why not? So he went to a class and was knocked out again, this time not by a fist or by the quality of the acting, which at this point he had no way of judging and didn't really care that much about, but by all the gorgeous young girls eager to learn how to emote. Acting might just be a good field for him after all. He did some fast checking and discovered that if he were accepted, he could attend for free under the G.I. Bill.

After sitting in on a few classes, he decided to call Sanford Meisner and find out how to get into the Neighborhood Playhouse. He and Meisner talked for a while, and Meisner asked Steven to come by for a personal interview. After a few minutes face-to-face, Meisner told Steven he was in. "That's when I became a man instead of a boy," McQueen later remembered. "Until he got after me, I understood nothing."

Although he didn't know it at the time, Steven had been accepted into a highly competitive group of seventy-two students, handpicked from more than three thousand applications. This was the beginning of what would become a phenomenon of style that would eventually alter the nature of the American stage, television, and film industries. It was the reblossoming of the Method, and as far as Meisner was concerned, Steven was a natural at it.

Method acting had been virtually unknown in commercial America until the 1930s, when the New York–based Group Theater introduced techniques that had been popularized in Russia by Konstantin Stanislavsky. His innovations in stage performing included such techniques as sense memory, improvisational character development, and moment-to-moment reality, all intended to bring a heightened—or as Stanislavsky called it, "theatrical" truth—to actors' performances.

The Method quickly caught on in America, until the jaws of politics gnawed away at the core membership for its leftist leanings (not at all uncommon among American artists in the thirties). The scent of communism proved irresistible to those American agents hunting so-called traitors, infiltrators, and spies for the Soviet Union in mainstream films, radio, and theater during the Depression. Those of the Group's founders who could no longer find work as actors and/or directors, which was most, turned to teaching as a way of making a living. Among them were Lee Strasberg, Stella Adler, Robert Lewis, and Sanford Meisner. Each eventually developed something of a cult following, blurring the lines between teacher and guru. Their approaches may have varied, but all were teaching, essentially, a method of acting derived from Stanislavsky.[4]

In 1947, Marlon Brando, eventually the ultimate American exemplar of the Method, made his breakthrough in Tennessee Williams's powerful, timely, and psychologically radical Broadway play *A Streetcar Named Desire*. Both the theatrical and later the 1951 screen version, which also starred Brando, were directed by Elia Kazan, who had begun his career as a stage manager and actor for the original Group Theater. Both times, Kazan's direction of Brando emphasized his beauty, strength, and animal sexuality so powerfully and successfully that Brando's appearance, speech, posture, and attitude became the obligatory accoutrements of Method acting, American style.

While Steven was on the make for pretty actresses, Meisner was in search of the Method's next Brando, and he thought he had finally found him in his young blond protégé. During an exercise Steven did one day in improvisation class with his assigned partner, Ellen Clark (later Hayers), she unexpectedly slapped him across the face, and he reacted in perfect Method fashion by punching her out. "We did scenes together where you couldn't tell what was going to happen," Clark later remembered. "Steven was always the most unpredictable person. One time he knocked me down to the ground in some scene and nobody expected it, not him or me, and the whole class stood up, shocked."

Steven remembered the incident this way: "They put me on the stage with a girl—a dilettante from Long Island—and we were supposed to improvise an argument. Well, she hit me. I didn't

---

[4] Strasberg, for instance, relied on the actor's recalling a parallel experience in his own life to find the essential reality in the character he was playing, while Adler relied less on sense memory than exploring the reality of the character's moment. Meisner's technique emphasized working off an actor's partner in a scene, to act by reacting—what he called "living truthfully under imaginary circumstances."

expect it. She hit me hard and I couldn't stand it. I hit back as hard as I could and knocked her cold. Man, it was Panicksville!" Afterward, an enthused Meisner urged Steven to stay with it, and told him that he would even help him try to get some acting work to help pay his rent.

By the summer of 1952 Steven, with Meisner's assistance, had landed a small role in a Jewish repertory company on the Lower East Side that featured the legendary Yiddish actress Molly Picon. He had four lines of dialogue—in Yiddish, which took him forever to learn. He never could master the accent and was fired after four performances, but it was a start, and not long after, with Steven's stint at the Neighborhood Playhouse coming to an end, Meisner urged him to try out for the prestigious and even-harder-to-get-into Herbert Berghof Studio.

Berghof, born in Vienna and educated at the University of Vienna and then the Vienna State Academy of Dramatic Art, where he had studied with the great Max Reinhardt, had been forced to flee from the Nazis in 1939. He relocated in New York City, where he became a Broadway star. In 1945 he created his acting school (joined later by his wife, the equally talented and successful Uta Hagen), intended as a lab for highly trained working professionals to practice their craft between gigs. Steven, the sum of whose professional acting consisted of a couple of nights badly impersonating a Jew in the Yiddish theater, not only was accepted by Berghof but, on the basis of his audition and Meisner's enthusiastic recommendation, was offered a full scholarship, all living expenses paid, which, of course, he eagerly accepted.

SUMMERTIME FOR New York actors in the 1950s meant summer stock. They spread out to rural towns and burgs where residents otherwise rarely got a chance to see live theater. In June 1953, Steven was cast opposite former child star Margaret O'Brien, a onetime Oscar winner, who found little demand for her services as an adult, in the J. Hartley Manners turn-of-the-century chestnut *Peg o' My Heart*.[5] Steven was her leading man. He listed himself as Steve in the program, the name he now preferred. On opening night stage fright got the better of him and he forgot most of his lines, leading him to think seriously about giving up acting and going back to being Steven.

He didn't, though, and continued to land summer acting jobs that often turned into national tours stretching into the fall and through the holiday season. After a handful of auditions in the spring of 1954, Steve landed a part in a show called *The Geep*, produced by Jack Garfein, a new play that never made it to Broadway.[6] A brief stint in a tour of Carson McCullers's *Member of the Wedding*, starring Ethel Waters, quickly followed, and that same year he was cast in the national tour of *Time Out for Ginger*, a comedy about a middle-class suburban family turned upside down when its teenage daughter wants to try out for the high school football team. The play starred Melvyn Douglas as the father. For $175 a week, Steve agreed to replace Conrad Janis as one of the football players. Janis had originated the small but effective part on Broadway but did not want to tour. The rest of the New York cast remained intact, including Douglas. In the first real review of Steve's acting, one local critic named Samuel Wilson wrote that "Mr. McQueen lampoons the star athlete of the school in a couple of turns."

However, things quickly turned sour for Steve because something about him—his cockiness, or perhaps his charisma—irritated Douglas, and the aging star insisted McQueen be fired. Steve was allowed to "retire" from the production and learned his first

---

[5] 1944—"Outstanding Child Actress" for her performance in Vincente Minnelli's *Meet Me in St. Louis*.

[6] Frequently and incorrectly reported as *Gep*, or *The Gep*.

lesson about star temperament, ego, and jealousy-fueled insecurity: that the star is always right. It was a lesson he would never forget.

⌣

IN 1955 Steve landed the male lead in a new off-Broadway production, *Two Fingers of Pride*, which co-starred Sam Jaffe, but it soon closed and with nothing else happening, Steve decided to return to class. Because he was now a "working actor," meaning he had actually earned money for his work, he was eligible to try out for the mecca of training schools, Lee Strasberg's Actors Studio, where the acceptance rate was about one out of two hundred.

For his audition, Steve put together a monologue from Clifford Odets's *Golden Boy*, a Group Theater production about a young violinist who really wants to be a prizefighter, a role that had made a star out of William Holden in the Rouben Mamoulian 1939 film version. The so-called park scene monologue was a popular one among young male actors, and it served Steve well; he was personally accepted into the Studio by Strasberg, who was impressed, as Meisner and Berghof before him had been, with Steve's easy, strong, youthful energy and a certain mumbling, indefinable quality that made him a perfect fit for the classroom stylistics of the Method.

For Steve, the Studio was a great place to study and find new girls and more work. Offers to work on live TV were plentiful, as agents regularly dropped in to observe classwork and were always impressed with his acting and presence, as they forever trolled the waters for the next Marlon Brando.

I'm not a prodigy of the beat generation. I've knocked around a lot, and there's nothing very romantic in it. Responsibility toward my profession is something I've learned just recently. . . . If I hadn't become an actor I might have gone the other way—into an anti-social life, possibly a life of crime.

—STEVE MCQUEEN

L IKE STEVE, RUBY NEILAM SALVADOR ADAMS, OR NEILE, as everyone called her, never met her father. She was the daughter of a Manila-based woman of German and Spanish descent by the name of Carmen Salvador, known professionally as Miami, a hula star. In 1932, when Miami was twenty, she met a handsome stranger of English, Filipino, and Chinese origin, became pregnant, and married him. Unfortunately, he was already married to someone else, and that was the end of that.

Whenever Miami worked the islands, she left Neile with relatives in Manila. The nine-year-old child was caught there when the Japanese attacked it and Pearl Harbor on December 7, 1941. A month later, the Japanese occupied Manila.

Six months after, Neile returned to school and soon became a child spy for the Philippine underground. "I spoke five languages so it was my job to carry messages from one band of guerrillas to another. Children were never searched and there was usually something to eat as a reward." In 1945, during the island's liberation by Allied forces, Neile suffered shrapnel wounds in one of her legs. After the war, Miami returned to Manila and sent Neile off to the States to attend Rosemary Hall, a private school in Connecticut, thanks to the generosity of Miami's newest "friend."

After graduating, Neile, who wanted to be a dancer like her mother (not *exactly* like her mother), landed a summer stock job in upstate New York, and in 1952, at the age of twenty, she moved to New York City, took a small apartment, and enrolled in the American Theatre Wing, the American President School of Acting, and the Katherine Dunham School of Dance, all located in the heart of the theater district. Her auditions had been good enough to win her scholarships. To pay her living expenses she began modeling for detective and crime magazine covers, in what were considered suggestive poses at the time. None of it bothered her because she felt the photo sessions were antiseptic and businesslike, and it was the easiest work around. Like Steve, whom she didn't know at the time, she did it strictly for the money.

And like Steve, she didn't have to do it for long. By the end of 1953 Neile had made it to Broadway as a featured dancer in *Kismet*, starring Alfred Drake. "I made the chorus as one of the three princesses of Ababu in *Kismet*," she later recalled. "I was singing in the elevator at the Ziegfeld going up to the dressing rooms after a performance—I sing everywhere—and Maurice Levine, the show's musical director, heard me and suggested I study voice."

Four months later she replaced Reiko Sato as the lead dancer and remained in the show for the rest of *Kismet*'s two-year run. After a 1955 summer of stock theater, she returned to New York and negotiated a major deal with the Versailles Club, at the time one of the biggest nightspots in the city, to be part of a revue that also featured the slick, good-looking, silver-haired Jack Cassidy. The revue ran for six months, and when it closed, legendary Broadway director George Abbott chose Neile to replace Carol Haney, the star of his current hit musical *The Pajama Game*.

During her days off she took singing and dancing classes in some of the many studios above Carnegie Hall. It was 1956, and

Midtown Manhattan was teeming with young actors and actresses appearing on Broadway, doing live radio and TV dramas, and working in a fair amount of movies (mostly in the outer boroughs of Queens, Brooklyn, and the Bronx, where there was ample studio space). Socializing among the performers was fast and easy in the glitter and flash of the Big Street, and they bounced into and off each other as if they all lived on the surface of one gigantic pinball machine. They were good-looking and talented, with great bodies and heavy hormones, and the bedroom action among them reflected their endless energy, onstage and off.

It was in this heady atmosphere that Neile first noticed the good-looking, slightly stooped, rough-around-the-edges Steve McQueen one night after class. "I was coming out of dance class at Carnegie Hall, coming out the door, and he was out front and saw me. He came towards me and said, 'Hi. You're pretty.' I said, 'You're pretty too!' He was starting to ask me what my name was when a friend of mine, another dancer, blonde Sigyn Lund, who he happened to be with that night, smiled, took him by the arm and said to me, 'See ya!'"

They didn't run into each other again for several weeks, until one late afternoon Neile, who was going with actor and jazz pianist Mark Rydell, stopped with him at Downey's Steakhouse at Eighth Avenue and 49th Street for a bite before her performance that evening in *The Pajama Game*.[1]

Downey's was one of a number of Midtown restaurants that serviced the theater district and was known affectionately as the poor actor's kitchen. Downey's, like Mama Leone's, Lindy's, and Howard Johnson's, had separate menus for "civilians" and "professionals." Steve loved Downey's steak and potatoes and pasta dishes

---

[1] Rydell would go on to a successful career as a film director. Thirteen years after that night at Downey's, he would direct McQueen in 1969's *The Reivers*. In 1981 Rydell was nominated for an Oscar for Best Director for *On Golden Pond*.

made only for theater regulars and ate there as often as he could. The afternoon Neile and Rydell stopped by, she happened to spot Steve sitting with Frank Corsaro, a Broadway director who currently had Michael Gazzo's *A Hatful of Rain* on the boards. Neile remembered Steve right away as the good-looking guy from outside Carnegie Hall. "As I sat down, Steve looked up from his table. He had just forked a mouthful of spaghetti and no sooner did he see me than it slopped back on the plate and into his lap! After that, every day for a week we had a silent mutual admiration society going at Downey's."

Corsaro, who had seen Steve in Chicago in the national touring company of *Time Out for Ginger*, had asked him to lunch to offer Steve the opportunity to take over the lead role of Johnny Pope in *Hatful*, about a Korean War veteran's addiction to heroin. *Hatful* had made a star out of its original lead, Ben Gazzara. A talented stage performer with a tough but vulnerable vibe and a face that always looked like it was about to break out in tears, Gazzara had also originated the role of Brick in Tennessee Williams's Broadway production of *Cat on a Hot Tin Roof* but had lost out in his bid to repeat the role on film. Instead, Richard Brooks cast another stage-trained actor creating an enormous buzz, Paul Newman, to play the role. Gazzara then returned to Broadway and *A Hatful of Rain*.

When his contract was up, Gazzara opted not to renew, to star instead in Otto Preminger's upcoming film *Anatomy of a Murder*, his breakthrough screen role after nearly a decade of television drama and stage work. To replace Gazzara, Corsaro wanted Steve, after seeing him in a number of live TV shows and in his first film, Robert Wise's just-released adaptation of prizefighter Rocky Graziano's memoir, *Somebody Up There Likes Me*, starring Paul Newman in *his* breakthrough role after James Dean, Wise's first choice to play Graziano, was killed in a car crash.

To fill out the background of tough, crooked street kids Graziano grew up with and left behind, Wise had cast the diminutive,

Bronx-born Sal Mineo, and Steve, who only appears in the first fifteen minutes of the film as a pool-playing, tire-stealing, fur-coat-hijacking, roof-top-jumping delinquent named Fidel. His part was not big enough for him to be listed in the front credits, but Wise liked him so much he expanded his role as much as possible (at $20 a day).

Steve and Newman knew each other casually from the several live TV appearances each had done, a rite of passage for New York actors hoping to graduate to the big screen. They often competed for the same role, although except for their both having startlingly blue eyes (something lost on the small black-and-white screens of the 1950s), the similarities between the two weren't all that apparent. Steve had a leanness that at the time made him look a bit emaciated, which was only accentuated by his shortness (he was five foot eight, though his height shrank and grew with the progression of his career, with reports varying from five-six to five-eleven; studio PR bios always listed him as five foot ten). Like Newman, Steve was extremely good-looking, but he had a haunted, suspicious cast about him, a hardness, and those slightly stooped shoulders. Newman, on the other hand, was classically handsome, his face a Greek god's, and while he, too, had to stand on tiptoe to reach six feet, his body was tougher, harder, and more cut than McQueen's. And Newman, ever the charmer, always seemed to have a smile on his face. It was precisely Steve's darker, offbeat edge that had landed him the role in *Hatful* over dozens of other hopefuls.

FINALLY, AFTER a week of Neile seeing Steve and Steve seeing her at Downey's, Neile, there again with Rydell, finally walked over to the table where he was eating and said "Hi!" to no one in particular. Steve smiled. According to Neile's memoir, after she excused herself to use the ladies' room, Steve got up, walked over to Rydell, and told him that he intended to go after his date, as in "Sorry, buddy, but all's fair in love, etc., etc." When Neile returned, Steve politely excused himself and left.

The next day Steve asked around and found out who she was and what show she was in, and, like the proverbial stage-door Johnny, showed up at six-thirty one night in Shubert Alley, where the actors and actresses from *The Pajama Game* came and went, now that the show had moved to the Shubert Theater from the St. James. When he saw her, he stumbled and stuttered his way into a date after the show. He came back that night dressed in black leather and jeans and rode his Harley right up to the stage door. When Neile came out, he sat her on the back, pulled her arms around him, and roared down Broadway to his place in the Village.

They stayed up talking all night, and by dawn, despite the fact that they didn't have sex (or maybe because of that), Neile believed she had finally found her soul mate.[2]

Steve believed he had found his too: "I wanted to marry Neile a few weeks after I met her." Unlike all of the women before her, Neile had tapped in to an emotional engine stronger than the one that usually drove Steve's sexual wants. Women were available to him anytime he felt like it; mothers, real or surrogate, were so much harder to find.

In her memoir, Neile wrote that she thought Steve wanted to sleep with her right away and she resisted because she didn't want to lose him that quickly. She had been around and knew the hit-and-run nature of most Broadway one-night stands. She saw something in Steve that she thought made him better than that. He was fascinated and intrigued that Neile seemed to find something of value in him above the waist. It was an entirely new

---

[2] Neile, perhaps choosing tact over fact, remembered their first real meeting a little differently. In an article she wrote for the March 1960 edition of *TV and Movie Western Magazine*, she said that "a mutual friend, actor Mark Rydell, couldn't take it any more—he took pity on us and arranged an introduction." Later on, in her memoir, she told the "all's fair" version of the story.

dynamic for Steve, who was the kind of man who didn't take no for an answer when it came to sex, and almost never had to. One night she showed him a long scar on her leg where Japanese shrapnel had ripped it open. "Poor kid," Steve said to her. Then he told her some things about his childhood, and his mother. "Poor kid," she said to him.

According to Neile's memoir, the mutual and heavy attraction they had for each other was rooted in shared childhood experiences. Both had mothers who had gotten pregnant too young. Steve's father had abandoned him in infancy; Neile had never known hers. Steve was raised in Missouri by his grand-uncle Claude; Neile was raised in the Philippines by a kind old man. Steve had gone to reform school; Neile had spent time in a Japanese concentration camp. Both eventually drifted to New York to pursue careers in show business. Steve was all-American and aggressive; Neile was Asian and submissive. To her, there was an element of predestination about them; they were meant to be together.

STEVE SHOWED Neile things about New York City she'd never seen before—late-night jazz clubs, midnight double features on 42nd Street, Fire Island. And always, back at her apartment, Steve would walk in first, throw his clothes off, and fall backward onto the bed while Neile efficiently picked up after him. She didn't mind that part; she was used to a neat and clean household. Nor did she mind that Steve had unofficially moved into her place. His walk-up could not compare with her spacious digs on West 55th Street, which was far better suited for both of them.

The only thing she really didn't like was Steve's pot smoking. He was a big-time pothead and had been ever since coming to the Village and discovering the joys of weed. Whenever she did bring it up, he would shrug it off and tell her that it was just his way of unwinding, but she could never get used to that pungent sour-sweet smell or the yellow clouds that invaded every room of her apartment.

IN SEPTEMBER 1956, Neile's run ended in *The Pajama Game*, the same night that Steve's did in *A Hatful of Rain*. His performance did not lead to any immediate career-lifting offers. He had never been able to fully immerse himself in the character of Johnny. Neile, on the other hand, could have stayed with the show longer, but Robert Wise, the same director who'd cast Steve in *Somebody Up There Likes Me*, was making a new movie, *This Could Be the Night*, and was looking for an actress who could do a killer strip. Veteran Hollywood film producer Joe Pasternak had seen Neile in *The Pajama Game*, been totally charmed by her performance, and when Wise asked Pasternak if he knew anyone who could play a stripper, he immediately recommended Neile. Pasternak was so enthusiastic about her that Wise flew Neile out to Hollywood to screen-test. That same day he gave her the role. It didn't make the news of her planned trip to L.A. any easier for Steve when he found out his co-star in *A Hatful of Rain*, Anthony Franciosa, had been cast as the male lead in the film opposite Jean Simmons.

With nothing to do and Neile away in Hollywood, Steve moped about her apartment for a week or so. Then, out of money, he went to a pawn shop on Eighth Avenue, casually hocked the gold watch that Uncle Claude had given him, and bought a ticket on a cross-country flight to L.A. He missed Neile and wanted to be with her, and that was worth more to him than any watch, even this watch. He called Neile and told her he was coming, and she said she couldn't wait to see him.

However, at the last minute he changed his mind and went to Cuba with his upstairs neighbor Lionel Olay, who had been to the island many times before and even interviewed Fidel prior to his becoming *el presidente*. Steve and Olay had hit it off from the moment they met. Both shared a love of smoking weed and often got stoned all day. When Olay told Steve about his upcoming trip to Cuba, Steve said he wanted to go, and when Olay said sure, he cashed in his L.A. ticket and bought one to Havana. Just before the flight took off, Steve called Neile to tell her about his change of plans. She wasn't happy about it.

When Neile's film was delayed by the pregnancy of its star, Simmons, Neile suddenly had a lot of time on her hands, and with Steve no longer coming, she decided she would return to New York and wait out the film's delay there. Then, two days before she was scheduled to fly back to L.A., she received a telegram from Steve—signed "Esteban"—telling her he loved her and that he was broke, and asking if she could wire him enough money so he could catch a flight home from Cuba.

Neile was less than thrilled, and let him know it. She sent him a wire back telling him she would be leaving New York the day after next, that she wasn't sending any money, and that she loved him, too. She figured if she sent him anything, he would only stay in Cuba longer. What she didn't know was that Steve and Olay had accidentally ridden their bikes too close to a rebel fort and been arrested as spies. The rebels threatened to send them in front of a firing squad, but instead took their bikes and let them go. By the time Steve's telegram arrived, he and Olay had somehow found enough money for plane tickets and were already on their way home.

When Neile resumed work on her film, Steve called her collect from New York almost every night. When he decided he didn't want to go through another city winter by himself, he scraped together enough money to buy a plane ticket to L.A. This time he didn't tell Neile he was coming.

One afternoon shortly after he arrived, Steve went to the MGM soundstage where Neile was rehearsing and waited until she was on a break, then swept her in his arms and asked her to marry him. His proposal came with a ring he had had bought in the Village (on which he'd put a down payment of $25, promising to pay the rest off, which Neile eventually did). Despite the warnings of friends, agents, and relatives, especially her mother, Neile said yes and the first weekend she had off they rented a Ford Thunderbird and drove to San Juan Capistrano. "The long-distance phone bills got so enormous we decided to get married instead," Neile recalled.

They were wed on Friday, November 2, 1956. With approval from the church, they settled on a justice of the peace, after which Neile rented a car and Steve drove them down to Mexico for a two-day honeymoon in Ensenada. Monday morning, Neile, now a married woman, happily returned to the soundstage where her movie was being filmed.

Steve, though, was not so happy. L.A. has always been hell for actors who aren't working. Every day he'd come by the studio where Neile was filming and hang out, generally making a pain in the ass out of himself. When Robert Wise finally told Neile to get rid of him or he would have Steve banned from the set, she smartly sent him out to buy a car for the two of them. With Neile's money he bought a brand-new Corvette. Her manager at the time, Hillard "Hilly" Elkins, took her aside and told her to have the marriage annulled before Steve cleaned her out and left her. Neile didn't want to hear any of that and instead asked Elkins to help find Steve a job. Elkins said no.

Steve, perhaps sensing he had worn out his welcome, decided to drive the car back east. As soon as he left, Neile realized how much she missed him, and she arranged to fly him out every weekend so they could be together on her days off. She also continued to press Elkins and her agents at the William Morris Agency, Stan Kamen, Leonard Hirshan, Sandy Glass, and Sy Marsh, to find work for Steve. As Elkins remembered, "She was doing very well, and then she brought this guy in who I thought was an obvious user, then I saw some of what he did on TV and the bit he did in *Somebody Up There Likes Me* and I thought, hey, whatever he is off the screen he's terrific on it."

Early in 1957, Elkins told Neile he thought he might have found something for Steve, a new two-part *Studio One* drama, "The Defender," that was going to be done live in New York City. The producer, Herbert Brodkin, and the director, Robert Mulligan, were looking for a young, good-looking actor for a major part on the show. Elkins promised Neile he would send Steve up for the part. He kept his word, and Steve got it.

Studio One was one of the jewels of CBS during the era of live TV (though many later episodes were either filmed or videotaped). It was a weekly anthology program that dealt with a wide variety of subjects and employed many New York theater-trained actors and actresses. "The Defender" centered on a murder trial. The defendant, Joseph Gordon (Steve, billed as Steven McQueen) is accused of murdering a psychiatrist's wife. The rest of the cast included Martin Balsam, Betty Furness, Ralph Bellamy, and William Shatner.[3]

This time Steve had no problem playing a disturbed young man, even without smiling. The TV camera did for him what the stage couldn't; it focused in on his intense eyes and his facial expressions during the testimony of various witnesses, effectively conveying that his character was a bit off-balance. It was his most effective performance to date and helped to spin "The Defender" into a highly successful lawyer series, *The Defenders*, which ran for four seasons Saturday nights on CBS.

The two-part pilot for "The Defender," which aired Febru-

---

[3] Clips from this episode appeared in a 2007 episode of Shatner's hit TV series, *Boston Legal*, as a flashback to the young version of Shatner's character talking to his father, Ralph Bellamy, about the legal definition of innocence.

ary 25, 1957, just shy of Steve's twenty-seventh birthday, featured Ralph Bellamy in what would become the E. G. Marshall role in the series, that of a conscientious lawyer in the years when such a thing was not immediately laughable. His son was played by Shatner; Robert Reed would play the part in the series. The hook of the pilot was that Bellamy believes the young grocery clerk (McQueen in a one-off) is guilty but still deserves the best defense possible.

The day after it aired, Sid Shalit of the New York *Daily News* wrote, "One thing must be said for the first half of 'The Defender,' the acting was uniformly expert. Bellamy, Martin Balsam (the prosecuting attorney) and especially McQueen." The second part was also well received; the ratings actually went up for it.

Herbert Brodkin, the producer of *Studio One*, was so pleased with Steve's performance he sent him a personal letter, dated March 5, 1957, written on official CBS Television stationery, thanking him for helping to make the show a hit, and to let him know that several women had called to find out who this Steven McQueen was. Stan Kamen, one of Neile's agents at William Morris, watched both parts of "The Defender" and was completely disarmed by Steve's performance. For the first time he thought the young man might have some real potential, and set out to find something for him.

Not long after, Kamen got Steve a small role in trash novelist Harold Robbins's upcoming film adaptation of his own first trash novel, 1948's *Never Love a Stranger*. One of the most-repeated stories about why publisher Pat Knopf bought *Never Love a Stranger* was because when he read it in manuscript form, he said it was the first time he "had ever read a book where on one page you'd have tears and on the next page you'd have a hard-on."

Despite its lurid style, the novel didn't do much in its original run, but Robbins's second one, 1952's *A Stone for Danny Fisher,* filmed before *Stranger,* went through the roof, and it appeared for a time that Robbins just might be the next Irwin Shaw.

Robbins, a self-styled swinging jet-setter, had come upon his fortune relatively late in life. Prior to *A Stone for Danny Fisher* climbing up the bestseller lists, the film rights to it had already been sold as a vehicle for Elvis Presley. As adapted by screenwriters Herbert Baker and Michael V. Gazzo (the latter had written *A Hatful of Rain*), for some reason, its locale was shifted from New York City to New Orleans and its name changed to *King Creole*. Veteran Michael Curtiz directed, and it was scheduled for a 1958 release, to keep Presley's name in the hearts and minds of his teenage fans while he did his time in the army.

The deal for *Danny Fisher* had infuriated Robbins because he had sold the screen rights to Paramount before the book came out and became a surprise bestseller. The studio paid very little money for it, with no back-end participation for Robbins. Vowing that such a thing would never again happen to him, Robbins personally renegotiated the film rights for *Never Love a Stranger*, which was having huge sales in paperback off the popularity of *A Stone for Danny Fisher*. Allied Artists paid Robbins $700,000 for *Never Love a Stranger* and an additional $50,000 for him to write the screenplay. Robert Stevens, a journeyman TV director who did a lot of episodes of *Alfred Hitchcock Presents*, was set to helm the production.

Allied Artists wanted the book as a vehicle for John Drew Barrymore, a young, good-looking inheritor of the famed Barrymore profile, if not the talent (the father of Drew Barrymore), and hoped it would turn him into the next James Dean. Also in the cast was actress Lita Milan. Kamen arranged for Steve to play one of the small but key parts in the film, Martin Cabell, a Jewish district attorney who discovers that his best friend, Frankie Kane (Barrymore), is not Jewish. It is all very complicated and very Robbins, for whom autobiographical New York–style Jewishness and universal anti-Semitism were present in virtually every novel he wrote. Because of it Allied Artists had to delay the film's release until deep into 1958, and almost didn't release it at all, because few southern theaters would book a film about Jews without a major non-Jewish star to bring audiences in. It was only after the huge success of *King Creole* (in which Danny Fisher—played by Elvis— is no longer a Jew) that *Never Love a Stranger* was widely released.

For his part, Steve was totally unimpressed with his work in the film and thought the whole thing was junk. "That turkey wasn't released for two years, and the only notice I got was from a critic who said my face looked like a Botticelli angel that had been crossed with a chimp."

Steve, however, did like Robbins. He especially liked the writer's macho posturing and his way with women. When Steve, still a newlywed, had an intensely sexual affair with Milan that everybody involved with the making of the film knew about, Robbins heartily approved. According to one observer, Steve and Lita "signaled to each other excitedly at night with torches from their adjacent suites and at one point Steve climbed into an empty maid's room to eavesdrop on a call between Milan and a girlfriend immediately below, later repeating the intimate conversation to her in bed. There was an abandon and fun, even frivolity" between the two. Not only did neither one of them try to hide their affair from anyone, but Steve proudly told his wife about it.

According to Neile, "Steve told me after the picture he had had a fling with her. She would be the first in a long line of 'flings' that would plague us—me—throughout our married life. . . . [O]kay, I thought, I can handle it—I have to—as long as he doesn't flaunt it. . . . [M]y combination Asian and Latin upbringing had taught me to separate love and marriage from feckless romps in the hay. I was so naive."

This pattern—Steve cheating and confessing and Neile forgiving him—would be repeated during the entire time they were married.

On their first anniversary, Neile gave Steven a gold St.

Christopher medallion. On the back of it she had engraved *To part is to die a little.*

It was something they both believed, something that kept them together. No matter what, they were kindred souls, two kids who had grown up alone, and somehow, had miraculously found each other. Together, they believed, they could take on the whole world.

Chapter 4

I like John Wayne and he's never had an acting lesson in his life.

—STEVE MCQUEEN

N EILE'S NEXT GIG WAS HEADLINING AT THE TROPICANA hotel in Las Vegas. To get to the Nevada desert gambling mecca, she took a cross-country road trip from New York City in the Corvette with Steve and his new dog, Thor, a German shepherd he had bought for himself as a present after *Studio One*. They took their time, enjoyed seeing the country state by state, and arrived in Las Vegas just in time for Neile to begin rehearsals for her scheduled September opening night.

As it happened, Steve couldn't be there for it because he had gotten a film. He sent her a congratulatory telegram, again signed "Esteban," though this time from St. Louis, where he had gone to chase down a small role in a teen horror flick called *The Blob*. He hated the script when he first read it because he knew he was far too old to play the teenage lead he was up for, a privileged suburban kid with a hot rod and a "let's go to the dance!" group of fresh-scrubbed friends who eventually have to deal with the arrival of the purply amorphous blob.

The film was produced by Jack H. Harris, a wannabe out of Philadelphia with little experience but lots of money who was looking for a way to establish himself as a player in Hollywood.

To do so, he invested $150,000 of his own money and borrowed an additional $100,000 to make this little horror movie. With that kind of budget, minuscule by studio standards, big-name players were out of the question. Steve, who had no money, no prospects, and little film experience, was the actor the producer wanted for the lead, based on his live TV work and brief appearance as a tough teen in *Somebody Up There Likes Me*. He liked Steve's good looks, his intensity, and the fact he was unknown, which meant he could get him for next to nothing.

To make the deal, Harris got in touch with Stan Kamen and gave him a choice: $3,000 cash up front for Steve, or no salary and 10 percent of the film's gross profits (10 percent of every ticket sold, before any production deductions or other disbursements). Kamen took the deal to Steve, who went for the up-front cash, which he needed badly. Besides, he thought the film was so awful it probably would never open, let alone make any money. After dropping Neile off in Vegas, Steve drove to Philadelphia and reported for duty.

There was another reason, besides the cash, that Steve agreed to do the film: the creeping desperation that comes with aging in the film business. Steve was pushing twenty-eight in 1958; while that may not have been too old in Hollywood years, he was definitely pushing the envelope for consideration in the only role that really interested him, that of the Next Big Thing. Paul Newman, four years older than McQueen, had grabbed that gold ring just in time, with *Somebody Up There Likes Me*. Steve didn't see anything like that about to happen for him, so he took *The Blob* to make a few dollars.

The Blob was part of a fifties film fad that saw many of these B horror movies unexpectedly earn huge profits. Don Siegel's 1956 *Invasion of the Body Snatchers*, the best of the decade's metaphorical, paranoid anticommunist films, turned into a sleeper hit, earning millions and making a star out of Kevin McCarthy (as well as typecasting him into Hollywood horror film hell). The other genre that *The Blob* happened to key into was the teen rebellion/delinquent movie, like Nicholas Ray's 1955 *Rebel Without a Cause*, which had helped make a sensation out of James Dean.

Harris's had all the key ingredients: a minimal investment, the obligatory monster, and frightened but good-looking teens who can't get any authority figures (police, parents, the school principal) to believe them, let alone help them, and wind up being their own heroes. Once the film was completed, Harris showed it to Paramount, who bought distribution rights with an advance of $300,000 against future earnings, meaning that Harris broke even before the film even opened. Sure enough, *The Blob* proved a huge hit, grossing more than $1.5 million in its first month and earning what was, for its time, an astonishing $12 million in its initial domestic release.[1] Had Steve accepted the initial deal Harris had offered (and urged him to take), he would have become a millionaire overnight.

But he didn't, and what was worse, he feared *The Blob* had turned him into the oldest kid in America, uncastable in anything but teen B movies. His fears looked as if they were coming true when, with no other offers, he took another B movie with another independent producer, this one called *The Great St. Louis Bank Robbery*. Shot on location and directed by Charles Guggenheim and John Stix, it was produced by Guggenheim, who managed to snag a distribution deal for it with United Artists.

Shot in black and white, *The Great St. Louis Bank Robbery* was based on a 1953 bank robbery attempt at the Southwest Bank of St. Louis. It was intended to be an art-house heist movie but lacked any stylistic appeal. It wound up doing little business outside of St. Louis, where the robbery attempt had become part of the local

---

[1] Film earnings are notoriously difficult to confirm. For this book, the author has relied on *Variety* and other reliable industry publications throughout.

folklore. In the film, Steve played the driver of a getaway car. The same day production ended, Steve, frustrated and fed up, jumped into the Corvette and drove to California to be with Neile, who had just finished her successful stint at the Tropicana and had returned to California in the hopes of getting her film career back on track.

Steve was frustrated, but didn't want Neile to know it. He put on a happy face for her that ultimately worked against him, because Neile was worried by his apparent lack of concern about acting, or anything else. She was making $50,000 a year to Steve's $3,000, and it bothered her that it didn't seem to bother him. Rather, she thought, he was content to spend her money as if it were his, buying new and expensive clothes, driving the 'Vette, and spending lavishly on hotels and long-distance phone calls. At one point she suggested they open separate bank accounts, and Steve told her she was crazy. *I married you, didn't I?* was the upshot of his response, meaning not just *Hey, that's a pretty fair amount of caring* but also *What's yours is mine.* Neile kept their joint account open, but her concerns about Steve continued to deepen—until his life took an unexpected and dramatic turn that changed everything.

By the late 1950s, westerns, a slowly fading movie genre, had successfully made the move from the large screen to the small one. By the fall of 1958, one-third of all network programming was original TV western series, and because of the necessity of shooting them outdoors, most television production relocated from New York to L.A. That is when TV began to change from a live tape medium to a filmed one, putting a gradual end to the so-called golden age of live TV.

Earlier that year, while in L.A. with Neile, Steve had received a call from Hilly Elkins, who invited him to have lunch at the famed Polo Lounge in the Beverly Hills Hotel to discuss a new project. Elkins had been approached by producer Vincent Fennelly, of Four Star Productions, about the possibility of creating a new western TV series on CBS and to test the pilot as an episode of the hit series *Trackdown*, which starred Robert Culp as a Texas Ranger who hunted bad guys. CBS wanted the new series to be as similar to *Trackdown* as possible, based on another bounty hunter, this one named Josh Randall. *Trackdown* was itself a spin-off of the western weekly series *Zane Grey Theatre*, another Four Star show. It was Culp who first suggested Steve to Elkins for the role of Josh Randall. Culp had known Steve from when they were both struggling actors living in Greenwich Village riding their motorcycles all around town. Elkins, who repped Culp and who was still eager to please Neile, jumped at the idea of using Steve in the pilot.

Four Star was headed by movie veteran Dick Powell, who had had a successful career as a youthful song-and-dance man at Warner's before gradually shifting into more dramatic parts. When Powell's film career began to wind down, he turned to television and, with three other actors having trouble finding big-screen roles, created Four Star Productions to develop scripts they could all star in and produce. Four Star quickly became one of television's powerhouse independents.[2]

"The Bounty Hunter" aired March 7, 1958, and audience reaction to Steve in the title role was so strong, he appeared as Josh Randall again in a hastily produced second episode of *Trackdown* called "The Brothers" that also did well. CBS then gave Four Star the green light to do the bounty hunter series *Wanted: Dead or Alive*.

---

[2] Four Star Television, also known as Four Star Films, Four Star Productions, and Four Star International, was created by Hollywood actors Dick Powell, David Niven, Ida Lupino, and Charles Boyer. It lasted from 1952 to 1989 and produced dozens of hit series.

Powell was happy to have a new show going into production at CBS but was hesitant about keeping Steve in the lead. Powell was concerned that Steve wasn't big or tall enough to be believable in the role of a tough-guy bounty hunter. Besides, Steve didn't know how to ride horses. However, when Powell saw some early rushes of the first episode of the series, his attitude changed. Once he experienced firsthand Steve's star power, he knew the show would be a hit. On July 24, Powell sent Steve a telegram that said "Dear Steve, Welcome to the fold. Glad you are with us. I know your show will be a big success." He arranged for Steve to be assigned a special horse, Ringo, to train on every day until he became a proficient rider, or at least *looked* like one on TV.

The only problem was, Steve hated horses. "I'd done one or two Western shows before and had just refused to get on one of those animals," Steve said. "But with this series I had no choice. They sent me over to a stable and I got up on a horse and he threw me two seconds later. I can ride pretty good now, but I don't have to like it. When a horse learns to buy martinis, I'll learn to like horses."

Powell also wanted Steve to have a trademark characteristic, something that would distinguish him from the dozen other TV cowboys currently on the airwaves, many of whom had fancy costumes and paraphernalia, like Paladin's calling cards in *Have Gun—Will Travel*, Bat Masterson's cane in *Bat Masterson*, and Lucas McCain's sawed-off Winchester in *The Rifleman*. It was decided that, besides a crushed cowboy hat that Steve had found in the prop department, Josh Randall, like Lucas McCain, would use a specially modified weapon, a model 92 Winchester .44-40 with lever action customized to a .45-70.

He wore it like a pistol, and to learn how to draw it off his hip, Steve looked up another old friend from his New York days now living big in Hollywood, Sammy Davis Jr., a great entertainer who also happened to be a pistol nut, the self-proclaimed "fastest gun in Hollywood." When not working, Davis spent hours every day practicing his quick draw and fancy turns with western-style pistols.

Because Steve's gun was not a fake prop but the real thing, it had to be listed with the LAPD as a lethal weapon. Steve could not take it out of the studio without a special permit, which he had to get in order to take it to Davis's house. Davis was happy to show Steve how to use the piece and after weeks of practice, Randall's "Mare's Leg," or "Laig" in Josh's drawl, became a natural extension of Steve's (Josh's) right arm. He was quite proud of his newfound skills and loved to brag about how proficient he had become: "Technical matters are quite beautiful to me. I love guns and gunnery, [too]. [Sammy Davis Jr.], who is a very good friend, is fast on the guns, extremely fast. I'm about the fourth fastest in California now. I can put a book of matches on the back of my hand, drop it from waist level, draw and fire two shots into it before it hits the ground."

THE FIRST half-hour episode of the series was produced on the 20th Century Fox back lot in West Los Angeles, now Century City, and on location in Arizona (the rest of the episodes were mostly shot at the Selznick Studio in Hollywood). It debuted at eight-thirty Saturday night, September 6, 1958, sandwiched perfectly for maximum ratings between the enormously popular one-hour *Perry Mason* (in the 1950s network TV began prime-time broadcasting nightly at seven-thirty) and a shipboard sitcom that anticipated *The Love Boat*, *The Gale Storm Show*, which in turn was followed by the number one show on TV, *Gunsmoke*, and opposite *Jubilee USA* on ABC and the second half of *The Perry Como Show* on NBC.

Wanted: Dead or Alive became the unlikely career changer that Steve had been so desperate to find. It was the instrument that catapulted him into the forefront of the new TV season, and his gimmicky "Mare's Leg" became the latest craze among kids who wanted one just like it. The promotional ads for the show emphasized both the gun and Steve's sulky style of acting: "Steve McQueen, as Josh Randall, bounty hunter, uses a sawed-off rifle with a trick firing mechanism for a weapon. The holster is an entirely new type especially-built for a fast draw. And the role he plays is a brand-new technique for avid western fans."

All the show's focus was on Steve and his portrayal of Josh Randall. He had brought something new and different to TV westerns: a contemporary, Method-driven style of acting that let his face and body, rather than his words, do the talking. As the syndicated TV columnist Erskine Johnson put it, "Stanislavski [*sic*] has come to the TV West." Steve liked to describe his character as "Brando on Horseback." When pressed about what he meant, Steve would only shrug and say, "When you're hot you can play it very cool."

As for Steve's diminutive size, he turned it into a character asset, a boyish toughness that made his villains bigger and meaner and therefore his conquest of them more heroic. Steve brought stature rather than height to the role of Randall, and that quality instantly clicked with viewers, as did the character's rebellious nature—he was a Confederate States of America Civil War veteran, which helped explain Randall's edge.

The series' single national sponsor, the standard practice in those days, was Viceroy cigarettes. Looking to link TV's newest hit character with its product, the advertising dubbed Josh Randall "the thinking man's cowboy" and Viceroy "the thinking man's cigarette" (although in real life Steve was a two-pack-a-day Lucky man).

The show consistently made it into the top ten and Steve's salary quickly went from $750 an episode to $100,000 a year, enormous money by 1950s TV standards. Just shy of his twenty-ninth birthday he was, as newspapers all over the country described him, America's newest "overnight star."[3]

Wanted: Dead or Alive was a top-ten hit despite reviews that were less than glowing, and all of them were focused on Steve. *Variety* called "Steve McQueen a new face in the electronic corral . . . not a huge hunk of man to set a maiden's heart fluttering." The *San Francisco Examiner* said, "The man-hunting hero, Steve McQueen, is a trigger-happy James Cagney type. In the first three minutes of the first show he shot a man in the back and broke another man's hand. Later there were two violent on-camera killings . . . for blood and thunder fans, great! For the squeamish, appalling!"

The show proved a perfect showcase not only for Steve but also for the ever-increasing number of out-of-work big-screen studio players now scrounging for anything to keep their names current and their paychecks steady. Betsy Drake, fresh from her divorce from Cary Grant (wife number three), landed on a January 1959 episode playing, according to the CBS press release, "a violent, sweet-faced, murderous dressmaker." Big-screen veterans Noah Beery Jr. and Lon Chaney Jr. appeared frequently, alongside many up-and-coming names soon to have their own successful film careers or hit TV series, including Jim Best (*The Dukes of Hazzard*), DeForest Kelley (*Star Trek*), Michael Landon (*Bonanza, Little House on the Prairie, Highway to Heaven*), Warren Oates (*The Westerner* and numerous independent feature films), and William Schallert (*The Patty Duke Show*), among dozens of others on both sides of the fame fence.

As Steve's TV star continued to rise, the machinery of Hollywood success began to take over. Until *Wanted: Dead or Alive*,

---

[3] In the Nielsen ratings for February 1959, of the top ten most-watched network programs, eight were westerns. That month, *Gunsmoke* was the number one show in the country, followed by *Wagon Train, Have Gun—Will Travel, Lucy Goes to Alaska* (special), *The Danny Thomas Show, The Rifleman, Maverick, Wyatt Earp, Zane Grey Theatre*, and, at number ten, *Wanted: Dead or Alive*.

Steve had mostly depended on Neile and her continual pressure on Elkins and Kamen to get him work. Now he no longer had to fight to get their attention, especially since Neile was no longer as ambitious as she had once been, knowing full well that dancers, even those who had some personality and could act a little, were in their prime at twenty, old at twenty-two, and ancient at twenty-seven. So she happily accepted it when the spotlight shifted from her to him, beginning with his full-time commitment to a major public relations firm, a sure sign as any that Steve's star had nowhere to go but up.

DAVID FOSTER was a graduate of the University of Southern California (USC) in the fifties, at the height of the Korean conflict, when the film school was still located in a bungalow and considered the academic slum of the university. Two days after he graduated, Foster was drafted into the army, where he became a speechwriter for General "Iron Mike" Daniels during the war, an assignment that first introduced him to the fine art of public relations. Upon his discharge, he found a job with Rogers & Cowan, a hotshot Hollywood-based firm that handled many of the largest names in film, including Gary Cooper and Cary Grant. After working there for two years, Foster approached one of the heads of the firm, Henry Rogers, and asked if there was any chance the company might one day be known as Rogers & Cowan & Foster. "He looked at me like I was a mad man and said no, but I would do very well there. So I quit. I went to work at another company where they promised me that if everything went well my name would be in lights after a year. The year ended and the owners just couldn't manage to put another name above the title, so, along with a couple of other guys, I left and we started our own company, Foster and Ingersoll, and the clients just came to us. My first client was Steve McQueen."

The functions of PR firms are many and varied. Sometimes they try to keep their clients' names out of the gossips, but more often they work to get them in. They help to build the persona that attracts fans; they maximize everything that is saleable and minimize everything that is not. Sometimes they advise actors on career moves, and sometimes, as was the case with Foster and McQueen, they also become lifelong friends.

In the beginning, Foster made sure that Steve's name was placed in major publications and always in the best possible light, and that when his credits were reviewed, *The Blob* was left off his resume. One Foster blurb, which appeared in dozens of newspapers on January 2, 1959, as *Wanted: Dead or Alive* was riding high in the ratings, had this nugget of information for Steve's fans: "Clara Bow wired Steve McQueen to tell him she's a *Wanted: Dead or Alive* fan." And when, in November 1958, Steve was cited for driving too *slow* on the Hollywood Freeway, Foster managed to get every newspaper article written about it to emphasize that the incident had nothing to do with speeding, drinking, or belligerence. Steve's car had developed engine trouble and dropped to 30 mph, and he was given a ticket, all the PR-driven stories emphasized, that was dismissed by the judge at the first hearing.

Foster's other chores for his client involved helping the regular roundup of syndicated Hollywood columnists to "explain" Steve's self-imposed, Village "hipster" language that he loved to use whenever he was interviewed, part of his "cool" image (largely a product of Foster's star development program for Steve). Some of the more colorful McQueen/Foster jargon: Steve owed his success to being married to Neile, "one of the reasons I'm in successville." As for his feelings of love for her, "She's a swinger, man. She belts me." When Neile brought Steve home to meet her mother, he later described it as "hatesville." Having a discussion was "beating gums with" someone. Foster was superb at explaining what Steve "really meant." Other times, Steve was quite adept at explaining himself.

When a reporter asked him if Steve McQueen was his real name, he exploded, "Of course! What do you want me to be called? 'Racy Danger' or something?"

IN THE midst of Steve's professionally coordinated drive to major stardom, Neile was thrilled to land a part in a new show that everyone involved hoped was bound for Broadway, *At the Grand*, a musical adaptation of *Grand Hotel*, co-starring the aging but still great Paul Muni. It was slated to play the Curran Theater in San Francisco for a six-week tryout, during which it fell quickly into disarray, with discord among the stars, director, producers. It quickly closed, effectively marking the end of Neile's professional career in show business. She would, from now on, have to be content being Mrs. Steve McQueen.

Steve, meanwhile, was raking in the bucks. During breaks in his grueling TV series shooting schedule—"I get up at 5:30 in the morning to be at the studio by 6:30. I come home at 9 [at night], dog-tired"—he managed to find time to put together a collection of cars and motorcycles that would eventually total 35 antique autos and 135 bikes worth millions.[4] Neile, meanwhile, decided to put her own considerable savings into what she felt was more practical use and bought a house for the two of them in the Hollywood Hills. "We can look down and see all of Los Angeles," Steve enthusiastically told gossip columnist Louella Parsons for an article she was writing about him at the time called "A Rebel Is Anchored." "The view is beautiful. We also killed a baby rattlesnake this morning and last week a centipede came through the wall."

"And we can see coyotes and deer practically every day," Neile added.

---

[4] He kept them his entire life. They were auctioned off after his death to satisfy a $1.5 million tax bill.

〜

DURING REHEARSALS for *At the Grand*, Neile had discovered she was expecting. According to her memoir, Steve was "ecstatic" that she was now going to be "barefoot and pregnant," corralled, as it were, while he was free to roam around Hollywood as its newest Mr. Cool. Neile made one brief appearance on *The Eddie Fisher Show* in November 1959, just before she began to show.

For Steve, it meant that he was now the family's breadwinner. No problem. He was delighted that Neile was home where she belonged, with "one in the oven." To celebrate her pregnancy Steve went out and bought another car, a black 1958 Porsche Speedster that happened to be a newer version of the same car that James Dean had been driving the day he died.

His other hobby besides his cars and motorcycles was really an old one kicked up a notch: bedding young and willing starlets and female fans. It was behavior he not only could not keep from Neile but did not want to. He made it easy for her to find out about each and every one of them via phone calls, lipstick smudges on his shirts (and pants), and hot notes in the pockets of his jeans she carefully washed along with the rest of his clothes. It was, to be sure, partly his own male peacock ego run amok, but it was also his way of testing Neile, making sure she loved him enough to accept the whole Steve McQueen package. And she always did, no matter how much it hurt.

As 1958 drew to a close, Steve's rise to stardom had perfectly positioned him to return to the big screen and finally become Hollywood's number one hotshot, not just another handsome leading man but the inheritor of the throne left vacant by the untimely death of James Dean.

In other words, the next Paul Newman.

PART TWO

Big-Screen Wonder

Chapter 5

One of the main reasons that I'm happier these days is my
wonderful wife, Neile Adams.

—STEVE MCQUEEN

L IKE EVERY OTHER ACTOR OF HIS GENERATION, STEVE placed James Dean in the same temple of worship he did Marlon Brando, but felt closer to the blond immortal because of the love he had for auto racing. Steve was so into it that he told Hal Humphrey of the *Mirror News*, "I may blow the whole thing and take a job racing cars in Europe. I'll bet you no actor has ever done that before. . . . It's a legitimate offer from a factory in Europe. . . . One of their representatives scouted me in that Santa Barbara race I won."

In truth, although he loved racing, he really was less interested in giving up his acting career than he was in putting the squeeze on Dick Powell with interviews like the one he gave Humphrey. With *Wanted: Dead or Alive* a hit and fatherhood looming, Steve wanted not just more money but, in a move that at the time must have sent palms slapping against foreheads all over Hollywood, script approval.

The reason, he told one reporter, was that the stories he was being forced to act out were not "compatible" with the character of Josh Randall. "I remember one script which had three big guys in a saloon telling me to get out of town. Believe me, if you had seen these guys, you'd know there was only one thing for me to do—go! But in this script I knocked all three of 'em down. Is that silly?"

The answer was yes, certainly, as were most scripts for TV series that had to grind out a new show every week, but rarely did any small-screen star demand script approval over this junk. But there were other reasons Steve wanted to push Powell's buttons. Steve had been offered a major role in a feature film that co-starred one of the biggest names in show business, Frank Sinatra, and despite a full TV shooting schedule of thirty-nine new episodes, the norm at the time, Steve dearly wanted to take it. Elkins had already managed to get Powell not only to agree to a salary increase but to let Steve do a feature if the right one came along. Now that one had, Powell was still reluctant to let Steve make it, fearing it would take away his aura as the mysterious bounty hunter. Elkins had anticipated that and made sure Steve's being allowed to make this movie was written specifically into the new contract. Once Steve finished filming the final scenes for the first season of *Wanted: Dead or Alive*, he was free to make the movie, as long as he could shoot it during the show's twelve-week seasonal production break that began March 1.[1]

FILMING ON *Never So Few* (the film's original, much inferior working title was *Sacred and Profane*) began in March 1959. The movie was based on Tom Chamales's 1957 novel about the World

---

[1] The terms of the deal between MGM and Canterbury Productions/Sol Siegel and Four Star stipulated that if production on the film ran into the production time of *Wanted: Dead or Alive*, Steve would be released three days every week from *Never So Few*, and if the show had to pay overtime to its crew for any added weekend days, Steve would have to personally cover the costs. Steve then took out a $700-a-week insurance policy with Lloyd's of London to protect himself in the event he became liable for those costs. To get that policy, Steve had to agree not to race his Porsche Spyder anywhere for the duration of the film.

War II battle that took place in the India-Burma-China the-ater to keep open the crucial Burma supply trail despite Japan's all-out offensive to take it over. Most of the fighting was done by Burmese guerrillas, supervised and supported by a small contin-gent of American troops led by a tough-as-nails captain, Tom C. Reynolds, played by Sinatra.

Throughout, Reynolds, who continually refers to the Japanese and the Chinese as "gooks," "Nips," "Japs," and "lice," turns into a one-man American militia when, two-thirds of the way through the film, he and his men are ordered to destroy a Japanese airfield near the Chinese border. Although undermanned, they succeed, but on the way back they are attacked by a renegade force of Chi-nese soldiers opposed to both the Japanese occupation and Chiang Kai-shek's republic. They support Mao Tse-tung, further com-plicating the already complicated situation. After wiping out the renegades, Reynolds finds evidence that these same insurgents had killed dozens of American soldiers. Upon his return to headquar-ters, he is brought before an American general and is personally lauded for his actions by, of all people, Chiang Kai-shek.

In the midst of seemingly out of nowhere comes Carla Vesari (Gina Lollobrigida), kept in splendor by older Eurotrash suavo Nikko Regas (Paul Henreid), wealthy, sophisticated, wise, and ulti-mately unable to keep her from the lecherous advances of Reyn-olds. Vesari angrily rebuffs Reynolds for half the movie before letting him see her nude while taking a bubble bath, which turns him into a salivating bulldog, at which point she falls inexplicably and completely in love with him.

From then on, she continually pops up in the most unlikely of places on or near the front lines, almost always in sleeveless night-gowns, for the sole purpose of being near Reynolds. At one point he explains to her that he is a war lover first and foremost and could never live a normal married life. However, after Reynolds is fully pardoned for killing the insurgents by the Chinese government, in the last scene of the film we see him with Carla; they have just been married and she is setting him straight on what their life together is going to be like. She has somehow successfully domesticated him, and, quite bewilderingly, turned him from that bulldog into a whipped pussycat, at which point the film mercifully ends.

Besides its sociological and historical aspects, the film, made as the Vietnam conflict was just beginning to percolate in the United States and public sentiment had not yet shifted into the polarizing mind-set of the next decade, failed most at what it was originally intended to be, a non-musical vehicle to show off Frank Sinatra's acting chops. Still chasing his 1953 Oscar-winning performance in Fred Zinnemann's gripping *From Here to Eternity*, and on the lookout for a role that could revive his dramatic legitimacy after an uneven series of performances (Otto Preminger's 1956 *The Man with the Golden Arm* the best, Stanley Kramer's 1957 *The Pride and the Passion* the worst), Sinatra had purchased the film rights to *Never So Few* prior to the book's publication. Woefully miscasting himself as a militant guerrilla warrior, he looks especially scrawny on-screen, with an unexplained jungle goatee. The rest of the film seems to be little more than a vehicle for Sinatra's so-called Rat Pack, with Peter Lawford in an otherwise meaningless role.

Another member of Sinatra's clan, Sammy Davis Jr., was supposed to play the role of Corporal Ringa, but shortly before the film was to begin production, during an interview Davis gave to Jack Eigen on a Chicago radio talk show, he broke a cardinal Sinatra rule and openly criticized him. "Talent is not an excuse for bad manners. . . . I love Frank, but there are many things he does that there is no excuse for. . . . I don't care if you are the most talented person in the world. It does not give you a right to step on people and treat them rotten. This is what he does occasionally."

Those comments cost Davis the role of Ringa and the $75,000 paycheck that came with it. According to Lawford, who was well aware of Sinatra's vindictive side, "That was it for Sammy. Frank called him 'a dirty nigger bastard' and wrote him out of the film."

Davis's agent happened to be Hilly Elkins, and once it became clear Sinatra was not going to forgive Davis, Elkins went to the film's director, John Sturges, and suggested Steve for the part. "Earlier that year," recalled Robert E. Relyea, Sturges's first assistant director on the film, "Stan Kamen, John Sturges' agent at the William Morris Agency, asked the director to look at a television show featuring a young actor Kamen was also representing. Sturges had a great eye for new talent, and after watching *Wanted: Dead or Alive*, he asked Stan to bring the young man in. Within minutes of meeting him, Sturges knew Steve McQueen would be a star. So when Sinatra canned Sammy Davis, Jr., Sturges brought in McQueen."

Prior to *Never So Few*, Sturges had made several mildly successful, prosaic mid-1950s movies that celebrated machismo and stamina as moral correlatives to freedom and democracy (though without the poetic depth of John Ford or the expansive vision of Raoul Walsh), most notably 1955's *Bad Day at Black Rock*, 1957's *Gunfight at the O.K. Corral*, 1958's *The Old Man and the Sea*, and 1959's *Last Train from Gun Hill*, the latter released earlier the same year as *Never So Few*. Sturges preferred rugged old-school leading men such as Spencer Tracy, Robert Ryan, Kirk Douglas, and Burt Lancaster. When Elkins first introduced him to Steve, Sturges was immediately struck by the young actor's strong masculine presence and great-looking all-American face, which fit the mold of a typical Sturges hero. He was, in fact, far more suited, both physically and in terms of his youth, to play Ringa than Davis was, but the final decision, as always, was Sinatra's. Fortunately, Sinatra liked Steve and okayed his replacing Davis—for $25,000.

Elkins didn't protest the salary differential, understanding that Davis was, at the time, a much bigger star than Steve. After three low-budget independent features that had done nothing for his career, this was his first major studio production, and it could be the big-screen career changer Steve had been searching for.

As a welcoming gesture, Sinatra and the film's producer, Sol C. Siegel, invited Steve and a very pregnant Neile to an April 14 cocktail reception to be held in the MGM Executive Dining Room "honoring Miss Gina Lollobrigida on her arrival at MGM Studios for her first Hollywood Motion Picture, *Never So Few.*" Not long after, when asked his opinion of Sinatra, Steve told a reporter, "I kind of dig him . . . he's a great talent. When I first met him recently he said to me, 'You gas me, pal.' I replied, 'That's funny. You gas me, too.'"

Although the publicity department touted the film's extensive on-location filming in Burma, less than 10 percent was actually shot there. Another 40 percent was done in Ceylon, Thailand, and Hawaii, with the rest filmed on MGM's expansive Culver City back lot, accounting for much of the picture's artificial-green-jungle look. During the MGM shoots, Foster introduced Steve to Hedda Hopper. Hopper was one of the last surviving Hollywood gossip columnists, who in the studio era's heyday had been one of the almighty arbiters of manufactured stardom. Like her biggest competitor, Louella Parsons, Hopper had made a name for herself as a gunslinger for the studios, patting "good" stars on the head when they behaved well and punishing "bad" stars when their studio wanted to rein them in, usually during a contract dispute or when trying to control political and/or sexual mavericks.

Through her syndicated column, Hopper's career-breaking power became so great she dubbed the palatial digs she bought with her considerable earnings "The House That Fear Built." (It has always been thought that the J. J. Hunsecker role Burt Lancaster played in Alexander Mackendrick's piercing *Sweet Smell of Success* was an amalgam of Parsons, Hopper, Walter Winchell, and Ed Sullivan, all of whom wielded considerable power and influence in Hollywood during the 1940s and '50s.) Foster warned Steve in advance to be on his best behavior with Hopper.

That April, for a Sunday newspaper feature that would be syndicated nationally in June following the completion of principal shooting on *Never So Few*, Hopper invited Steve and Neile to the Fear Palace. Neile, too big now to fit into the Porsche Spyder, let Steve have it for the night and she drove to the house in a Ford Mustang convertible. She arrived before her husband. In a story that may be apocryphal, when he arrived, Steve flashed his great smile at Hopper, who personally went to the door to meet him, and asked her in a whisper—so that Neile, who was already inside, couldn't hear him—if she wanted to screw. Supposedly Hopper, who was known to be quite vain, was utterly charmed by this.

During the interview, Steve told Hopper: "I could never find a level with society. I came from poor people who worked hard to stay alive. I got into situations I wasn't bright about. I didn't have any concept of what I was like, so I existed in it, so I got into trouble. It was never anything serious, really—just hassles. The guys I was living with were all goofing off. Now I have a beautiful wife. I'm putting money into stock and bonds, own my own home, and am carving myself a career. I'm going to toe the line from now on."

Although almost none of it was true—the only stocks and bonds Steve had were his cars and motorcycles, and the home had been purchased by Neile—that day Hopper became an enthusiastic lifelong supporter of Steve and his career. When her piece on him came out, it read more like a gushing love letter than a comprehensive profile. Steve knew how to turn on the charm when it benefited him.

During filming, Sinatra became increasingly fond of Steve, and a bit envious of his seemingly effortless acting abilities. Sinatra huffed and puffed his way through his scenes, trying whenever he could to telegraph his feelings to the audiences—"indicating" his emotions, Method actors would say—rather than organically connecting to the character and letting the emotional results come from that connection. Sinatra's idea of projecting toughness in the film was talking tough (which actually had the opposite effect, making his character seem a bit of an empty barrel) and in his jungle love scenes he acted like he was trying to pick up Lollobrigida at the bar at Jilly's.

Sinatra always liked "real men" and expressed his affection for Steve in typical boys-will-be-boys fashion. Sometimes on set he would sneak up behind McQueen and set off a firecracker near Steve's ass, or stick a dud in his gun belt, light it, and wait for the fun to begin. The first couple of times Sinatra did it, Steve jumped like a scared rabbit, which sent Sinatra into convulsions. Soon enough, though, Steve taught himself not to jump at the cracker sounds, and that made Sinatra even more envious of him. And to get even, one time Steve grabbed one of the prop machine guns, called out Sinatra's name, and when he turned around, shot a round of blanks directly at him. Sinatra stared at Steve for several seconds, during which the entire set went quiet. Steve stared back, unblinking. "Everybody was watching Frank to see what he'd do. He had a real bad temper, and I guess they all figured we were gonna end in a punch-out. I wasn't sure myself, as we stared at each other. Then he just started laughing and it was all over. After, we got along just fine . . . you back down to a guy like Sinatra, he never respects you." According to Steve, it was the turning point of their relationship. After that, "Frank Sinatra kept saying, 'Give the close-up to Steve.' He went out of his way to give me the breaks. 'It's your picture, kid.'"

Only it wasn't. *Never So Few* didn't turn Steve into a star or compartmentalize his career the way it did for another member of the cast, Charles Bronson, whose portrayal in the picture of a defensive tough-guy Native American became the character template for much of the rest of his highly successful career. It did, however, introduce Steve to a larger audience who liked what they saw, even if they didn't exactly know who he was. So did Sinatra, who now wanted to make Steve a card-carrying member of the Rat Pack. Steve turned him down, claiming he was a family man now and that had to be his first priority.

On June 5, Neile had given birth to a beautiful baby girl they named Terry Leslie. Steve just made it home in time that day from the MGM soundstage to take her to the hospital.

Fatherhood triggered a sudden desire in Steve to find out what had become of his own father. He soon discovered that Terrence "Bill" McQueen's last known whereabouts were in Los Angeles, somewhere in the Silverlake section, not very far from Hollywood. Like a detective in a movie thriller, Steve went to the places where his father most likely would have been known, the bars and pool halls. Sure enough, someone recognized the name and told Steve she did indeed know a Bill McQueen. That same night Steve drove to Echo Park, to a nondescript apartment building, where an elderly woman who described herself as Bill's "lady friend" told him that he had recently passed, having suffered a fatal heart attack. At the end of this visit, she gave Steve a silver lighter that bore the initials WMcQ. It had belonged to Bill and she thought Steve would like to have it, along with a photograph of his father as a young man, in which he bore a remarkable likeness to Steve. She told him that his father had also been a marine and had worked for the Flying Tigers, stationed in China during World War II.

It was the last time Steve ever talked about Bill.

AT THE party following the film's first preview in December, held in New York City, Sinatra came up to Steve, slapped him on the back, and told him, "It's all yours, kid!" Later that night, Sinatra and Steve threw a couple of live firecrackers out of Steve's hotel window.

Never So Few was originally planned as a summer release but officially opened December 7, 1959, and received generally good reviews, the best going to Steve. The *Hollywood Reporter,* an influential industry publication read by everyone in the business, didn't think much of the rest of the film but noted that it "provides a catapult to stardom for Steve McQueen, hitherto known principally as a television actor." Bosley Crowther, the *New York Times* film critic at the time, was far less kind to both the film and Steve: "It looks as though Frank Sinatra has been tapped to succeed Errol Flynn as the most fantastically romantic presentation of the warrior breed on screen. . . . And John Sturges has directed it for kicks. Those who will get them are the youngsters who can be lightly carried away by the juvenile brashness of Mr. Sinatra, and by the swashbuckling antics of his pals, played almost beyond comprehension by Richard Johnson, Peter Lawford, and Steve McQueen." On the other hand, Paul V. Beckley, writing in what was then one of the other New York broadsheets, the *New York Herald Tribune*, liked Steve's performance more than he did the film: "Steve McQueen looks good as a brash, casual G.I. He possesses that combination of smooth-rough charm that suggests star possibilities."

Commercially the film didn't do much at the box office and is not remembered as either classic Sinatra or essential McQueen, but it did mark the auspicious start of the ongoing professional relationship between John Sturges and Steve.

Even before the film opened, Sinatra had been trying to get a film made called *The Execution of Private Slovik*, about the only American soldier executed for treason during World War II, and now he wanted Steve to play Slovik. However, the project fell through even as Steve was trying to decide whether or not to do it; no studio would touch the subject, and Sinatra finally turned to something that fit more easily into his comfort zone, the Rat Pack wet dream *Ocean's Eleven*, about a bunch of aging hipsters attempting to simultaneously rob five of Las Vegas's biggest casinos.[2]

---

[2] *The Execution of Private Slovik* was eventually made into a 1973 TV movie, starring Martin Sheen in the title role. Sinatra had nothing to do with the project. When he first announced his intention to make the movie, both he and it were met with outrage in Hollywood, led by both Hedda Hopper and Louella Parsons. At the time, Sinatra was actively involved in JFK's run for president and was heavily pressured by Joe Kennedy to drop the project, which he did.

Sinatra wanted Steve for that film as well, and this time Steve wanted to do it, until Hopper heard about it and summoned him to her home for dinner and a career summit. She warned him that he would be throwing his career away if he became one of Sinatra's Rat Pack flunkies. Steve took her advice and turned Sinatra down, using his second-year, more prohibitive contract with CBS for *Wanted: Dead or Alive* as the reason he had to bow out.[3] Sinatra let it rest there, but never again asked Steve to appear with him on film.

THE RATINGS success of the first season of *Wanted: Dead or Alive* gave Steve more power and control on the set, and to those who had to work with him, both in front of the camera and behind it, it made him a royal pain in the ass. Although he had absolutely no experience in screen or television writing and had had no hand in the first season's scripts, he now demanded rewrites—as his new contract allowed—with scenes in which he was to have more dialogue and fewer shootouts. The demands were made with a belligerence that previously no one had seen from him. He was not alone in complaining about the quality of shows; most sitcom and western stars routinely complained about everything from their salaries to their co-stars. What made Steve different and gave him an added boost was that between seasons he had made the transition to A movies, and knew that he now had real power. Ironically, while he was never one to trust authority, once he tasted it he became exacting and controlling, and as a result, gained a reputation for being difficult.

Nonetheless, high ratings meant bigger budgets per episode and more characters. Several up-and-coming actors willingly did

---

[3] The network actually did prevent him from appearing in at least one other big-screen movie that year, Blake Edwards's 1961 adaptation of Truman Capote's novella *Breakfast at Tiffany's*. The male lead, the aspiring writer who falls in love with Holly Golightly, instead went to George Peppard.

guest shots, some returning in different roles from the first sea-son, among them tall, rugged-looking James Coburn, whom Steve especially liked. Coburn had appeared in dozens of live and filmed TV shows and one movie, Budd Boetticher's 1959 *Ride Lonesome*, a star vehicle for perennial Hollywood cowboy actor Randolph Scott that co-starred future TV *Bonanza* star Pernell Roberts. Coburn's good looks and his friendship with Roberts resulted in three guest shots on *Bonanza*, after which he became a guest staple of TV west-erns. From *Bonanza* he went to *Rawhide* with Clint Eastwood, then two *Laramie*s, five *Klondike*s, two *Lawmen*, two *Zane Grey Theatre*s, four *Death Valley Days*, and finally, three *Wanted: Dead or Alive*s. To pass the time between setups on *Wanted*, Coburn and Steve would retire to his trailer and get stoned.

WHILE FILMING the second-season episodes, despite turning down Sinatra, Steve worked on several other projects, although as his contract stipulated, no feature films. In the late fall of 1959, just before *Never So Few* opened, Foster hit a home run when he arranged for Steve and Neile to be invited to join Bob Hope's annual Christmas show to entertain the troops in Alaska (although much of it was actually shot at the Air Force Academy in Colorado). When Steve asked for CBS's permission to do it, even though it cut into the series' production time, which would inevitably mean overtime paychecks to virtually everyone who worked on it, the network, recognizing the PR value in it, said yes. That opened the floodgates. He did a guest spot on Perry Como's musical hour, at the time one of the highest-rated shows on NBC. And then it was on to an episode of *Alfred Hitchcock Presents*, on CBS.

"Man from the South," which originally aired January 3, 1960, was based on a short story by Roald Dahl and adapted by John Adams into a twenty-two-minute teleplay set in Las Vegas about a bet between Gambler (Steve) and Carlos (the venerable Peter Lorre) that Gambler can't light his cigarette lighter ten times in a row. If he does, he will win Carlos's brand-new car. If he doesn't, Carlos will chop off one of Gambler's pinky fingers. Gambler easily lights his lighter seven times, and then Carlos's wife (Katherine Squire) intervenes. It seems she is well aware of her husband's "games." What happened with the Gambler's last three tries made the show memorably Hitchcock (although Hitchcock did not direct this episode, veteran Hitchcock actor and producer Norman Lloyd did). Neile played the smaller part of a character called Woman, who is a witness to the action of the bet, and whose face is used mostly for reaction shots.

It is difficult to pinpoint the exact moment in Steve and Neile's marriage when they officially became players in a real-life version of *A Star Is Born*. In the McQueens' case, his star turn compared with her bit part in "Man from the South" was probably it.

EARLY IN March 1960, a few weeks shy of Steve's thirtieth birthday, with production winding down on the second-season episodes of *Wanted: Dead or Alive*, independent feature film producers the Mirisch brothers offered John Sturges the chance to remake Akira Kurosawa's 1954 Japanese classic, *The Seven Samurai*, as an American western for United Artists. The new version, to be called *The Magnificent Seven*, was, like so many 1950s westerns, something of a tribute to the dying breed of gunfighters-for-hire of the Old West (as well as its ironic real-life counterpart, the dying breed of big-screen Hollywood studio westerns that were being replaced by those on the small screen, like *Wanted: Dead or Alive*). As director John Carpenter put it, "It was the beginning of the end of the great American westerns. In 1959 you had [Howard Hawks's] *Rio Bravo*. In 1960 you had *The Magnificent Seven*. Literally four or five years later you had Sergio Leone coming on the scene with his Clint Eastwood 'spaghetti westerns' that were the death knell of the [Hollywood] western by transforming it into something else. *The Magnificent Seven* was kind of the last hurrah."

Yul Brynner claimed to have actually been the first to want to remake Kurosawa's classic samurai film as a vehicle for himself but had been beaten to the draw by independent producer Lou Morheim, who had acquired the rights to the film before Brynner with the intention of making it with the fiery Anthony Quinn. However, by the time Walter Bernstein was assigned to write the screenplay, Quinn was out and Brynner was back in as the star.

Bernstein, who had been blacklisted for much of the fifties, wrote a script for Brynner that was a parable reflecting the dying days of the studio system and his own feelings of being branded an "outlaw" because of his political views. In *The Magnificent Seven*, there are good outlaws and bad outlaws; the bad outlaws have all the power, while the good outlaws are heroic veterans of the Civil War who now have to scrounge for their living. Chris Adams (Brynner) is older than the others, a kind of wise old man closer to Kurosawa's original vision.

By the time Bernstein finished his draft, the rights to *The Magnificent Seven* had passed from Morheim to independent producers Walter, Marvin, and Harold Mirisch, who had a production deal with United Artists at the time, one of the few independent studio/ distribution houses in Hollywood.

In 1959, UA, which was struggling, cut a multiple-picture deal with the Mirisch brothers in the hopes they could help revitalize the company. Walter Mirisch happened to have been an ardent fan of Kurosawa from the time he had first seen *The Seven Samurai* (which, interestingly, was originally released in America as *The Magnificent Seven*), and when the chance came along to get the rights away from Morheim, he jumped at it.

To play the lead gunfighter, Mirisch retained an immensely

satisfied Brynner, even though he was about to marry his fiancée, Doris (which he insisted on doing on the set during a break in the film). Mirisch then hired John Sturges, whose *Bad Day at Black Rock* and *Gunfight at the OK Corral* had convinced Mirisch that Sturges was perfect for *The Magnificent Seven*, to direct. Sturges, in turn, wanted Steve McQueen to be one of the film's "seven."

THE ONLY problem was, CBS would still not let Steve make any features (especially westerns), and it appeared that he would have to pass on the film, as he had already done with *Breakfast at Tiffany's*. Steve threw a fit and called on Hilly Elkins to intervene.

Elkins wasted no time in getting Dick Powell to agree to a sit-down meeting. Powell, however, was having none of it. He had a hit TV series and a star that he had created, and wasn't about to give him away to the movies. No matter how Elkins tried, Powell would not budge. Later that day, Elkins called Steve and told him, calmly, to have "a little accident."

Steve understood what Elkins meant. After a scheduled promotional stop for *Wanted: Dead or Alive* in Hartford, Connecticut, Steve took Neile up to Boston for a quick holiday in his studio-supplied rented Cadillac. According to Elkins, "He promptly took his rented Cadillac and ran it into the Bank of Boston and came out of it with whiplash, which everybody gets when hitting something hard when driving. Most Hollywood insiders thought it was a staged act even with Steve's neck in a brace. He was a racing car driver. He knew exactly what he was doing and understood what I was asking him to do. The car had a few dents in it."

When Steve returned to Los Angeles, his neck was indeed swathed in a stiff white brace. Powell was not amused. He knew Steve was faking, using his "injury" to hold up production on the series until he received the okay to star in *The Magnificent*

Seven. He had to settle this before Steve's contract expired. An industry-wide strike was about to hit Hollywood and shut down any new projects (including negotiations on Steve's new contract for another season on the series) but not affect any existing contracts or any film already in production. Powell tipped over his king and allowed Steve to make the movie.[4]

Elkins, however, wanted more. "Not only did Powell let him do the picture, but I also demanded they double Steve's salary before he would return to the series." Infuriated, but fighting against the strike clock, Powell agreed to that as well. The next day Steve signed on to play the part of Vin, one of the other six behind Brynner, who would only allow lesser-name actors to appear in the film with him.

Sturges, meanwhile, wanted a whole new script written and suggested Walter Newman for the job. Newman's previous screen credits included Billy Wilder's *Ace in the Hole*, written with Lesser Samuels and Billy Wilder, and which had been nominated for a Best Screenplay Oscar. Newman had also written the first episode of the enormously popular TV western *Gunsmoke*. The Mirisches promptly hired him.[5]

Sturges wanted something else as well—sole producing credit on the movie. That ignited a lawsuit between Sturges and Morheim. Walter Mirisch then approached Morheim and asked what it would take to make him and his lawsuit go away. According to

---

[4] This was the first strike in SAG history and it had to do with the issue of residuals. Only those contracts that were signed before March 7, the strike deadline, were considered valid (the Writers Guild was already on strike for a month and pressuring SAG members to go out as well, to strengthen the industry's union movement). Hence, Powell needed to renegotiate and sign Steve's contract before the strike, and Sturges needed to get his film cast and into production to beat the deadline as well.

[5] Walter Newman, angry over rewrites to his version of the script, would later insist on having his name removed from the credits.

Morheim, money was paid, he agreed to change his credit to associate producer, and he had no involvement in the making of the film. Then Anthony Quinn sued Brynner and UA for $650,000, claiming he had been promised the leading role, but he lost in court.

Sturges then set about casting the rest of the film. He had been impressed with Charles Bronson's work on *Never So Few* and signed him on, as well as Brad Dexter, who had been in Sturges's *Last Train from Gun Hill*. Sturges cast Horst Buchholz, a German film star still largely unknown in America, as Chico, a move that upset Yul Brynner, who didn't want another European "exotic" in the picture. As a result, Brynner kept his distance from Buchholz during the entire production. Another surprise move by Sturges was casting Eli Wallach, who at this point had made only a handful of films, most notably Kazan's 1956 *Baby Doll*, and was considered primarily a New York stage actor, for the key role of the Mexican outlaw leader Calvera.

To this day Wallach claims to be "mystified" by the choice, but nonetheless threw himself into the role. "In all the cowboy pictures I saw as a boy, the bandits held up trains, robbed banks, stole cattle, but no one ever knew what they did with the money. That was the key I needed to create my character; I would be a dandy spendthrift. I asked Sturges and he smilingly agreed, if I could have a beautiful horse, a silver-studded saddle, red silk shirts, silver rings on all my fingers and two gold caps for my teeth." To add a level of depth to Calvera, and also to save some money, according to Sturges's assistant director, Bob Relyea, the production went into the hills of Mexico and hired forty real bandits to play Calvera's gang. None of them spoke English or knew anything about making movies. Relyea remembered that "Eli became as attached to the bandits as they were to him. Eli's wife, Anne Jackson, accompanied him to the set everyday. If she moved ten feet, here were several bandits there to make sure she had a clean chair and adequate shade. On Sundays when we weren't shooting, the bandits came to Cuernavaca early in the morning to take Eli and Anne on all-day adventures. . . . As Eli correctly pointed out, he was the only American working on *The Magnificent Seven* who truly saw Mexico."

Robert Vaughn, who had just been nominated for an Academy Award for his supporting role in Vincent Sherman's *The Young Philadelphians*, a star vehicle for Paul Newman, was also being considered for a role. Sturges liked his performance in that film as an intelligent if bent sophisticate and wanted him to bring those same qualities to *The Magnificent Seven*, but had no definite part in mind. It wasn't until after the film began shooting that Sturges cast Vaughn in the role of Lee, a suave outlaw on the run who signs on with the seven, figuring Mexico is as good a place as any to hide from the law.

Sturges asked Vaughn if he knew of any other actors who might be right for a part in the film, someone who was tall and handsome and didn't talk a lot, like Gary Cooper. "After that, I ran into Jimmy Coburn," Vaughn later recalled, "and I told him they were casting for *The Magnificent Seven* and he should try out for it. Jimmy and I were old friends from school." They had, in fact, both attended Los Angeles City College, generally acknowledged at the time as the best off-studio training ground for actors (Clint Eastwood also went there), and when Jimmy found out that Steve was going to be in it, he figured he had a decent shot, especially since Sturges was running out of time before the big union stoppage.

According to Coburn, "The film had to be cast by that Saturday night because of the impending strike. I went to see John and he told me there was only one of the seven that had not yet been cast, Britt, the knife-wielding killer, the counterpart for *The Seven Samurai*'s greatest swordsman in Japan. Well, I said to John, that's the part I want to play. 'I'll let you know,' he said, and I went home, thinking I had a chance. At 3:30, Sturges called and told me, 'Okay, come on over and pick up your knives!' It was like Christmas, Valentine's Day, and my birthday all rolled into one."

Sturges had managed to complete his casting a week before the March 7 strike deadline. Production began March 1, 1960, in Cuernavaca, Mexico, where much of the entire film was shot on two main sets—the border town at the beginning of the film and the Mexican village where most of the subsequent action takes place. Both were constructed on the outskirts of Cuernavaca.

Sturges then faced another and more difficult obstacle: the government of Mexico. While it allowed the film to be made because of the enormous amount of money the production would spend in the country, there were still a lot of bad feelings that lingered from another American film shot in Mexico, Robert Aldrich's 1954 *Vera Cruz*. Upon its release the Mexican government felt the film had portrayed Mexicans in a bad light. To try to smooth things over, Sturges hired as many locals as he could afford to work as extras and on the crew, and then had to walk a fine line with the Mexican censors, who did not want the Mexican peasants terrorized by Calvera to appear to be unable to fight for themselves. This resulted in a key change from the original Kurosawa film: in *The Seven Samurai* the village hires the fighters, while in *The Magnificent Seven* they intend to buy guns and fight themselves, until Adams (Brynner) convinces them to let him and his boys do the job for them. It is a subtle but important plot shift that ultimately defines the difference in the two movies' structures.

However, Sturges's biggest problem was his bickering cast members. According to Elkins, bad chemistry between Brynner and Steve continually threatened to shut down production. "The film was important because it popped Steve heavily into the limelight. The problem was the rest of the cast was a unit, all friends, and then there was Yul Brynner, who was very busy being a star and Steve knew what he was up against."

Not just Steve, but all the newer, less well-known faces resented Brynner's black limo and separate trailer, and broke up into their own groups—Steve, Vaughn, Buchholz, and Coburn; Brynner and Dexter; and, always the loner, Bronson, who remained aloof. (On the last day of shooting there was a big wrap party and the Mexican casting director did impressions of the American actors. Everyone fell down laughing except Bronson, who angrily stormed out, slamming the door behind him.)

On-screen, everyone was determined to be noticed. But the worst of it, as Elkins confirmed, was between Steve and Brynner. According to Robert Relyea, the assistant director on the film, the scene stealing began with the very first sequence that was shot— the seven gunmen riding in single file across a narrow creek. "We only had three or four rehearsals, with the men just riding and looking about from side to side, but when film was going through the camera, Steve on horseback [who was directly behind Brynner in the formation] swung out of the saddle with his hat, scooped up water from the stream and doused himself. Next I think was Charlie Bronson who unbuttoned his shirt, stretched and turned his bandana around, and then Brad Dexter who did three acts of *Hamlet*. Poor Yul didn't know what was going on behind him while everybody was trying to stake their ground."

In his memoir, Robert Vaughn recalled the incident a little differently. "In one scene, several of us, including Yul and Steve, were sitting on our horses next to a stream and debating our strategy for retaking the village from the *banditos*. In the midst of the scene, Brynner suddenly doffed his black Stetson, revealing his famous bald pate glistening in the afternoon sun.

"Between takes, McQueen drew me aside. 'Did you see what that bastard Brynner did?' he hissed. He couldn't take this act of scene stealing lying down. A few minutes later, we shot another take. Once again, Brynner doffed his hat. This time, McQueen took off *his* hat, leaned way over from his perch in the saddle, lowered his hat into the stream and filled it with water. Then, without missing a beat, he replaced it on his head. Water cascaded down his head and shoulders, soaking him thoroughly. He looked like a fool, but at least no one was looking at Yul Brynner."

More than the others, throughout the entire production, during scenes Steve continued to wave hats, play with his gun, and do everything he could to take the audience's eyes off Brynner, who was known to have a very short fuse. He grew increasingly frustrated and noticeably angry over what he considered to be Steve's obstinate disrespect. Inevitably it came to a head between the two. According to Dexter, who witnessed the incident, after Steve took his hat off while he was in the background of a three-shot that featured Brynner in the forefront, "Brynner turned around and said to Steve, 'Do this one more time, and in any scene you have all I have to do is take my hat off and you won't be seen anymore.'"

Steve remembered the tension between him and Brynner this way: "No, we didn't get along. Listen, I'm a pretty fast draw. I'm a farm boy, man, I grew up around horses and guns. I know how to handle them. When we were making *The Magnificent Seven* Brynner came up to me one day in front of a lot of people and grabbed me by the shoulder. He was mad about something—I don't know what. He doesn't ride well and he knows nothing about guns so maybe he thought I represented a threat. I was in my element. He wasn't. Anyway, I don't like people pawing me. 'Take your hands off me,' I said. What had I got to lose from a little fight? I've got a busted nose and teeth missing and stitches in my lips and I'm deaf in the right ear. . . . When you work in a scene with Yul you're supposed to stand perfectly still ten feet away. Well, I don't work that way. So I protected myself."

Off the set, Steve and Vaughn became close friends, and on Good Friday 1960, when all work had to be shut down because of the strictness of the Catholic-dominated Mexican government, the two of them, at Brad Dexter's invitation, decided to visit what Dexter told them was "one of the finest brothels in North America." Steve was all for it; he had loved hookers before he was married and saw no reason why he shouldn't love them now. When they arrived they were greeted by a blond madam who treated the three movie actors like foreign dignitaries. They all quickly got drunk on margaritas; Brad disappeared with two girls, and Steve and Vaughn shared seven others, together in one silken-pillowed room.

At around midnight, Vaughn reminded Steve they had to film the next day. "I said to Steve, let's pay our bill and get out of here," Vaughn later recalled. "I hadn't yet heard about Steve's famous habit of *not* carrying any money. He replied, 'Hey, man, could you loan me some *dinero?*'" The bill came to something like seven hundred dollars. They split up and Vaughn managed to get back to the hotel, and didn't see Steve again until he showed up the next morning forty-five minutes late for his first scene, badly hungover. He told Vaughn not to worry, he had talked his way out of the situation. Vaughn did not pursue the matter.[6]

The Magnificent Seven, shot in Panavision, opened with great fanfare in America on October 23, 1960, but surprisingly little business. Put into general release rather than road-show distribution—reserved seats for two-a-day screenings—the film was a box office dud until it opened in Europe, where it became a pop sensation. It then made its way back to the States and became one of the highest-grossing films of the year. However, because

---

[6] According to Relyea, they weren't the only bad boys on the set. "Being a newlywed didn't stop Yul from being Yul. On a few occasions during the shoot, Yul summoned the beautiful young Mexican actress, Rosenda Monteros, to his trailer after Doris drove off in their Cadillac."

of its unusually high budget, $3 million, it didn't earn its money back in its initial theatrical release.[7]

But its cultural impact was huge, beginning with Elmer Bernstein's thrilling, hoof-pounding, string-dominated score (it was nominated for an Oscar but lost to Ernest Gold's score for Otto Preminger's *Exodus*; it was the only Oscar nomination *The Magnificent Seven* received). Its rousing melody line later became the Marlboro theme in television commercials that ran for years, and also anticipated Ennio Morricone's sweeping musical scores for Sergio Leone's groundbreaking spaghetti westerns of the second half of the decade. Thirty-three years later, when asked what he thought the most recognizable piece of music he had written was, Bernstein said, "I was in Spain last year doing some concerts near Barcelona. We were in this tiny town. I sat down at a little sidewalk café. There was a mechanical horse that kids like to ride, you put a quarter in. All of the sudden it starts to play *The Magnificent Seven!*"

The film spawned three mediocre sequels inspired as much by Leone's 1964 *A Fistful of Dollars*, a remake of yet another Kurosawa film (*Yojimbo*), as the original *The Magnificent Seven:* Burt Kennedy's 1966 *Return of the Seven*, with Yul Brynner the only returning cast member from the original; Paul Wendkos's 1969 *Guns of the Magnificent Seven*, and 1972's *Magnificent Seven Ride.* There was also a moderately successful TV series that ran for two seasons (twenty-three episodes) on CBS. It also was responsible for countless "ensemble" action movies, most notable among them Robert Aldrich's 1967 *The Dirty Dozen*, J. Lee Thompson's 1961 *The Guns of Navarone*, and, two years later, Sturges's own *The*

---

[7] It finished out of the twenty top-grossing movies of the year. The top-grossing film of 1960 was Ken Annakin's *Swiss Family Robinson* (Disney Studios), which took in $20,178,000. Exact figures for *The Magnificent Seven* were not made available.

Great Escape, which brought back many of the same cast members of *The Magnificent Seven*, including Steve, Bronson, and Coburn. The film's lasting popularity is such that to this day, only Michael Curtiz's 1942 *Casablanca* is screened on TV more often than *The Magnificent Seven*.

For Brynner, the film marked the last of his "big" movies, which had begun with his Oscar-winning appearance in Walter Lang's 1956 screen version of *The King and I*, in which Brynner reprised the role he had originated on Broadway, and for which he won a Best Actor Oscar. A string of big successes followed, including Cecil B. DeMille's 1956 *The Ten Commandments* and Anatole Litvak's *Anastasia*, also released in 1956, but despite appearing in another thirty movies after *The Magnificent Seven*, Brynner was never again able to duplicate his earlier successes.

Eli Wallach would remain a stage actor with occasional forays into film, until his appearance as the Ugly in Leone's 1966 *The Good, the Bad and the Ugly* established him as a major movie star. Brad Dexter's acting career continued to decline, and he eventually became a successful film producer. Charles Bronson appeared in big action films and became a box-office sensation in the 1970s playing a murderous vigilante in the cultural touchstone urban-nightmare *Death Wish* films. James Coburn went on to appear in more than seventy movies and won a Best Supporting Oscar for his role in Paul Schrader's 1997 *Affliction*. Robert Vaughn appeared in several more movies but made his name as the star of the popular 1960s TV series *The Man from U.N.C.L.E.* Horst Buchholz returned to Europe, where his film career thrived.

And Steve McQueen was able to use *The Magnificent Seven* to put himself on the road to superstardom, going "from name to face to star," as Andrew Sarris put it. His visual charm was underscored by his lean, muscular frame, his beautiful blue eyes and moppy blond hair, and his fluid way of moving. In the climactic shootout, he turns, twists, dives, shoots, and rolls with such balletic grace and precision it often brought cheers from the audience.

AFTER THE film's release, thirty-year-old Steve went on a spending spree, purchasing a $300,000 Japanese-Danish–style house on Solar Drive in Nichols Canyon, once owned by Howard Hughes's paramour Terry Moore, with floor-to-ceiling windows offering a panoramic view; a ranch house in Palm Springs with a fifty-five-by-thirty-five-foot swimming pool; and fifty acres of open land near Carmel, California.

Returning for a third season of *Wanted: Dead or Alive*, Steve had both his manager, Hilly Elkins, and his agent, Stan Kamen of the William Morris Agency, continue to aggressively search for another big-screen role for him, but not in another ensemble cast. And no more Yul Brynners. He wanted the audience's focus only on him.

At the same time, just before the start of production on *The Magnificent Seven*, Neile had been slated to test for the role of Anita in Robert Wise's upcoming film version of *West Side Story*, which she hoped would serve as something of a comeback for her. That plan was short-circuited when she learned she was pregnant again. The part went instead to Rita Moreno, who won a Best Supporting Actress Oscar for it.

Also in 1960, Steve was named Rookie of the Year by the American Sports Car Association for his participation in several races, something that brought him a sense of relief from all the pressures of his acting career. According to Steve Ferry, a friend of Steve's at the time, "He races to get the garbage out of his system."

BACK IN production on *Wanted: Dead or Alive*, Steve began to complain again, this time to the show's new producer, Ed Adamson, a Four Star employee, that the new scripts didn't make sense and weren't being shot correctly. He was also angered by what he considered the show's continual rotation of directors not always familiar with either its premise or, more important, the idiosyncratic nature of the Josh Randall character.

Things came to a head when Adamson hired TV director Richard Donner, who had learned his craft directing commercials for Westinghouse that featured many of independent TV studio Desilu's best-known players, including its founders, Lucille Ball and Desi Arnaz. What bothered Steve was that Adamson had hired Donner without running it by him, and he took it out on Donner. On the first day of shooting Steve got in Donner's face over things that wouldn't have bothered anyone else. By the end of the day, Donner had had enough and announced he was quitting. Steve took that as an insult and confronted him. The director agreed to stay on, and he completed that episode and five more, but the chemistry between him and Steve was not good. During their sixth episode together, Steve stopped a scene to go to the toilet, and Donner announced that everyone had to wait for Steve to finish taking a shit. When Steve returned, he fired Donner and told him he would never work again on the show. That was fine with Donner, who soon moved on to the big screen, and directed some of the biggest movies of the seventies, eighties, and nineties, including *Superman* (1978) and *Lethal Weapon* (1987) and its three sequels (1989, 1992, and 1998).

Steve now wanted to leave the series for good and put pressure on Elkins and Kamen to get him another "big" movie, insisting to both that "I'm going to be the biggest fucking movie star since Brando."

WHILE WAITING for the arrival of his second child, Steve took to driving around in his brand-new Jaguar prototype XK-SS, for which he had paid the then hefty price of $5,000. The problem was, he liked to drive it day and night at speeds well above the hilly canyon's limits, with an engine that did not benefit from any kind of effective muffler system, the growl it produced being one of its attractions. It was the noise that got Steve into an altercation with his new neighbor, fifty-eight-year-old Edmund W. George, an electrical supervisor, already furious at Steve because his dogs barked continuously twenty-four hours a day. George had already called the police several times to complain about the noise, something the police did nothing about.

On November 21, 1960, with Neile close to delivering, Steve took his sixteen-month-old daughter and his dog for a walk along the canyon's twisty road. According to Neile in her memoir, because it was the Christmas season Steve wanted to smooth over the bad feelings that had developed between him and George. Late afternoon, Steve knocked on George's door. According to Neile, Steve extended his hand and said, "Hi, let's be friends," to which George responded, "Get off my land, you coward." Steve was stunned by the response, figuring that George had called him that because he, Steve, was holding his daughter in his arms. Steve put her down and punched the neighbor in the face. George put his hand to his chin and said in disbelief, "You hit me!"

"Right, motherfucker, and I'm gonna hit you again!"—and did. By the time George got up, his wife had come running out of the house, and Steve accidentally hit her in the face instead of George.

When the police arrived, they listened to both sides of the story, including George's insistence that Steve had hit him first. Claiming they saw no visible signs of a physical fight despite the wife's bruised face, they left without pressing charges.

On December 28, 1960, Neile gave birth to a baby boy they named Chadwick Steven McQueen. "I knew I wouldn't be pressured to have another child," Neile later wrote, "since we now had what Steve wanted most. A son."

This tumultuous year officially came to an end New Year's Eve with the late-night delivery of a Western Union telegram from Florida that read, "Happy New Year happy new baby."

It was signed Doris and Yul Brynner.

I've been through stageville, hatesville and successville, and finally it's added up to what I've been looking for—a degree of privacy that allows me to live in my home on a hill with my wife and the children and doing the best I can at my work. My idea of having it made.

—STEVE McQUEEN

NINETEEN SIXTY-ONE KICKED OFF WITH AN UNEXPECTED *Wanted: Dead or Alive* ratings crash and an accompanying celebratory whoop from Steve when the series was canceled. Its ninety-fourth and final episode aired March 29, 1961. The show was the victim of a new time slot, Wednesday evenings at eight-thirty, product of a poorly thought-out network programming strategy that put it opposite the classic sitcom and perennial ratings winner *The Adventures of Ozzie and Harriet* on ABC and the prime-time version of the popular NBC daytime game show *The Price Is Right*, which itself benefited enormously from the blockbuster western series *Wagon Train*, which preceded it, and *The Perry Como Show*, a fixture on the network, which followed.

Moreover, *Wanted: Dead or Alive* was now slotted to follow something called *The Aquanauts*, which did not do well at all and was quickly canceled, and lead into *My Sister Eileen*. CBS may have actually wanted to kill the show because of its increasing cost, due primarily to Steve's ever-expanding contract. Whatever the reasons, Steve celebrated his last scene onset by doing a jig in front of everyone. When asked by a reporter if he was going to miss the show, Steve sniffed, "Now I don't have to lean on Josh Randall and his shotgun. I'm up for recognition now. . . . I stole that shotgun when I checked out. I'm gonna have it made into a cigarette lighter." Later on, whenever he was asked about the show's cancellation, he would shrug and say that Josh Randall had been killed trying to capture some bad guys. Translation: he would never play that character again.[1]

Even as *Wanted: Dead or Alive* was winding down, Stan Kamen and Hilly Elkins were putting the final touches on a deal that would bring Steve to MGM for his first starring role in a major studio production, Richard Thorpe's *The Honeymoon Machine* (the title refers to an electronic computer aboard a navy vessel that some of the sailors aboard want to use to beat a roulette wheel in a casino in Venice, Italy).

Although he had signed on to do it, this was not the project Steve saw as the best follow-up to *The Magnificent Seven.* He had wanted to play Dave the Dude in *Pocketful of Miracles,* Frank Capra's remake of his own 1933 *Lady for a Day,* at UA, but it hadn't worked out. The part had originally been offered to Frank Sinatra, who turned it down, as did Dean Martin. Steve was then offered the role and wanted to take it, but by then he had signed an exclusive three-picture deal with MGM, and they wouldn't let him out of his contract.

Steve was actually the second choice for the lead after Cary Grant in *The Honeymoon Machine.* Originally called *The Golden Fleecing,* it was based on a Broadway comedy that had closed after only eighty-four performances. When Grant said no, Elkins put Steve up for the role, and MGM signed him for it and two future films to be named later. However, *The Honeymoon Machine* laid an atomic bomb at the box office. It was so bad, even Steve walked

---

[1] There was a film version of *Wanted: Dead or Alive* that was made in 1987. It was set in the present time and directed by Gary Sherman, with Rutger Hauer playing Josh Randall's grandson Nick Randall.

out during the first public sneak preview, and despite owing MGM two more pictures, he vowed he would never work for the studio again. "I take full credit for that one," Elkins later said. "It was a dumb move for both Steve and me." MGM, not looking to lose any more money with McQueen, quickly voided the rest of the contract.

The film's failure also damaged both Steve's personal and professional relationship with Elkins, whom he blamed for bringing his career to a screeching halt after the success of *The Magnificent Seven*.

To lick his wounds, Steve took Neile and the two children to their house in the desert. Whenever Steve was at the Palm Springs house, even if it was to get away from everyone, his friend Tom Gilson could be counted on to show up. Gilson had had some success as a TV actor, most notably for his role as an Elvis-type soldier—Elvin Pelvin—in a hilarious episode of the Phil Silvers *Sergeant Bilko* sitcom. He was then signed to a movie contract by 20th Century Fox and made his best-remembered film appearance as another Elvis-like character in Leo McCarey's 1958 *Rally Round the Flag, Boys*, which starred Paul Newman and his wife Joanne Woodward. After that he became something of a desert rat, part of his appeal for Steve.

According to Neile, Gilson and Steve would "go to the high desert, pick up peyote from some Indians they knew, and then bring it home." Ever the helpful wife, Neile would "put the stuff in boiling water, let it simmer for approximately thirty minutes, pour in salt and enough pepper to kill an elephant and then I would watch as they gulped it down. Although the stuff was vile, the end result of being totally stoned was worth it to them."

Their desert drug intake was not limited to peyote. They often took LSD together, and there was always grass at the McQueen house. Neile, in her memoir, recalls the constant smell of grass permeating every room, and how she became adept at drying Steve's weed, getting the seeds and stems out, and then helping

Steve hide it in case the house was ever raided. Back in L.A., most of this was done on the days when the household staff was off. In the desert, there was no staff.

Steve and Gilson remained close until, at the age of twenty-eight, Gilson was shot and killed by his estranged wife after he broke into her home on the night of October 6, 1962. Steve served as a pallbearer at his funeral.

For his next film, hoping to regain the lost moment of *The Magnificent Seven*, Steve returned to the ensemble action genre. The project he chose was a war film sent to him by Paramount, called *Separation Hill*, the story of an ill-fated American squadron, understaffed and poorly armed, trying to hold off what seemed like the entire German army in 1944. It was written by Robert Pirosh, a studio veteran whose career highlight was the script for the 1949 ensemble cast picture *Battleground*, directed by William Wellman. It told the story of the Ardennes, one of the most intense war fields in the crucial World War II Battle of the Bulge. Pirosh won an Oscar for *Battleground*, after which he became an "expert" at making studio war films. He pulled out *Separation Hill* from his trunk of unproduced manuscripts, brought it to Paramount, and said he wanted to direct it as well. When Stan Kamen put the word out he was looking for a new film project for Steve, Paramount sent it to him.

Separation Hill appealed to Steve because it was an action-oriented war film. As a Method actor, he could call upon his marine experiences much more easily than searching for his inner cowboy. Pirosh's screenplay told the story of seven men (a lucky number for Steve) who must hold a strategic position while waiting for the rest of their company. Steve liked it well enough, but when he met with Pirosh he told him to make his part—that of the troubled Private Reese, a sullen loner who winds up paying the ultimate price in an act of unexpected bravery—even bigger and more dramatic.

Fine, Pirosh said, as long as not a single word of his script was changed. Steve then went to Marty Rackin, the newly appointed head of Paramount, and told him it was either him or Pirosh and there was no compromise possible. Pirosh was out as director, and Rackin called veteran Don Siegel to offer him the film. Siegel's directing career had begun in 1945 with *Star in the Night*, a two-reeler intended to open the double-feature programs at neighborhood movie theaters. When it won an Oscar for Best Short Subject, Siegel moved up to features and became a solid B-movie director, with an occasional outstanding moment, such as 1956's classic sleeper hit *Invasion of the Body Snatchers*, which he made as a one-off at Allied Artists. His taut 1958 *The Lineup*, shot on location on the streets of San Francisco, helped relaunch the film career of Eli Wallach, and Siegel's direction caught the eye of Clint Eastwood. With Steve and Pirosh locking horns over *Separation Hill*, Rackin thought Siegel was the right director to save the project.

At first, Siegel said no, because Pirosh had been one of his best friends ever since they had worked on *The Big Steal* together in 1949. When Rackin persisted, Siegel called Pirosh to find out exactly what had gone down. When Pirosh said he couldn't get along with anyone connected to the film, Siegel said, "What the hell's the matter with you?"

"One word," Pirosh said. "McQueen. Second word: Rackin."

"You're getting a royal screwing," Siegel told him, "but at the same time, you're stupid. So you don't direct the picture—but at least produce it and write it. I can take some of the pressure off as the director. How about it?"

"I don't want anything to do with [*Separation Hill*]."

"Bob, have you anything against my directing your picture?"

"On the contrary, good luck—you'll need it."

Only then did Siegel agree to do the film and meet Steve for the first time in Rackin's office. As Siegel recalled in his memoir,

"Others were there. Dick Carr, a writer brought in by Rackin specifically to develop and improve Steve's role, Al Manuel, Rackin's associate, and Hilly Elkins, who Steve was still angry at over having lost *Pocketful of Miracles* and the subsequent flop *The Honeymoon Machine*. With the exception of a very tight McQueen, everyone else was positively beaming."

A still-furious-at-Pirosh McQueen spoke, and it wasn't pretty. "I don't understand all this happiness," he said, referring to the cordiality among those in the room. "My name goes on the picture and I still don't like the project." He then chewed out Rackin for having bought an inferior and unfinished script from Pirosh. Next on his hit list was Carr, whom he dismissed in front of everybody as a hack. And Elkins came in for his share as well, according to Steve, for not properly looking after the McQueen franchise. Finally, Steve looked straight at Siegel and said that he hoped the director wouldn't mind if he looked through the camera on every shot, to make sure it was right. Siegel replied in an even tone, "I don't mind. The cameraman might, though."

Steve, realizing he had made a silly gaffe, tried to regain his composure. "Now, I throw ideas at the director all the time," he continued. "Maybe four or five hundred. I don't say they're all good. Maybe only one hundred and fifty are usable."

Siegel came right back at him. "I don't care who I get the ideas from—the grip, the electrician. My name goes on the screen as the director. But there's one thing you better be damn sure you understand." Siegel than banged the table for emphasis. *"I'm the director! Come hell or high water."*

According to Siegel, Steve was so stunned at the outburst, he had what appeared to be an epileptic attack. His face contorted and he had difficulty breathing. At that point, Siegel excused himself and went down the hall to where his agent, Marty Baum, was waiting, to tell him he thought he had blown it. Baum told him to go back in and save the deal. When Siegel returned, a recovered

Steve came up to him and said quietly, "Don't ever do that again." At that point, Elkins looked at his watch, announced it was lunchtime, and suggested everyone eat together. They all agreed, except Carr, who curtly excused himself.

A few minutes later, in the Paramount commissary, Steve opened up to Siegel, telling him all about the trouble he had had so far with this picture. Rackin then turned to Steve and, assuming (or hoping) the deal was set, told Steve to get his wardrobe together and prepare for some publicity photos. In response, Steve shoved the lunch table hard against Rackin and said through clenched teeth, "Don't push me, Marty."

After lunch, everyone's deal was finalized and the film was scheduled to go into production.

THE FIRST thing Steve wanted changed was the title of the film. *Separation Hill* didn't do it for him. He told Siegel it didn't make any sense, and Siegel came up with *The War Story*. Better, Steve said, and then suggested *Hell Is for Heroes*. It was a great title, one that surprised and impressed Siegel, who was all for it until he quickly discovered that Paramount already had a film in production with that title— something that no doubt Steve had heard about on the lot. When Siegel said it couldn't be used, Steve threw a fit and went directly to Rackin, who was in no mood to have any more confrontations with his temperamental star. Rackin changed the name of the other film, an Edmond O'Brien melodrama that the highly respected but fading actor was both producing and directing, to *Man-Trap*. O'Brien was furious but could not do anything about it. He had by this time lost any clout he might have once had as one of Hollywood's better character actors. In the Hollywood rulebook, character actors enriched movies, but leading men brought in the money.

The film's ensemble cast was filled out with an unusual mix of actors and personalities. Fess Parker was a struggling B-movie actor (Gordon Douglas's 1954 atomic ant horror flick *Them*) before gaining enormous popularity and becoming an icon of 1950s TV for his portrayal of Davy Crockett in Walt Disney's weekly television series, but was still trying to make a name for himself on the big screen. He was a large, strong, handsome man, and based on his ability to act as a leader, as demonstrated by the Crockett TV show, Siegel wanted him to play the squadron's company sergeant.

For the role of Pvt. Corby, a moody, volatile personality, Siegel chose Bobby Darin, another fifties pop sensation ("That Darin young man!"). A Bronx-born product of New York City's Brill Building school of singers and songwriters, Darin had done okay with a series of original hit tunes until in 1959 he recorded a version of "Mack the Knife" from Kurt Weill's *The Threepenny Opera* that catapulted him into superstar status. He was suddenly being compared to Frank Sinatra (Darin boasted he would be a bigger star), and moved into film. Five uneven pictures later, Darin, at twenty-five the youngest member of the cast, accepted a role in *Hell Is for Heroes* hoping it would be the film that would indeed make him as big as Sinatra. Darin would die twelve years later of heart disease, never reaching the level of success in either music or film that Sinatra had.

Troubled actor Nick Adams, who had appeared with James Dean in Nicholas Ray's 1955 *Rebel Without a Cause* and then starred for two years in a TV western series, *The Rebel*, a role he won after appearing in an episode of *Wanted: Dead or Alive*, was someone Steve suggested and Siegel okayed. Steve and Nick knew and liked each other from their TV days, and though persistent unfounded rumors in the late 1950s and early 1960s that he was bisexual plagued Adams and hurt his career, Steve never believed them, because they had, on several occasions, shared women and drugs. After *Hell Is for Heroes* Adams's career appeared to be on the upswing until his untimely death in 1968 from a drug overdose. In *Hell Is for Heroes*, he plays a Polish refugee eager to kill Nazis.

Bob Newhart, a former accountant turned entertainer who had scored big with his comedy records, made his film debut in *Hell Is for Heroes* in a role that tried to cash in on his specialty, funny phone monologues; his character is assigned to send a false report over a phone that has been bugged by the Germans. A perfect example of opportunistic miscalculation, Newhart's appearance in the film only added to its oddball no-chemistry mix of pop-stars as characters. In his memoir, Newhart claimed that during the making of the picture, because of his hit albums his fees for nightclub appearances increased, and he looked for an excuse to get out of the film. He routinely went to Siegel with ideas on how his character could be killed off.

James Coburn, Steve's pot-smoking buddy, was cast as a mechanical genius able to help fool the Germans by rigging a jeep to sound like a tank. Coburn brought his easygoing charm to a film that greatly needed anything to keep audiences awake.

Brooklyn-born Harry Guardino, who appeared in numerous 1950s TV shows and was also in the original cast of *A Hatful of Rain*, was cast by Siegel to play tough-guy Sgt. Larkin. Guardino and Steve did not get along well, partly because Guardino was a real-life Italian street kid from New York City and thought that Steve was not big enough to be as tough as he tried to come off onset. There was also some residual hostility from Steve because of *A Hatful of Rain*. Steve resented anything and everything from the original cast, and that put an X over Guardino's name in Steve's book. The rest of the ensemble included Joseph Hoover, Bill Mullikin, L. Q. Jones, Michele Montau, and Don Haggerty.

Steve was not very popular with the other cast members during the making of the film and, besides Guardino, found himself embroiled in a personality clash with Darin, who thought he was the bigger name of the two and the obvious star of the film. One visitor to the set during filming, veteran columnist James Bacon, witnessed some of the tension between Darin and Steve, took

Darin aside, and tried to ease the hostilities by telling him that McQueen was his own worst enemy. "Not while I'm still alive," Darin muttered back.

HELL IS FOR HEROES, set in Germany in 1944, tells the story of seven un-magnificent soldiers assigned to hold a single position for two days while waiting for their company to return from another battle. What's interesting about the film is the interaction between the men in the company, their private mini-battles meant to illustrate their character differences, before the apocalyptic ending. As Steve intended, he died a star-status hero's heroic death.

Underbudgeted at $2.5 million, a victim of Paramount's hard times and Rackin's lack of faith in it after his difficulties with Steve, *Hell Is for Heroes* became a perfect Hollywood-style example of Murphy's law—anything that could go wrong did. Most of the props had a cheap, phony look about them and gave the picture a live-TV look rather than a widescreen film feel. Prop firearms routinely malfunctioned during battle scenes, and a closer look reveals that the same actor playing a German soldier is killed at least three times during the course of the action. In the film's final battle scene, Steve's M3 "grease gun" malfunctioned, something that Siegel caught on film and decided to leave in because the anger it brought out in Steve's character was something he could never duplicate again. Siegel thought it added some much-needed realism to the picture.

Despite that one time, Siegel later talked about all the trouble he had trying to get Steve to perform the way Siegel wanted him to: "For one scene I wanted a close-up of Steve crying. I had a long talk with him about his motivations for breaking down. We both had worked with the Stanislavski [*sic*] method, and I felt confident that Steve, face set, eyes straight ahead, military bearing, when he walked from an extreme long shot into a huge close-up, would start crying. We shot it. Nothing, absolutely nothing in those bitter blue eyes. Not a glimmer of a tear. We didn't give up. When Steve walked into his close-up, we blew chopped onion shreds directly below his eyes. It might as well have been chopped liver.

"Steve probably had the strongest eyes in the world. I decided on a desperate measure. This time when I yelled 'Action,' as steely-eyed Steve started walking I slapped him sharply across the face—then dived over an embankment, expecting him to tackle me. Instead, he walked on and, as usual, nothing happened. My eventual solution wasn't what I wanted, but it worked. We put drops into Steve's eyes to make him look as if he was crying. I made a one-foot dissolve from the huge close-up to an insert of his eyes crying."

The production dragged on for four months, which further stretched the film's already minuscule budget. Much of it was shot in the woods in Redding, California, where the temperature often reached 117 degrees. Steve had a stipulation in his contract that provided him a rental car. His frustration trying to find the handle on the character of Reese probably added to his lack of off-set concentration and he wound up crashing three cars, after which Coburn, who had accompanied him every day, refused to ride alongside him anymore on the way to the set.

Despite all the film's preproduction problems and on-set mishaps, Steve's dramatic death scene gave him the chance to show what he could do. The critics, at least, saw what Steve wanted them to see, and reacted in kind when the picture finally opened on June 26, 1962. Reviewing the picture for the *New York Post*, Eugene Archer wrote, "An arresting performance by Steve McQueen, a young actor with presence and a keen sense of timing, is the outstanding feature [of the film]. McQueen sharply outlines a provocative modern military type." The *New York Times* said, "Steve McQueen is extraordinarily good." The New York *Daily News* called the film "an unstintingly honest depiction of the hell of war.

Among the more memorable men in the squad is Steve McQueen, whose word-at-a-time speech indicates an undercurrent of hostility." Andrew Sarris, in his groundbreaking *The American Cinema*, perhaps best explains what made the film such a good vehicle for both McQueen and his director: "Siegel's most successful films express the doomed peculiarity of the anti-social outcast. The director's gallery of loners assimilates an otherwise anomalous group of actors [including] Steve McQueen in *Hell Is for Heroes*." The film set the table for cinema's most ambitious loner of all, Siegel fan Clint Eastwood, whom Siegel would later direct in such films as *Coogan's Bluff* (1968), *Two Mules for Sister Sara* (1970), *The Beguiled* (1971), and the cinematic landmark *Dirty Harry*.

Hell Is for Heroes did nothing at the box office, despite a rarely seen introduction by John F. Kennedy, in his first year as president of the United States (the introduction was cut after Kennedy's assassination). Perhaps the final blow came when the film censorship board tried, unsuccessfully, to have the word *hell* removed from the title. The outcome had been all but guaranteed by Rackin, who had had enough of the film and everyone associated with it. In the end, Rackin had decided it was nothing more than a B movie and released it as the bottom half of a double feature with Ronald Neame's *Escape from Zahrain*, a fugitives-in-the-desert-trying-to-escape film starring . . . Yul Brynner.

Time would be good to the film, and, because of the appearances of Darin, Newhart, and, above all, Steve, it became something of a cult favorite, so much so that decades later, an episode of the series *Deep Space 9*, "The Siege of AR-558," was loosely based on the plot of *Hell Is for Heroes*, right down to the characters' names. And it remains among the most frequently requested screenings at Steve McQueen film festivals.

When it was first released, one young director Steve did not know personally took the time to send him a telegram congratulating him for his work on the film: "Dear Steve, I want to congratulate you for your performance in *Hell Is for Heroes*. It's the most perceptive and realistic performance of any soldier in any war film I have seen. Best regards, Stanley Kubrick." Years later Kubrick would make his own homage of sorts to the film, his 1987 ensemble-cast war picture *Full Metal Jacket*.

But at the time, neither *The Honeymoon Machine* nor *Hell Is for Heroes* failed to propel Steve's career. According to Hilly Elkins, "*Hell Is for Heroes* benefited from Siegel, no doubt. But it was the same deal as far as Steve's career went as *The Honeymoon Machine*— a neutral."

EVEN BEFORE *Hell Is for Heroes* opened, Steve signed on with Columbia Studios for $75,000 to star in yet another war movie, his third in nine films (his fourth if you count *The Magnificent Seven*), in a role that Warren Beatty had just turned down. In September 1961, he and Neile packed their bags and with their two young children flew to London, England, where production was set to begin on *The War Lover*, based on the novel by John Hersey and adapted for the screen by Academy Award winner Howard Koch, with British-born Philip Leacock (famed documentary filmmaker Richard Leacock's brother) set to direct.[2]

The film's producer, Arthur Hornblow Jr., arranged for Steve and his family to stay at 80 Chester Square, in fashionable Belgravia, a six-floor town house complete with a Greek butler, a full staff, and a private key to the park in Chester Square. The manse belonged to

---

[2] Koch won Best Screenplay with Julius and Philip Epstein for Michael Curtiz's 1942 *Casablanca*. He also wrote the radio adaptation of *The War of the Worlds*, broadcast in 1938, that began an invasion panic across the country. Other noteworthy credits include the screenplay for Max Ophüls's 1948 *Letter from an Unknown Woman*.

Lord and Lady Russell, who leased it to Columbia Studios for the McQueen family at $300 a week for the duration of the shoot.[3]

It was intended as a great perk, a welcoming gesture by the studio for the McQueens, but Steve was far more excited about the close proximity of his living quarters to Brands Hatch auto racetrack. London was, after all, the home of Stirling Moss, one of the most famous Grand Prix racers in the world, and an old friend from the *Wanted: Dead or Alive* years, when Steve first seriously got into racing. No sooner had Steve arrived than he looked up Moss, who was more than happy to show Steve the track and offered to teach him some of the championship-level intricacies of high-speed racing, an offer Steve enthusiastically accepted. Recalled Moss, "Steve and his wife were living in a funny little house at the back of Hollywood when I first met him, he had hit the high spots. He had a D-type Jag, among other things, and a fantastic house. I considered him a cool type of guy. . . . I can remember that night we had together in London around that time. I think Sammy Davis came into it at some stage. If you ask me the kinds of things we talked about, that's fairly simple—girls and cars. Yes, in that order."

STEVE HAD arrived in England in August, a month before Neile and the kids and his co-star, Robert Wagner, to be able to get in some racing time with Moss before *The War Lover* went into production. Rather than check into the mansion without his family, he quietly took a suite for himself at the Savoy, visiting the Brands Hatch racetrack every day with Moss, getting friendly with several other racers, and driving the track as often as he could. (Columbia

---

[3] Steve never got used to life in the Russell mansion. About the park, he told one reporter, "Man, what a thing. You let yourself in, relock the gate and sit there looking through the bars. I'd be caged like some kind of a nut off his streetcar going 'toot, toot,' and saying, 'Man, look who is going by on a double-decker bus.'"

was not happy about any of this and made him sign an agreement that he would pay the studio $2.5 million should he have an accident that interfered with production; it also forbade him to race between the first day of production and the end of shooting, something that in turn made Steve even more unhappy with the studio.)

On the last night of his stay at the Savoy, before his family was scheduled to arrive, Steve threw a wild party in his hotel suite for his racing buddies and their girls—and a few extra girls for good measure. It quickly got out of hand, a small fire broke out, and Steve had to run into the hallway in his underwear to find an extinguisher to put it out. The next day the Savoy made a point of evicting him, even though his stay was officially over. He quickly packed his bags, threw them in his car, and drove to the airport to pick up Neile and the kids and take them to Lord Russell's house.

When the story hit the British and American newspapers the next day, the forever loyal Neile, who was still on the other side of the pond when the events of that night had taken place, angrily denied the published story about Steve "getting gassed and bounding around the hotel in his briefs."

"Balderdash," she said. "Somebody hollered 'fire,' and Stevo lunged out of their room minus his Levi's to find an extinguisher!"

A month later, Steve dropped a note to Hedda Hopper suggesting that British hotels in general were the problem. "The servants make me nervous as hell. I find myself wanting to get up as soon as they come into the room."[4]

❧

[4] In October 1963, after the film's release, Steve changed his story slightly when asked about it again by *Variety:* "My friends and I were trying to make toast on a hot plate. The curtains in the room caught on fire. I ran out in shorts into the hall for a fire extinguisher and there waiting for an elevator were two Dame May Whitty types. . . . Maybe I have the reputations for getting into so much trouble because I'm in the public eye; also I get around quite a bit. Actually I feel that I'm a home guy. I'm married, have two children, and don't run around."

PHILIP LEACOCK was primarily a TV director who made a handful of mostly undistinguished and forgettable films in the 1950s
and early '60s, of which *The War Lover* was his penultimate
big-screen adventure, and by far the best of his features.[5] Leacock was hired by Columbia to make the film on location in London. Although it is often referred to as a foreign film, *The War
Lover* was actually an American film shot by Columbia Studios
on location at the Royal Air Force (RAF) air stations at Boving-
don in Hertfordshire and Manston in Kent, in Cambridgeshire,
and at the legendary Shepperton Studios in England. Leacock
insisted that no miniatures be used for the flight sequences, the
essential visuals of the film—that, in fact, all the planes to be
used had to be rebuilt from their original plans and fully capable
of flying.

To accommodate him, Columbia hired Captain John Crewdson of the RAF, working for Aviation Services, Ltd., an organi-
zation originally created for Alfred Hitchcock's *To Catch a Thief*,
when the rotund director wanted to use helicopters to film the
famous rooftop chase and needed special equipment to do it. Captain Crewdson was now charged with resurrecting three Boeing
B-17 "Flying Fortresses" that had been sitting disused for a decade
outside of Dallas, Texas, and getting them to the RAF base at Bov-
ingdon for refurbishing.[6] All the production values, including the
costumes and props for *The War Lover*, were a vast improvement

---

[5] His other films include, among others, *Life in Her Hands* (1951), *The Brave
Don't Cry* (1952), *The Little Kidnappers* (1953), *Let No Man Write My Epitaph*
(1960), and his final feature, a year after *The War Lover*, *Tamahine* (1963), after
which he returned to American episodic television.

[6] *The War Lover* has other connections to Hitchcock. Leacock was British and
worked primarily in America, as did Hitchcock once he crossed the pond, and
the musical score was conducted by the prolific Muir Mathieson, who conducted the great Bernard Herrmann score for Hitchcock's 1958 *Vertigo*.

over the tacky ones used in *Hell Is for Heroes*, with several rare stock shots of actual aerial combat used to flesh out the battles that gave Robert Huke's black-and-white wide-screen cinematography a greater elegance.

The plot of *The War Lover* is deceptively simple. The film is set in 1943. A squadron of American bomber pilots are stationed in England, from where they conduct frequent bombing raids into the heart of Germany. The story centers around the lives of two pilots, a captain and his co-pilot, McQueen and Hollywood pretty boy and former Fox contract player Robert Wagner. In the film, they are not-so-friendly rivals, with Wagner by far the more "normal" and conventionally attractive of the two. Here, for one of the very few times in his career, Steve's wild and haunted eyes took on a thematic value; his character, Buzz Rickson, links violence to sex, and sex to violence. In one fantastic scene in *The War Lover,* his body convulses orgasmically during one of the early bombing raids in the film, displaying a degree of recklessness that ultimately causes the death of another pilot; Rickson takes great pride in the fact that his "Flying Fortress" has a sexy cartoon of a woman painted on its side who is happily dropping bombs. Back at headquarters, his wall is covered with photos of female conquests, and in one scene he closes his eyes and goes on a "raid" with his fingers to decide whom he will be with next.

The film has a great deal going for it. There is a major if somewhat ironic antiwar theme that goes much farther than the overacting school hysterics of *Hell Is for Heroes* by cleverly intertwining it with a doppelganger relationship between the relatively well-balanced, handsome Lieutenant Ed Bolland (Wagner) and the severely unbalanced and not-as-handsome Rickson; it is as if Bolland is not just Rickson's healthier "other" but the spur that kicks Rickson into trying to prove he is both a better bomber and a better lover, if indeed there is a difference, to Bolland (really, of course, to himself).[7]

All of this comes into sharper (and deeper) focus when both men meet Daphne Caldwell (played extremely well by the beautiful British stage, TV, and film actress Shirley Anne Field), another type of war lover. She was previously involved with at least one other American pilot, who was killed in action, and the film suggests she has since become a serial lover of Americans in uniform. When she socially tests both Bolland and Rickson, and chooses Bolland as her next lover, the stronger, interior plot of the film emerges. Rickson becomes so jealous and enraged that he sets out on a course of mass destruction in the air and sexually perverse revenge on the ground that irrevocably links sex, violence, and war as a continuum of rage, destruction, and death.

Quite surprisingly for a mainstream war movie of the early sixties, Caldwell is the sexual aggressor. She initiates the affair with Bolland when he brings her home and at her suggestion she stays the night. This triggers a series of events that clarifies Bolland's disillusionment with Rickson. As the film races toward its exciting climax, an aerial raid makes Rickson even more desperate, and he brazenly tries to steal a not-unwilling Caldwell from Bolland by following her home one night and practically raping her. Her defense against him is yet another interesting twist: she preaches nonviolence to him, with a sermon on the couch about the meek inheriting the earth. We do not see what follows, but the strong suggestion is that a sexually violent or violently sexual encounter has taken place, perhaps even a murder.

On his next mission, Rickson's plane is hit, and after forcing everyone else out to save themselves, he tries what might be a

---

[7] Hitchcock had often used a similar technique, most prominently in *Notorious* (1946), *Strangers on a Train* (1952), *Dial M For Murder* (1954), and *Vertigo* (1957), and most spectacularly in *Psycho* (1960).

consciously impossible and therefore suicidal emergency return-to-base landing that results in his crashing head-on into the white cliffs of Dover, where he dies in an apocalyptic explosion. With a final scene (that feels tacked on), Bolland is reunited with Caldwell in a happily-ever-after embrace. Before this mission, Bolland, whose tour of duty is coming to an end, had shown no prior interest in carrying his relationship beyond a wartime fling. Partly a concession to the censors, this ending also suggests that with his own darker side eliminated (Rickson), he can now pursue a healthy and long-term relationship with Caldwell; hence, the deeper and more complex meanings of "war lover" become apparent.

In the film, Steve played a character closer to who he really was, less charmingly romanticized and rougher than any he had previously attempted; Vin in *The Magnificent Seven*, Sgt. Ringa in *Never So Few*, and Private Reese in *Hell Is for Heroes* are more cardboard cutouts than flesh and blood. His strong portrayal of Rickson is three-dimensional; the character is overtly sexual, angry, nonredemptive (his final act of heroism aboard the doomed B-17 is less about saving others than about needing to die in a solo reverie of imagined immortality, the ultimate orgasm), rough and tough and utterly believable. *The War Lover* was by far Steve's most challenging adult role and his best performance to date. For the first time he eschewed the protective layer of his pretty-boy exterior for the harder edge of his more complex interior.

To ensure the realism of his portrayal, Steve fell back into Method 101 and antagonized Field offscreen, admonishing her and all the British for their externalized acting, while at the same time buddy-buddying with Wagner, who was decidedly not a Method actor and who welcomed Steve's friendship on an uncomplicated level that helped the two avoid any ego clashes over who was better-looking, a better ladies' man in real life, and so on.

As for Leacock, Steve liked him because he wasn't very forceful and didn't demand a lot of takes. The affable director, in turn, admired Steve's rough edges and even consented to letting him race cars once in a while on his days off, even though it was specifically prohibited by Steve's contract. One rainy day when exterior shooting was canceled and there was only one major scene left to film, Rickson's doomed last flight, Leacock gave Steve the go-ahead to take a modified Formula Jr. Cooper he had just purchased out to Brands Hatch, where he promptly smashed it into a wall, leaving his face banged and bruised. Fortunately, in that final scene in the cockpit Rickson is wounded and bloody, which made it easy to incorporate Steve's real-life injuries.

As the days of production wound down to pickups and second-unit shoots, Steve had very little to do and often spent his afternoons writing to the industry journalists he had liked best, Hedda Hopper and Sidney Skolsky. To Hopper, he confessed "England's fun, Hedda, but I miss California very much. I am an American and I never realized how deep-rooted this was until I was a foreigner in someone else's land. . . . [S]ometimes when I get home from work if I have got a few hours to spare, Neile and I go down to the market along the Thames and have fish and chips. . . . I should be back home about the middle of January and I'm going to make a bee-line for Palm Springs and do nothing as hard as I can."

To Skolsky, he was a little more graphically descriptive about the native food that was far less appealing to him than a home-grown menu: "Sid, we are just finishing up with the movie and I'm going to be damn glad to get home. I would give my left nut right now for a hamburger, a chocolate milk shake and some French fries from Schwab's. Fish and chips are coming out of my ears."

This resulted in Skolsky anointing Steve as the subject of his December 23 nationally syndicated "Tintype" column, an appearance in which was a boost for any Hollywood actor. According to Skolsky's column, "He has an insatiable appetite and never gains a pound—thinks nothing of ordering two helpings of potatoes and a couple of sandwiches for lunch . . . all his spare time is spent tinkering with his Porsche sports car . . . he sleeps in a double bed in the nude and has one luxury. Neile often brings him coffee before he gets out of bed—after all, you can't walk down to the kitchen like that!"

THE WAR LOVER opened in October 1962, just four months after *Hell Is for Heroes*, and received mixed-to-negative reviews. The first hint that the film was not going to do well was the review in *Daily Variety*, a paper that had an uncanny ability to predict the taste of the moviegoing public, even if, in this instance, it totally missed the essential meaning of the film. It said, in part, "This production of John Hersey's novel *The War Lover* is accomplished in all respects save one: lack of proper penetration into the character referred to by the title. The scenario seems reluctant to come to grips with the issue of this character's unique personality—a 'war lover' whose exaggerated shell of heroic masculinity covers up a psychopathic inability to love or enjoy normal relationships with women. . . . [T]hat the central character emerges more of an unappealing symbol than a sympathetic flesh-and-blood portrait is no fault of McQueen, who plays with vigor and authority, although occasionally with too much eyeball emotion. Robert Wagner and Shirley Anne Field share the film's secondary, but interesting, romantic story. Wagner does quite well, and Field has a fresh, natural quality."

The *Washington Post* was even less impressed: "*The War Lover* goes to remarkable trouble to avoid what it is talking about. One would have thought Steve McQueen ideal for the title role, and he might have been so, had he been imaginatively used."

None of the critics really liked the film, their reviews did nothing to stir the public's interest, and it failed at the box office. A growing antiwar sentiment in America didn't help. With civil rights issues hanging in the air and the aftermath of the Korean War still quite pungent in the hearts and minds of Americans, World War II films seemed slightly dated and out of touch.

The film's disappointing box office left Steve dangling from a career tightrope. One more false step now and he would undoubtedly fall into the chasm of failed stardom, while one smart move toward safety would ensure his place in the pantheon of name-above-the-title performers. Few TV stars to date had successfully made the transition to the movies. It usually happened in reverse: Lucille Ball, Phil Silvers, Perry Como, Jackie Gleason, and dozens of others who had worked steadily in films but never made it to the top of that world had become genuine television sensations, as the small screen made their small-scale talents seem that much bigger.

Back in L.A., Steve did nothing very hard as he buried himself in auto racing. He was so much better at it after having been with Moss in England, that he was invited by John Cooper to become an active member of the British Motor Corporation (BMC), which meant he would always be able to race professionally in Europe. He had one weekend to decide. According to Steve, "It was a very tough decision for me to reach, because [at this point] I didn't know if I was an actor who raced or a racer who acted. But I had Neile and our two children to consider, and that made a difference. I turned down the BMC offer but I came very close to chucking my film career. I [knew] I hadn't done anything really important or outstanding on the screen, and I was tired of waiting for the 'big picture,' the one that hopefully would break me through."

However, plans were already being made for him to star in yet another war picture, but this one would be very different; this one would finally make him a superstar.

⌄

HE HAD been given the script to read before he'd left England by Hilly Elkins, who himself was growing weary of the Hollywood scene. The studio system was crumbling, leaving the film business in something of a shambles, and Elkins was eager to return to New York and Broadway. He already had a project for Sammy Davis Jr.: a musical version of *The Golden Boy*, the Clifford Odets play that had been turned into a movie in 1939, making William Holden a star, and was now, under Elkins, being reconceived into a song-and-dance stage drama for Davis.

As a final gesture of goodwill to Steve, with whom he would remain friends for the rest of his life, Elkins encouraged Stan Kamen at the William Morris Agency to continue to rep him, despite Steve's string of unimpressive box office returns, which normally would be the kiss of death in Hollywood. As a parting gesture, Elkins had sent Steve the script for *The Great Escape*, which already had John Sturges attached—something that made the decision to be in it very easy. That, and the fact he was being offered top billing, something he had never had before.

However, as always, Steve held his cards close to his vest and tried to hedge his bets. Steve had been considering several other projects. He had tried but failed to buy the TV rights to "Beauty and the Beast" (that would one day become a Disney animated feature and Broadway stage musical), and he had been turned down by director George Roy Hill for the leading role of Ralph Baitz in Hill's screen adaptation of Tennessee Williams's *Period of Adjustment*, a minor neurotic war-between-the-sexes drama, the type of play that Williams could write in his sleep (and which played like he had). The role went instead to Anthony Franciosa. Steve turned down a role in Carl Foreman's *The Victors*, an antiwar movie by the once-blacklisted producer-writer of such great films as Fred

Zinnemann's 1952 *High Noon*. *The Victors*, set in World War II and, like *The War Lover*, was an American film that was going to be made in England, but so blatantly antiwar it made *The War Lover* seem by comparison a romantic comedy. Steve had first become interested when he heard that Foreman had gone after Ava Gardner, Simone Signoret, and Sophia Loren for the female roles in the film, but when none of them signed on and Steve could not get the percentage of the profits that he demanded, he turned the project down as well. Eventually the role went to George Peppard (and the female parts went to Romy Schneider, Melina Mercouri, Rosanna Schiaffino, Jeanne Moreau, and Elke Sommer). It turned out to be a prescient choice for Steve. *The Victors*, a very good film, was considered far too prole in its anti-American sentiment—Frank Sinatra's version of "Have Yourself a Merry Little Christmas" is sung over the U.S.-ordered execution of an American soldier for treason—and bombed big-time at the box office.

Besides Sturges's involvement, the other things that appealed to Steve about *The Great Escape* were the $100,000 fee and the fact that he would be part of another ensemble cast, which he was ready for. It meant after two flops he wouldn't have to take all the credit or get all the blame. In the right ensemble, he knew, he could shine, as he had in *The Magnificent Seven*, thanks in no small measure to the rough-and-ready Sturges, whose directing style he liked and whose toughness he appreciated.

After announcing to the public that he was going to be in *The Great Escape*, and while Sturges was putting together the rest of the cast, Steve tried to recover some of his emotional balance after having thrown himself so heavily into the role of Rickson. He told Hedda Hopper, "It really twisted me up, so I decided to knock off for a time. But I think it's a magnificent picture. It's the best work Bob Wagner has ever done and Shirley Anne Field, the English actress, is good in it too. . . . I'm trying to regain some of the weight I lost before I go back to Europe for *The Great Escape* in June. I'm not an actor who can go on the set and just turn it on when the cameras start to roll; I have to live with it and it's very uncomfortable."

To relax, Steve kept busy with his racing. He'd brought back two new race cars from England, the repaired Cooper and a souped-up Land Rover. That April, barely a month after having returned to the States, Steve raced the Cooper at Del Mar and scored a sweep on successive days. A week later, at Cotati in Northern California, a crack in the combustion chamber robbed the Cooper of the thrust it needed to win. "Everything went wrong," he said later. "I tried to stay in the race by slipstreaming, following in the vacuum or suction of another car, the first day. So I caught a rock in the eye, which shattered my goggles. The second day I pushed too hard through the corners to make up for ground lost in the straights and wound up off the track and into some tall weeds. That was quite a scene! The Cooper sits pretty low and I nearly drove out of sight. There I sat looking up into the face of a big sun flower."

STURGES HAD been trying to make *The Great Escape* for thirteen years, ever since 1950, when he first read the newly published novel by Paul Brickhill, based on his own real-life experience flying for the RAF during World War II, being shot down by the Luftwaffe, and being sent to the prison camp Stalag Luft III, sarcastically called Göring's luxury camp by Allied prisoners of war. During his more than two-year confinement, Brickhill took part in the planning and execution of a massive escape plan. Out of the seventy-six soldiers who attempted the escape, only three made it safely to England. British-born Brickhill was one of them, and in 1950 he put down on paper, with great accuracy and enormous detail, the events leading up to, during, and following his imprisonment.

A lesser-known fact that was in the book but not the movie

was the role the escapees played in helping the Allied invasion of Normandy on D-Day to succeed—so many Germans were sent to recapture the officers that they were not available to help repel the Allies (in fact, this was one of the reasons the escape had been planned). Many of the Nazis who were involved in the mass execution of fifty of the escapees later stood trial for it at Nuremberg, and the book carried the dedication "To the fifty."

Sturges immediately saw in the book the possibility of a "big" movie, and he took it to the studio he was with at the time, MGM, which promptly turned it down. Sturges then insisted on a private meeting with the top man, Louis B. Mayer, during which he told him the story of the film and how exciting he thought it could be. Mayer still didn't go for it, asking who would go see a movie where only three people out of seventy-six make it out alive. Then Mayer asked what the budget for the film would be. When Sturges told him $10 million, an enormous amount for 1950, Mayer said the deal was dead. Sturges later said, "I tried to make it for about eight years before I became an independent, and everybody just smiled and changed the subject."

It was only after Sturges left MGM and made *The Magnificent Seven* that he was able to resurrect the project. In 1961, the Mirisch brothers took a meeting with Sturges. Even though *The Magnificent Seven* had not been an instant box office hit, the film had steadily made money overseas and eventually become profitable, and to the Mirisch brothers that made Sturges a very desirable director. According to Sturges, "If I wanted to direct the telephone book they would have at least given me a hearing."

They listened to his pitch and gave him the green light if— and they underscored the word *if*—he could bring it in for under $4 million. According to one observer, "After *The Magnificent Seven* Sturges believed he could save an enormous amount of money by recreating the German prison camp Stalag Luft III built in Geiselgasteig just outside of Munich in Palm Springs and using locals as extras to play the other prisoners and soldiers not directly involved with the story. And if there were unforeseen problems, once the film was in production, he knew the Mirisches, who had gotten UA to agree to be partners on the project and put up half the money, would have to put up the cost of the overrun rather than losing everything by shutting down the picture."

The only problem left for Sturges was to actually acquire the rights to the book, which to this point he had not done—a tiny fact he left out of his pitch to the Mirisches. What he thought would be the easiest thing in the world turned out to be anything but. As it turned out, Sturges had not been the first director or producer to try to buy Brickhill's story. All previous comers had been turned away because of the author's disdain for Hollywood-style movies that to his mind glorified true war stories with unrealistic battle scenes and always had beautiful women popping up in impossible places just to sell tickets.

Brickhill initially said no to Sturges, but the director kept after the writer, refusing to take no for an answer. He finally convinced Brickhill to at least come to Hollywood from England to talk about it in person, all expenses paid. During their meetings, always at less flashy, more traditional American restaurants like Musso and Frank's, Sturges poured on the charm, impressing the author with his vast knowledge of World War II and assuring him that the film would remain true to his book.

After winning a conditional okay from the author, Sturges set about getting a treatment written that Brickhill insisted he had to read before he would give final consent. Sturges turned to William Roberts, who, for a hefty fee, wrote a sixty-four-page draft that Brickhill disliked, feeling it was not faithful enough to his book. Walter Newman did the second draft, but never finished, and, still not over what had happened with his script for

The Magnificent Seven, bowed out and refused to do any further work on it.

Sturges then hired veteran screenwriter W. R. Burnett, whose previous credits included Raoul Walsh's 1941 *High Sierra* and John Huston's 1950 *The Asphalt Jungle*, the former a film about an ex-con who can never escape the imprisonment of his soul, the latter a great ensemble piece that set the standard for American heist movies. Both had been adapted from original novels that Burnett had written.

Burnett's major contribution, at the urging of John Sturges and over Brickhill's loud objection, was to add American soldiers to the planning and execution of what had been essentially a British-conceived and -executed escape. According to Robert Relyea, who was once again serving as Sturges's first assistant director: "He thought [adding Americans] would make it a great picture, because it was really about nobility and honor. . . . I think there's always a concern to make a picture as accurate as you can, and then you have to have some creative license to adjust to make it entertainment. I think we held to this very close, although, maybe in some cases, characters were altered a bit." And, of course, it would widen the film's box-office appeal in America.

The finished script was sent to Steve, who immediately signed on, along with two other alumni from *The Magnificent Seven* Sturges wanted in the film: Charles Bronson for the role of Danny, "the Tunnel King," and James Coburn for Louie Sedgwick, "the Manufacturer." (Sturges had to keep some of the major characters European to keep Brickhill, who had finally approved the script, from having a nervous breakdown, and so both actors used awkward accents to try to help convince audiences they were not "American.") Also signed was real-life Korean War veteran James Garner as one of the made-up Americans, Bob Hendley, "the Scrounger," whose job it was to somehow come up with

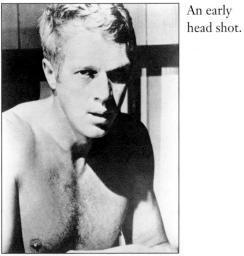

An early head shot.

Wanted: Dead or Alive, 1959.

With Hilly Elkins, Steve's first manager, going over a script.
COURTESY OF HILLY ELKINS

The Blob, 1958.

Hell Is for Heroes, 1962.

With Robert Wagner in *The War Lover,* 1962.

Breaking out of camp
on his motorcycle in
The Great Escape, 1963.

A movie poster for
The Great Escape.

In one of his few romantic roles opposite Natalie Wood in Robert Mulligan's *Love with the Proper Stranger*, 1963.
AP Photo/David Pickoff

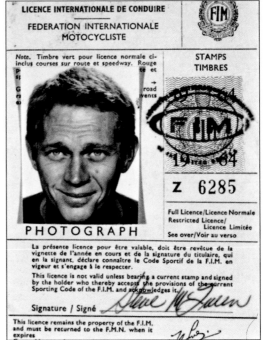

LICENCE INTERNATIONALE DE CONDUIRE

FEDERATION INTERNATIONALE
MOTOCYCLISTE

Note. Timbre vert pour licence normale ci-inclus courses sur route et speedway. Rouge

STAMPS
TIMBRES

Z 6285

PHOTOGRAPH

Full Licence/Licence Normale
Restricted Licence/
Licence Limitée
See over/Voir au verso

La présente licence pour être valable, doit être revêtue de la vignette de l'année en cours et de la signature du titulaire, qui en la signant, déclare connaître le Code Sportif de la F.I.M. en vigueur et s'engage à le respecter.

This licence is not valid unless bearing a current stamp and signed by the holder who thereby accepts the provisions of the current Sporting Code of the F.I.M. and acknowledges it.

Signature / Signé

This licence remains the property of the F.I.M. and must be returned to the F.M.N. when it expires

Steve's international motorcycle license acquired in France, 1964.

Faking it on guitar in *Baby, the Rain Must Fall*, 1965

The Cincinnati Kid, 1965.

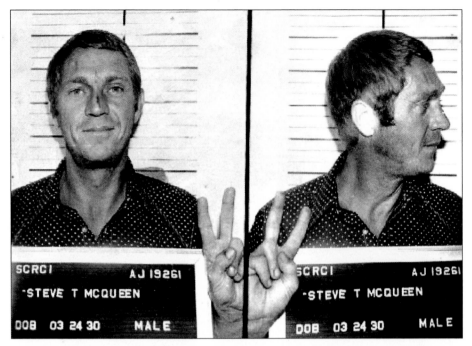

Steve's mug shot for speeding and drunk driving while on vacation with his family in Alaska prior to the release of *The Sand Pebbles*, 1966.

With Candice Bergen, *The Sand Pebbles*.

The Sand Pebbles.

Placing his handprints and signature at the famed Grauman's Chinese Theatre on Hollywood Boulevard, with Neile by his side, March 21, 1967.

Nominated for Best
Actor for *The Sand
Pebbles*, Steve arrives
with Neile at the
Academy Awards,
April 10, 1967.
AP Photo

The famous kiss from
*The Thomas Crown
Affair*, 1968.

Quintessential Steve
as Bullitt.

With Robert Vaughn in
Bullitt, 1968.

A change of pace—as Boon Hogganbeck in *The Reivers*, 1969.

Junior Bonner, 1972.

Steve with the founding members of First Artists, the producers of *The Getaway*. It was one of the only First Artists films to make money.

LEFT TO RIGHT: Steve, Paul Newman, Barbra Streisand, and Sidney Poitier.

The Getaway, 1972, paired two of Hollywood's biggest stars.

With producer and close friend David Foster, who surprised Steve with a birthday cake during production of *The Getaway*.

Relaxing with Ali MacGraw, as they were both falling in love.

Controversial ad for *The Towering Inferno*, 1974. Steve's name came first, but Paul Newman's was higher.

Steve, in full beard and glasses, with director George Schaefer, in the never-released *An Enemy of the People*, 1978.

In the biopic *Tom Horn*, 1980, which he also executive produced.

The Hunter, 1980, was
Steve's final film.

Steve and his third wife, Barbara Minty, arrive for the premiere of *The Hunter* in Oxnard, March 1980. It was his final public appearance.

An ad for an estate auction following his death.

the necessary equipment needed to build the secret escape tunnels. Steve and Garner were, by far, the two biggest American names in the film, the only ones Sturges might be able to count on for any box office clout. To retain at least some of the original British flavor of the novel, Sturges cast British actor Richard Attenborough (after Richard Harris bowed out), for the key role of Roger Bartlett. He filled out the rest of the principals with Brits James Donald, Donald Pleasence, and Scottish-born David McCallum.

Sturges then hired Australian writer James Clavell to polish the script. Clavell's previous screenplays included Kurt Neumann's 1958 *The Fly* and 1959's *Five Gates to Hell*, which Clavell also directed. Sturges especially liked Clavell, who later would gain fame as a novelist dealing with romanticized versions of Asian history (*Shogun*, *Tai-Pan*), for *The Great Escape* because he too had actually spent time in a prison camp, albeit a Japanese one, during the war, and Sturges felt that would help him keep the script as accurate as possible.

With cast and screenwriter in place, Sturges set about finding the perfect desert setting to replicate Stalag Luft III. As Sturges's assistant director, Robert Relyea, later recalled, "Besides the wire and the fences, there was this enormous forest that surrounded the camp that further prevented any prisoners from escaping. I found six very crummy, scrawny pine trees—six—between the barren stretches of Idyllwild and Palm Springs, and I told John I had found 'the Black Forest.' He was fighting laughter as we looked at these six trees, but agreed that we could build the camp around them and somehow make it work."

Before production could begin, however, the Screen Extras Guild refused to allow locals to play extras in the film unless they were brought in from Hollywood, more than a hundred miles from the six trees. Realizing that that would be just as expensive as going to Germany to make the film there, Sturges sent Relyea to Europe to scout locations, and on his advice decided to construct a replica of the original prison camp in Munich, just outside Germany's Bavaria Studios. To play the other prisoners and soldiers, Sturges hired local students instead of using professional extras.[8]

When Steve was told about the locale change, he was both excited—he had, since his merchant marine days, always loved to travel to new countries—and concerned. He enjoyed being overseas, but it meant he would be away from Hollywood for a solid year, except for the few weeks following the completion of *The War Lover*. He didn't want to become one of those American actors who only worked abroad. Sturges calmed his fears by reminding him he had top billing for the first time in his career and assuring him that he and the family would be put up in a beautiful chalet in Deining, Bavaria. Plus, Sturges pointed out, there were no speed limits in Germany. Technically that wasn't true—only the autobahn had no speed limit; limits on local roads were strictly enforced—but it was enough to get Steve to consent to the German shoot. To prevent Steve from speeding anywhere besides the autobahn, and potentially being arrested and delaying the production, Sturges hired a private escort to make sure he stayed within the legal limit when he drove. It was an unintentional boost for a Method actor playing a POW in Germany.

Six writers and eleven drafts later, on location in Germany with a script that was still mostly improvised from setups the director gave his actors, it became increasingly clear that as far as Sturges was concerned, this was Steve's picture, despite his smaller role of the American Captain Virgil Hilts. "The Cooler King," as he was

---

[8] The original camp was in occupied Poland. Sturges and Relyea tried to visit the actual site prior to filming but Poland was, since the end of World War II, part of the Soviet Union and they could not get permission to enter the country. Instead, they used photographs and original blueprints to re-create Stalag Luft III.

known, was an amalgam of several of the relatively few American POWs detained at the camp. Hilts spends most of the film in solitary confinement—a prison within a prison—throwing a baseball against his cell wall and catching it in his mitt, a nice image of the meaningless monotony of prison life. According to James Coburn, "Steve's performance was perfect in the film. He represented everything about the indomitable spirit these guys had."

All well and good, but Steve quickly grew frustrated with what he perceived was, in fact, a secondary role, and, as he had with Yul Brynner in *The Magnificent Seven* and Bobby Darin in *Hell Is for Heroes*, he quickly got into a contentious relationship with the actor he perceived as his biggest competitor in the film—not Attenborough, who played the leader of the escape, but James Garner, the American who was by far the most charming actor in the cast. Darkly handsome, with a warm smile and an easy manner reminiscent of middle Cary Grant, Garner had come up through the TV western series ranks as Steve had, starring in the offbeat weekly one-hour series *Maverick*. Whereas *Wanted: Dead or Alive* had been all business, with simple by-the-book stories that highlighted the sullen personality of its star, *Maverick* was a goofball comedy-drama about a slick, slightly cowardly gambler whose winning personality immediately connected with audiences and made Garner a TV star. Like Steve, Garner too was in the midst of an uneven transition to the big screen, having appeared the year before in Michael Gordon's comedy *Boys' Night Out* and, as soon as filming was completed on *The Great Escape*, was scheduled to star opposite Doris Day in Norman Jewison's romantic comedy *The Thrill of It All*.

As far as Steve was concerned, however, Garner was less a charmer than a schemer, doing his best to make the movie his own. He had the bigger, more interesting role, and his character actually takes part in the "escape." To turn the focus back on himself, Steve came up with the idea for the sequence that everyone remembers far more than anything Garner did in the film.

"We got to Germany and Steve's part was still not defined," recalled Neile. "Nothing to say, 'Ah, that's a Steve McQueen film!' Then, when Jimmy [Garner] came on with his cap, and white tee-shirt, Steve said he wasn't going to continue unless they fixed his part."

"When Sturges and film editor Ferris Webster foolishly showed a rough-cut to the cast of the first six weeks' worth of shooting," according to Donald Pleasence, "Steve McQueen walked out, insisting that his part had to be rewritten." Steve meant what he said, and the next day refused to show up for his scheduled scenes.

For several days Sturges waited around for two more screenwriters to arrive from Hollywood to try to find a way to make Steve's part more acceptable to him.

But it didn't happen as quickly as either Sturges or Steve had hoped, and Steve's refusal to participate in any more filming threatened the entire production schedule. To try to improve the situation, the always-cool James Coburn and an increasingly disgruntled Garner got together with Steve to try to hash things out and come up with a solution. According to Garner, "Coburn and Steve came over to my place in Munich and I said, 'What's your problem, Steve?' It turned out after a few hours of talking, Steve wanted to be the hero [in the film] but he didn't want to do anything heroic. Turned out there were a lot of things that were suggested to him but he turned them all down, saying they were corny. Finally, we simply told him he was a hero and he liked that. If you remember, he escapes by himself. They capture him and he becomes a hero, and that's what he wanted. Or at least that's what Coburn and I convinced him he wanted."

Despite volunteering to help solve the impasse, Garner never liked Steve's professional manner or style of acting. Years later, while being interviewed by Charlie Rose, Garner remained critical of Steve's abilities, especially during the filming of *The Great*

Escape: "Steve was a little out-of-hand always. He had a great persona that people loved, but I could always see him 'acting,' and that was the kiss of death."

Steve's behavior offset also caused the production problems. He drove himself to the production every day from his hotel in Munich in a souped-up Mercedes that was always followed closely by the German police who, despite Steve's "bodyguards," during the course of the shoot gave him thirty-seven tickets—for speeding, for nearly hitting stray farm animals, and once for wrapping the car around a tree. In court for that appearance, he was almost sent directly to jail when the judge discovered Steve had left his driver's license back in the States. Steve's self-presented defense was that he used his driving time to help him prepare for his role in the film—mental Method acting. The studio lawyers were in court nearly every day trying to keep Steve from being locked up. Their most effective argument, and the one that kept him free, was that if Steve couldn't work on the film, the production would shut down and the local economy would lose millions (this despite the fact that Steve had been on strike for several days before he ran into his legal problems).

Up until now, despite all of Steve's disruptive behavior, Sturges's belief in his star's ability had never wavered. "When you find somebody with that kind of talent, you use him. Steve is unique, the way Cary Grant is unique, or Spencer Tracy or Marlon Brando. There's something bubbling inside of him . . . that's why you can't take your eyes off him on screen."

But after the script was revised and Steve was still grousing, Sturges finally gave up and told Steve not only that was he going to write Virgil Hilts out of the script but also that Garner's role would be enlarged. "We're going to blend McQueen's character into Garner's," an enraged Sturges shouted to the entire set. "Steve McQueen is no longer on this picture!"

Furious, Steve called Stan Kamen and William Morris Agency head Abe Lastfogel in New York, both of whom immediately caught a plane and arrived in Germany the next day, hoping to get Steve and the film back on track. After several hours of negotiations between the four parties, Sturges agreed to try to build up Steve's character even more than he already had. The first thing Sturges did was to promise that the baseball-and-mitt routine would run through most of the film. The second thing Sturges okayed was something Steve had from the first lobbied to get into the film: the motorcycle escape scene that became its most unforgettable moment, a surge of sheer visual excitement sorely needed in a film that had far too much talky exposition before the actual great escape and capture sequences.

In the revised script, Hilts also was always trying to escape by himself, a motif established in his very first sequence when he tosses his ball too close to the prison boundary and nearly gets machine-gunned to death by a guard. Later, Hilts breaks out of the compound and steals a uniform, a helmet, and a motorcycle from a German soldier and makes his break. Hilts eludes pursuer after pursuer in the breathtaking chase sequence until he fails to make a jump over a barbed-wire fence and is brought back to the camp once more and put into baseball-and-glove solitary. The sequence ratcheted up the dramatic arc of the film by reducing the cumbersome plot to the essence of what it was supposed to be, an attempt to escape that becomes an exercise in futility and a metaphor for the going-nowhere-while-having-nowhere-to-go POWs.

Audiences were always thrilled by this chase, which was directed by Relyea, and it became one of Steve's career signatures, but in fact, he didn't even do much of the riding. Rather, Hilts's riding was done by Steve's close friend from the San Fernando Valley, Bud Ekins, a sometime stunt rider and full-time motorcycle builder who, at Steve's urging, had been hired by Sturges to perform any stunts that the insurance companies would prevent him from doing himself. In the scene Steve plays one of the German pursuers, in effect, movie-magically chasing himself.

Ramps were built for the final, thrilling sixty-foot jump that lands Hilts (Ekins) into barbed wire (stretched and wrapped rubber that the entire company, actors and crew, worked on during their spare time). The sequence was so perfectly put together it earned Ferris Webster an Oscar nomination for Best Editor and Steve a reputation as an extraordinary physical film actor, able to perform unbelievable stunts that were impressive and, equally important, added needed depth to the character he played.

FILMING OF *The Great Escape* ended in October 1962, and back in America, postproduction took another six months. Sturges hired Elmer Bernstein to do the score, which turned out to be another great one, complete with a whistle-out-the-door, drum-heavy military-style theme that floated throughout the entire film. There were distinct echoes in it of Kenneth Alford's "Colonel Bogey's March," a World War I whistle tune that had driven David Lean's *The Bridge on the River Kwai* a decade earlier. (That film was also essentially a true British World War II story populated on-screen with Americans to make it more commercially appealing in the States.)

Despite all the problems with the production, *The Great Escape* had allowed Steve to finally find his Hollywood star footing, escape the bonds of B-movie hell for good, and take his place alongside Hollywood's hottest rebel superstars.

The minute a picture is over, I run like a thief. . . . I'll put the old lady and the kids in my Land Rover and take off. Up in the mountains, out in the desert, anywhere . . . man, I don't want to be bugged by anybody.

—STEVE MCQUEEN

ONCE HE FINISHED FILMING HIS SCENES, STEVE WENT BACK to California. Feeling certain that *The Great Escape* couldn't miss, he and Neile confidently bought a beautiful new $300,000 stone house in Brentwood that overlooked the city of Santa Monica and the beautiful Pacific crescent. They affectionately nicknamed it "the Castle."

The first thing Steve added to it was a sophisticated home gymnasium where he could work out daily, or "fanatically," as Neile described his then-obsessive body conditioning in her memoir. Prior to this he had worked out three times a week at a Beverly Hills club, where Neile often went along and took jazz dancing classes. He also invested even more heavily in his two favorite non-film-related hobbies, fast cars and fancy handguns, and added to his already impressive collection of both.

As they settled back into the Southern California lifestyle, a welcome change from the long, dank European winter, David Foster arranged for *Life* magazine to do a cover story on the now very hot Steve that emphasized his passion for cars and racing as well as his acting to run that summer to coincide with the American release of *The Great Escape*. The cover was a color close-up of

Steve and Neile riding double-saddle on a motorcycle, with only the handles visible. Lest Steve come off as too much like Brando, another Method actor with a penchant for bikes, Foster made sure Steve and Neile looked clean-cut, smiling, cute, and happy: Mr. and Mrs. Perfect Young Couple, movie-star style.

At the same time, with much less fanfare, Steve quietly presented the first of what was to be the annual Steve McQueen College Scholarship at the Boys Republic in Chino, a fund he had set up to help other lost boys like himself. He kept his participation determinedly low-key, and except for a very occasional mention by someone else in the press, it was not something he talked much about.

Steve, meanwhile, despite his strong feeling the film would be a hit, was still smarting from his experience in *The Great Escape*, which had left him feeling like a combination of powerless employee, mannequin to be moved as the director saw fit, and slave to the dictates of the corporate machine. He decided to form his own independent company, so that no one could ever again push him around or tell him what to do.

He named it Solar Productions (the original name was Scuderia Condor, but Neile urged him to choose something a little easier on the tongue, and suggested Solar to commemorate their first house in Nichols Canyon on Solar Drive). Solar was meant to be the initial step toward producing the kind of films he wanted to make.

Interestingly, Steve hit upon the notion of owning his own production company five years before Clint Eastwood formed Malpaso. For his first venture, Eastwood chose *Hang 'Em High*, directed by Ted Post. What motivated Clint to create Malpaso was exactly the opposite of what drove Steve to form Solar. Clint was thrilled with the success of the Sergio Leone trilogy of spaghetti westerns that had made him an international star. The character was golden for him, but the payoff wasn't. Clint wanted to own his pictures so he could maxmize his profits. He figured, correctly, that he could make any picture he wanted if he was also the executive producer. Eventually this led him to directing. Malpaso became a factory, and its major (and almost) exclusive product was Clint Eastwood as director, producer, and star. Once his image had been set in gold with the Leone movies, he would make films with that winning character over and over again—and make a fortune doing so.

Steve, however, had no such iconic character and no such grand ambitions. He created Solar primarily as a tax shelter that would give him creative control and pay him a salary of $300,000 a film plus a percentage of the profits while building up a solid bank account that he could call upon as his acquisition fund when he finally found a movie he wanted to produce for himself.

He began looking for that script, something of high quality and not very expensive that would show off his acting and make money for both him and Solar. He came across *Soldier in the Rain*, a 1960 novel by William Goldman that the author had turned into a screenplay. Steve read it, liked it, and made it Solar Productions's first acquisition. He was able to get it relatively cheap because the original book had not been a big hit and the author was still relatively unknown.

With new property in hand, Steve struck a one-off deal with Allied Artists, which agreed to put up the money to make the movie in return for distribution rights if Steve agreed to star in it as well as executive produce. To commemorate their new partnership, Allied Artists gave Steve Gary Cooper's old dressing room to use while he made the film.

He quickly put together a production team for *Soldier in the Rain* that included Ralph Nelson, an up-and-coming film director Steve knew from his days in live TV. To produce and direct, he chose Blake Edwards, who'd made 1961's *Breakfast at Tiffany's*, a film Steve particularly liked (he was still smarting over Dick Powell's refusal to let him star in it because of the production schedule of *Wanted: Dead or Alive*).

And for what he thought was the cherry on top, Steve signed Jackie Gleason to co-star in the film. Gleason's relatively late but fabulous comedic run-up on live television had made him hot enough to return as a star to the big screen, where he had struggled as a nameless character actor before moving to TV. Gleason's film career had had a spectacular relaunch when he appeared as Minnesota Fats in Robert Rossen's 1961 *The Hustler*, playing opposite Paul Newman, after which the rotund comic actor appeared in a number of increasingly less significant movies, including Nelson's 1962 film version of Rod Serling's teleplay *Requiem for a Heavyweight*. By the time Steve asked him to co-star in *Soldier in the Rain*, Gleason was eager to work again in a "big" film.

Soldier in the Rain had a military setting that was a familiar and welcome one for Steve—no doubt one of the reasons he chose this novel to produce and star in—but with a major difference that separated it from his other war movies, *Never So Few, Hell Is for Heroes, The War Lover,* and *The Great Escape*. Goldman's novel, like so much of his early work, was a light comedy drenched in romanticized autobiographical melancholia. Comedy was something with which Steve had never been successful. The last time he had tried it, in *The Honeymoon Machine*, both he and the film were a disaster. Who better than Gleason, "the Great One," to ensure *Soldier in the Rain* would be, if nothing else, appealingly warm and fuzzy?

Soldier in the Rain concerns the intertwining lives of Sergeant Eustis Clay (Steve)—Goldman liked to choose characters' names to describe their personality—a not-too-bright southern soldier (the type that TV would find its epitome in with *Gomer Pyle*), and Master Sergeant Maxwell Slaughter (Gleason), a lifer who is brighter than Eustis and therefore more cynical about life. As the plot unfolds, it becomes clear that Eustis sees his future tied to Max's, and wants them both to resign from the service when their time is up. Eustis figures Max will help him succeed in private business. Max, in turn, sees his own misspent youth in Eustis, and agrees to take the boy under his wing. As their relationship progresses, women and failed schemes come and go, until one night all of Eustis's hopes and dreams come to a shattering end in a barroom brawl during which Max is killed. Eustis then gives up his dreams of becoming rich and living the good life and, older and bitterer, reenlists, in effect becoming Max.

All of this reads funnier and far more poignant in Goldman's thin novel than it played on the screen, where Steve came off as an uninteresting country bumpkin and Gleason got a chance to show off an unfunny dullness playing a boring loser (wordy scripts, as Goldman's was, that talk endlessly about the past and the future are anathema to physical comedy). Even the luscious Tuesday Weld was wasted in the film; in the original novel, the character of Bobby Jo was a true nymphet, but in the film she was aged and tamed in a tailored-for-the-censor script.

The film went into production in September 1963, and by the time it wrapped a month later, Steve knew he had a loser on his hands. The script never gelled, the director's pace needed crutches, and not even a search party could find Gleason's comic timing. There were rumors that Gleason and Steve didn't hit it off on the set, that Steve did not appreciate Gleason's star turn of using a golf cart to get around, and objected to his constantly showing up late to calls, a form of self-imposed star-tripping that Steve as executive producer felt did the production no good. In the end, Steve hoped the eighty-seven-minute final cut could somehow just disappear, go away, and never see the silver screen light of day.

He plunged straight into yet another movie, this time strictly as an actor for hire (Solar had no more cash reserves and Allied Artists wanted to wait for the results from *Soldier in the Rain* before extending its commitment). This one was a romantic comedy that was, unfortunately, heavy on the romance and light on the comedy. *Love with the Proper Stranger* was written by Arnold Schulman, another veteran of 1950s live TV dramas who had since written a couple of decent movies, including George Cukor's 1957 *Wild Is the Wind* and Frank Capra's 1959 *A Hole in the Head*, and earlier in 1963 the book for a Broadway musical, *Jennie*.

Love with the Proper Stranger came to Steve via Alan Pakula, a producer who had started in the cartoon department of Warner Bros. in the 1950s and had hit it big in 1962 at Paramount with the multiple Academy Award–winning screen adaptation of *To Kill a Mockingbird*, from the superb Harper Lee novel. That film was directed by Robert Mulligan, yet another live TV alumnus, who'd helmed his first movie in 1957 (*Fear Strikes Out*) and won the Oscar for Best Director for *Mockingbird*. Mulligan and Pakula then formed their own production unit at Paramount and searched for the right project to follow *Mockingbird*, something dramatic that resonated with a layer of social consciousness. They believed they had found it in Schulman's *Love with the Proper Stranger*. On paper it had all the makings of one of those 1950s kitchen-sink TV dramas they both had cut their teeth on. *To Kill a Mockingbird* had dealt with race and rape; *Love with the Proper Stranger* confronted the issue of illegal abortion.

The plot concerns a young, single, struggling union night-club musician, Rocky Papasano (Steve), who has a one-night affair with a shopgirl by the name of Angela Rossini (Natalie Wood). She lives with her Italian working-class family in cramped everybody-shares-one-bathroom city quarters. They meet during a weekend getaway each took separately. In the style of fifties movies, she was a "good girl" looking for love that would eventually lead to marriage and freedom from her physically and emotionally repressive home life, while he was simply looking to get laid (we don't see any of this; we learn about it later). They run into each other again not long after (this we see), only this time she is pregnant, the result of their weekend fling (it is when we learn they actually slept together). They agree she should get an abortion, still illegal at the time, but at the last minute, in a scene that is horrifically realistic, Rocky decides he can't go through with it, presented to us as he can't let *Angela* go through with it. They break up but eventually come together again, and the film ends with an uncertain hopefulness that they will somehow move beyond their initial physical attraction and together find real, committed love, marry and live happily ever after.

Steve wanted to play Rocky Papasano for several reasons (even if he could not pass for Italian in a million years): he wanted to work with winning talent, and Pakula and Mulligan were at the top of their game; he was familiar with the New York street milieu in which the film was set; and he wanted to do a one-on-one romance opposite a beautiful leading lady, something he had not yet attempted on-screen.

But perhaps the thing that made it most irresistible to Steve was that Paul Newman, who had pushed through to the stratosphere in *his* kitchen-sink drama, Robert Rossen's 1961 *The Hustler,* had considered taking the role in *Love with the Proper Stranger* before turning it down to play the devastatingly good-looking, coldhearted bastard in Martin Ritt's *Hud.* Newman had previously worked with Natalie Wood in Victor Saville's awful sandals-and-robes *The Silver Chalice* (1954), in which Newman was crucified by the critics and his film career nearly ruined. Wood had had only a small part in *Chalice*—she was still considered a juvenile at the time—but already had a reputation as a Dietrich-like mankiller who had to sleep with every leading man.

Steve, as always, wanted to outdo Newman, his self-perceived biggest rival, and he was certain Rocky Papasano was the perfect role for that. Steve was always more "street" than Newman, both in real life and in the way he came across on-screen. He had always looked a bit haunted, eyes a bit hollow, with owl-like rings under them when shot from certain angles. And his shoulders were hunched, as if he walked with a combination of perpetual fear and

STEVE McQUEEN ♦ 131

manic distrust. All of this had been minimized in his previous features by Hollywood's obsession with emphasizing classic male beauty in its leading men. Now, through Papasano, he wanted to portray a young man the camera would clearly show had been beaten down by loneliness and failure.

Whereas Newman's portrayal of pool-hall savant "Fast Eddie" Felson in *The Hustler* was that of a young and beautiful loser longing to leave his existential hell, Steve's Papasano meandered aimlessly through those no-exit depths. Newman's Felson was a passionate artist with his pool cue, while McQueen's Papasano was a cold wanderer with his music—the crucial character difference between these two otherwise similar-looking black-and-white films about the pursuit and consequences of love.

Steve wanted to be in the film so much that he readily agreed not to do any racing during its on-location shoot. Much of *Love with the Proper Stranger* was shot in New York City in March 1963, with five days' worth of interiors added in Hollywood that April. The New York production schedule gave Steve and Neile a chance to revisit the early days of their romance in the place where they each had made their professional breakthroughs. However, for all the energy the city had, as the film worked its way through production, it became depressingly clear to Steve the script had no pulse. It was choked off by its overly sociological treatise on the evils of abortion that all but killed the better story of two working-class kids struggling to find love among the ruins.

And while Steve, despite his ethnic shortcomings, otherwise fit perfectly into Papasano, Natalie Wood, even with her dark hair, looked even less Italian, and far too glamorous to be believable as plain-Jane Angela Rossini, a working-class salesgirl at Macy's.

Moreover, throughout the shoot, off-set, Wood kept trying to seduce Steve, all but drawing red arrows on the floor of the set from the soundstage to her dressing room. He didn't bite because he considered Bob Wagner, her husband, whom he had starred with in

The War Lover, a good friend. And Warren Beatty, her present lover, was as well. But even if he had wanted to he couldn't. Throughout the production, Neile clung to Steve like a tick to a dog's neck.

She needn't have worried; there was no real heat between Wood and Steve. Natalie had to rely on her feelings for Beatty to get herself into character. According to actor Tom Bosley, who played Natalie's father in the film, "She was able to use, obviously, her relationship with Beatty in some of the scenes with McQueen, there's no question about it." And Edie Adams, who played Steve's regular girlfriend in the film, remembered that "she was vulnerable to anything at that point. She was more fragile than people thought." But if Wood suffered from an unsatisfying sexual transfer fantasy with Steve, she seemed blissfully unaware of it. Quite the opposite. As Wood remembered, or preferred to remember, "Making *Love with the Proper Stranger* was the most rewarding experience I had in films, all the way around. . . . [M]y personal life was quite meager then, and the picture was 'it,' we were like a family."

IT TOOK a year of postproduction before Sturges felt *The Great Escape* was ready for release. Fittingly, in tribute to the soldiers whose escape had made them something of a legend, the film's world premiere was held in London on July 4, 1963. To Sturges's surprise, the film received at best mixed reviews. Many there felt the story had been too Americanized and took much of the deserved glory away from the British. Respected British film critic Leslie Halliwell called it nothing more than a "pretty good but overlong POW adventure with a tragic ending." After the lukewarm London reception, MGM, which had signed on late as the film's American distributor after Dore Schary, the studio's new head, decided it should be involved with the film after all, pushed back its release date to August 7, well after the summer's surefire blockbusters.

But when it finally did open in the States, it proved the blockbuster Sturges had hoped and Steve knew it would be, grossing $6 million in its initial domestic release (against the $4 million it cost to make), becoming the ninth-highest-grossing film of 1963 in America, and earning an additional $12 million worldwide.[1] The U.S. box office no doubt was bolstered by American reviewers less sensitive to the factual liberties Sturges had taken with the story. Judith Crist, in the *New York Herald Tribune*, called *The Great Escape* "a first-rate adventure film, fascinating in its detail, suspenseful in its plot, stirring in its climax and excellent in performance. Steve McQueen plays a familiar American war-movie type—brash, self-interested, super-brave emoter. For sheer bravura, whether he's pounding a baseball in his catcher's mitt in solitary or stumping cross-country on a motorcycle with scores of Germans in pursuit, Steve McQueen takes the honors."

Time said, "The use of color photography is unnecessary and jarring, but little else is wrong with this film. With accurate casting, a swift screenplay, and authentic German settings, Producer-Director John Sturges has created classic cinema of action. There is no sermonizing, no soul probing, no sex. *The Great Escape* is simply great escapism."

And yet, despite its ample commercial success, the film was for the most part dismissed by the major studio–dominated Academy, which at the time still looked down its nose at elaborate independent films, even (or especially) those that made money. It was therefore not surprising that *The Great Escape* was nominated for only one Oscar, for Ferris Webster's editing, who lost to Dorothy Spencer and Elmo Williams for Fox's disastrous *Cleopatra*.

Audiences, however, loved the film and especially Steve, the

---

[1] The others in the top ten were, in order, Joseph L. Mankiewicz's *Cleopatra*, John Ford's *How the West Was Won*, Stanley Kramer's *It's a Mad, Mad, Mad, Mad World*, Alfred Hitchcock's *The Birds*, Tony Richardson's *Tom Jones*, Walt Disney's *The Sword in the Stone*, Terence Young's *Dr. No*, Stanley Donen's *Charade*, and George Sidney's *Bye Bye Birdie*.

reason many people went to see it, so much so that in Hollywood it elevated him from a star to a type, as in "Get me a Steve McQueen," an action movie star who could also act and bring huge numbers of men into theaters to see him do it.

However, Steve knew he would never be considered a true A-list star until he became a romantic leading man and was able to attract a large female audience. It was why he had wanted to do *Love with the Proper Stranger.*

But before *Love* was released in December 1963, six months after *The Great Escape*, he had to live through—or live down—the quiet opening and even quieter closing a month earlier of *Soldier in the Rain*. Not surprisingly, the reviews for it were awful. What did surprise Steve was how he, not Gleason, was singled out for all the tongue-lashings. Bosley Crowther wrote in his *New York Times* review that "McQueen is simply callow with his striking of foolish attitudes, his butchering of the English language, and his sporting of hick costumes." Judith Crist, one of Steve's most loyal critical supporters, wrote in the *New York Herald Tribune* that "McQueen, one of the more exciting actors around, is totally suppressed as a mush-mouthed stupid devoted to dawg and buddy to the point of tears." Wanda Hale, writing in the *Daily News*, was less poetic: "McQueen, with phony accent, jumps around as if he had ants in his pants, overdoing it so much that I could hardly recognize the fine comedian of *The Great Escape* and *The Honeymoon Machine.*" To Hale, *Soldier in the Rain* was so bad it made *The Honeymoon Machine* look good. And Archer Winsten, writing for the *New York Post*, put it this way: "The film should set back [Steve's] blossoming career one giant step."

What saved *Soldier in the Rain* from doing any real damage to Steve's career was the timing of its release. It opened November 27, 1963, five days after the assassination of John F. Kennedy, and virtually nobody went to see *any* movie that week. The film mercifully disappeared after a very brief run and has rarely been seen since.[2]

By the time *Soldier in the Rain* had opened and closed, *The Great Escape* was still playing in theaters everywhere. Steve, confident that the upcoming *Love with the Proper Stranger* was going to be a huge success and quite possibly bring him the ultimate in official validation, an Academy Award, quickly agreed to appear in another Mulligan/Pakula production. Based on a 1954 Horton Foote stage play, *The Traveling Lady*, the film originally had the title *Highway*, which, following the rise to number twelve on the *Billboard* charts of an Elmer Bernstein song written for the film and recorded by folksinger Glenn Yarbrough, was changed to *Baby the Rain Must Fall*.

The film focuses on the life of Henry Thomas, a just-released ex-con and highly unlikely would-be folksinger. (Steve did his own singing for the film, which made the premise even more improbable. To say that he couldn't sing, despite an enormous amount of postproduction overdubbing supervised by guitarist Billy Strange, would be a major understatement. He learned the guitar just for the film and played like it.) The story begins as Thomas, sent to prison for stabbing a man during a drunken brawl, returns to civilian life in Texas and to the waiting arms of the young and beautiful wife (Lee Remick) and small child he left behind. At this point, the plot has all the makings of a good, if not great, small-budget film. But then the unlikeliest of complications arises, turning the film into fourth-rate Tennessee Williams as if made by *Psycho*-era Hitchcock. It seems that an aging spinster, Miss Clara (Ruth White), who had mentored Thomas in his pre-prison days, now refuses to let him live with his wife. A drunk Thomas gets involved in a knife fight and faces a return to prison unless he does what the spinster

---

[2] It was released on DVD in 2009.

wants. Miss Clara lives in a Gothic-style house similar to the one Mrs. Bates did in *Psycho*. (At one point, when Thomas comes to visit her on her deathbed, there is even a foreboding climb up the stairs that strongly resembles Detective Arbogast's in Hitchcock's film, right down to the overhead camera angle.) As this story spins on interminably, the spinster dies, and Thomas must go back to prison; while saying goodbye to his wife and child, he makes one final and futile attempt to escape on the back of a speeding truck, but fails to make it and dies on the highway.

The film is a mess. The black and white looks both faded and tired (this was the last black-and-white film Steve would appear in). Steve looks tired, too, in a script that, in addition to every other hanging plotline, never connects Thomas to his music (at a time when singer-songwriters were the most connected-to-themselves performers of their generation). The acting is overheated but doomed by Horton Foote's tepid script. Foote, who had won an Academy Award for his adaptation of *To Kill a Mockingbird*, would go on to win a Pulitzer for his play *The Young Man from Atlanta*, and would eventually write a legitimately great movie about a failed singer, 1983's *Tender Mercies*. But his screenplay for *Baby the Rain Must Fall* failed on every level. And Mulligan, Pakula, and Columbia (and probably Foote, too) knew it, and agreed to push back its release to January 1965. It was the month following the big Christmas holiday season when studios dumped their worst films.[3]

Neile, who had come to New York with Steve for the duration of production on *Love with the Proper Stranger*, had little use for Steve's co-star, suspecting (rightly, as it turned out) that Remick

---

[3] The Mulligan/Pakula team lasted for three more movies before breaking up, having never been able to regain the level of success they had had with *To Kill a Mockingbird*. The three were 1965's *Inside Daisy Clover*, which starred Natalie Wood; 1967's *Up the Down Staircase;* and 1968's *The Stalking Moon*, with Gregory Peck and Eva Marie Saint.

and Steve were having an affair during its making. According to Neile, Steve came home during production of *Baby the Rain Must Fall* one night and simply, almost matter-of-factly, told her that he had been sleeping with Remick. Neile forgave her husband and blamed Remick, against whom she would hold a lifelong grudge. Years later, according to Neile, when Steve wanted to use Remick in another film, Neile prevented it from happening.[4]

And finally, after completing work on the film—his fourth of the year and the thirteenth of his career, plus ninety-four half-hour episodes of *Wanted: Dead or Alive*, several live-TV one-offs, and his stage work—Steve, feeling burned out, exhausted, and disappointed by what he perceived was his failure at becoming a bigger movie star, and believing now he never would be, at the age of thirty-three years old, stunned Hollywood by announcing he was retiring from film.

---

[4] Remick, who died relatively young in 1991 at the age of fifty-five from cancer, always denied the affair.

PART THREE

Big Wheel

The word "cop" isn't written all over him—something more puzzling is.

STEVE
McQUEEN
AS
'BULLITT'

A SOLAR PRODUCTION

Not many freaky cops like
BULLITT around. You look at the
Italian shoes and the turtleneck
and you have to wonder. You
listen to the official beefs about
"personal misconduct,"
"disruptive influence," you figure
he's got to be up for trade.

But when some rare
Chicago blood starts spilling in
San Fransisco, they give BULLITT
the mop. They weren't exactly
doing him a favor. But they've
done a great big one for you.

CO-STARRING
ROBERT VAUGHN

JACQUELINE BISSET · DON GORDON · ROBERT DUVALL · SIMON OAKLAND · NORMAN FELL

TECHNICOLOR® FROM WARNER BROS.-SEVEN ARTS

PREVIOUS PAGE: *Bullitt*, 1968.

It's very expensive to act, in both time and money. I don't advise [it]. . . . Be prepared to give all else up and live a straight life. That includes eating and sleeping right. You should see some of life so that you can feel life, and put it into use in your acting. Learning stuff on the streets helped my acting a lot.

—STEVE MCQUEEN

*L*OVE WITH THE *PROPER STRANGER* OPENED ON CHRIST-mas Day 1963 to mixed-to-negative reviews but did critic-proof blockbuster box office. Bosley Crowther, at the time the bearer of the cinematic standard for the *New York Times*, the culture-and-arts paper of record, was not a Steve McQueen fan and let him have it with both ink-stained barrels: "He's a face-squinching simpleton, for my money."

Archer Winsten, one of the more literate New York film critics, wrote in the *New York Post*, "McQueen does not strike one as belonging too successfully to this Italian family."

Andrew Sarris in the *Village Voice*, never a big fan of Richard Mulligan despite the director's having been anointed by François Truffaut to be the American keeper of the French-originated auteurist flame, was not impressed by the politics (as opposed to *les politiques*) of Mulligan's films. He found *To Kill a Mockingbird*'s antiracist themes racist in their condescending treatment of Tom Robinson, the black innocent played by Brock Peters (if, for example, Robinson had been found guilty rather than killed escaping, the film might have been more compelling) while overlooking the children's point of view, which made the film so memorable (Sarris, childless in real life, was rarely impressed with children's films, or children in films). Sarris dismissed McQueen's performance as overly mannered. Himself a product of New York's outer boroughs, he found Mulligan's neorealist film of working-class romance much too forced and fatally artificial.

Newsweek, meanwhile, had no such problems with Steve's performance; acknowledging not just his work in *Love with the Proper Stranger* but his four star turns that year, it declared, "Steve McQueen's splendid amalgam of blinks, furrowed brows, smirks, quick smiles, pursed lips, shyness, catlike grace and occasional clumsiness is one more explosion of the four-part firecracker of his career for the year."

The joint power of Natalie Wood and Steve McQueen was enough to make the film one of the top moneymakers of the year, where it settled in as the thirteenth-highest grosser, with an initial domestic theatrical take of nearly $6 million, solidly profitable, if not an all-out blockbuster. By contrast, the top-grossing film of the year was *Cleopatra*, which earned nearly $26 million but whose costs drastically exceeded that. Compounded with the Elizabeth Taylor/Richard Burton scandal, the film all but put 20th Century Fox out of business.[1]

Perhaps even more impressive were the five Oscar nominations *Love with the Proper Stranger* received. Natalie Wood got the only one of the "big-four" nominations (actor, actress, director, picture), for Best Actress, but lost to Patricia Neal, who won for her

---

[1] The domestic gross for the top twelve films of the year were *Cleopatra*, $26 million; *How the West Was Won*, $21 million; *It's A Mad, Mad, Mad, Mad World*, $21 million; *The Birds*, $18.5 million; *Tom Jones*, $12 million; *The Sword in the Stone*, $12 million; *Dr. No*, $8.4 million; *Charade*, $6.7 million; *The Great Escape*, $6.4 million; *Bye Bye Birdie*, $6.2 million; *Hud*, $5.8 million; *55 Days at Peking*, $5.7 million.

performance opposite Paul Newman in *Hud*. Hal Pereira, Roland Anderson, Sam Comer, and Grace Gregory were nominated for Best Black and White Art Direction/Set Decoration, Milton R. Krasner was nominated for Best Cinematography, Edith Head for Best Black and White Costume Design, and Arnold Schulman for Best Writing (Story and Screenplay Written Directly for the Screen). Despite *Newsweek*'s strong lobbying for Steve to get a Best Actor nomination, it didn't happen, and even with his much publicized "retirement," he was openly disappointed about it. (Earlier in the year, he had been nominated for a Golden Globe for Best Actor, awarded by the Hollywood Foreign Press Association, for his performance in *Love with the Proper Stranger*, but lost to Sidney Poitier in *Lilies of the Field*.)

That year the Oscars themselves were in one of their downward arcs of popularity, as evidenced by the low ratings for the broadcast hosted by Jack Lemmon and the general disinterest among the younger members of an industry coming apart at its corporate seams. Where once attendance was all but mandatory for those nominated, a total of fifty-seven failed to show up on April 13, 1964, at Los Angeles's Santa Monica Civic Auditorium. The widespread absence was due in part to the industry dismay at the *Cleopatra* debacle, which had put another wound in the belly of the dying studio beast, and the embarrassment of its nine nominations (it won four minor awards but was shut out of all the major categories).

Steve, although not nominated for any of his four pictures, was among those who did show up. He was asked to be a presenter despite having recently injured his hand in a motorcycle mishap. Looking resplendent in black tie and bandages, he handed the Oscar for Best Sound Recording to Franklin E. Milton for *How the West Was Won*. Afterward at the exclusive Governor's Ball, Hedda Hopper made a point of telling him how wonderful he looked in tails, but Steve remained steadfast in his decision to retire and had already turned down dozens of offers that had come his way since his announcement. For the remainder of that year, Neile later recalled, "we devoted ourselves exclusively to traveling, racing, furnishing our house, and other worldly pleasures." These were good times for Steve. He was grateful for all the success that had come his way, and the money that came with it.

And then, suddenly and without warning, his mother, Jullian, showed up unannounced on Steve and Neile's Brentwood doorstep.

Although Steve had always kept her at arm's length, he'd allowed Neile to communicate with her and for his mother to occasionally talk to the children, either by letter or telephone call. Jullian had since inherited a little bit of money and wanted to relocate to Los Angeles to be closer to her "family." Steve would have none of it. Instead, he helped her buy a house in the North Beach section of San Francisco and open a little boutique. That would keep her near, but not too near, and far but not too far.

As soon as he had Jullian settled in San Francisco, he and Neile planned an extended trip to Europe. Before they left, they threw a huge belated housewarming and bon voyage party that also had some of the feel of a farewell to film acting for Steve, and invited all their friends. Steve arranged to have live entertainment provided by Johnny Rivers, one of the house performers at the Whiskey a Go-Go on the Sunset Strip, one of his favorite hangouts, where rock and roll was just beginning its West Coast surge.

Behind the rise of rock on the Strip was Lou Adler, a former songwriting partner with pop trumpeter Herb Alpert in the late fifties before leaving to become a West Coast agent for Columbia Screen Gems. In 1963 Adler left Screen Gems and formed Dunhill Production Company, whose first big client was Rivers. At twenty-two years old, Rivers was a native New Yorker who'd grown up in Louisiana, moved to L.A. at the onset of Beatle-mania, and put himself under Adler's shrewd guidance. His 1963 album, *Johnny Rivers: Live at the Whiskey a Go-Go*, rose to number twelve on the charts, and "Memphis" went to number seven on the singles charts. Rivers then signed a one-year exclusive deal to be the star attraction at the Whiskey, and returned regularly to play there for the rest of the decade. He was a crucial part of the growing L.A. music scene that came out of the Whiskey.[2]

Steve easily fit in with the Whiskey club crowd, which was mostly celebrities (in many ways it anticipated the star hangout that Studio 54 became in New York City in the seventies). Rivers and Steve quickly became friends, and whenever Steve went down to the Whiskey, always without Neile, he and Rivers would hang out between sets until closing. Rivers was more than happy to be Steve's house band for the big party at the house.

Also at the bash were Tuesday Weld, whom Steve knew and liked from working with her on *Soldier in the Rain*; George Hamilton; the Kirk Douglases; and an as-yet-unknown pretty blond starlet by the name of Sharon Tate, on the arm of her frequent companion, Jay Sebring, an up-and-coming hairstylist who was making a name for himself among Hollywood's performing set. Douglas was especially fond of Sebring, perhaps seeing a younger version of himself in the good-looking ladies' man. While making Stanley Kubrick's 1960 *Spartacus*, Douglas had called Sebring "a genius with hair," adding, "Jay was a charismatic little fellow. Good-looking, well-built. Quite a ladies' man. Jay came up with the distinctive look for the slaves' haircut—butch on top, long in back, with a tiny ponytail."

---

[2] In the late 1960s, Rivers stopped performing and formed his own publishing company. Two of the first acts he signed were Jimmy Webb, the prolific songwriter, and the 5th Dimension, whom he recorded on his Soul City Label.

Steve was also close to Jay. They had met one night at the Whiskey and had become such good friends that Steve let Jay restyle his blond hair into the look of the day—short, flat, and combed to one side—and lighten it a bit to give him more of a California beach-boy look.

Natalie Wood showed up alone; Ben Gazzara brought his wife, Janice Rule. Steve had taken over for him on Broadway a few years earlier in *A Hatful of Rain* and now Steve was a much bigger movie star. The two had remained friends. Gazzara's pal John Cassavetes and his wife, Gena Rowlands, also came along with dozens of other members of the young Hollywood pop-culture elite.

The next day Steve and Neile and their two children left to spend the entire summer traveling around Europe, backpacking it and camping whenever they could. On days it got to be too much with the kids, they would check into hotels. Or Neile would— Steve wanted to avoid any chance of reporters or paparazzi knowing where he was.

Upon the family's return to the States that August, Steve and Natalie Wood were invited to co-host a cocktail party given for President Lyndon Johnson to help invigorate his reelection campaign by tapping in to a little JFK-style Hollywood glamour. If Johnson couldn't draw the Rat Pack (who avoided him like the plague), he had Steve McQueen, one of the hottest actors in the country. Neile came along, just to make sure that Steve and Natalie didn't dance too close. She needn't have worried. Steve danced all night with Johnson's younger daughter, Luci Baines Johnson. The party, with accompanying photos, was featured in newspapers around the world.

After that, it was back to Europe for a trip that combined pleasure and racing. This time it was just Steve and Neile. The fun part was Steve joining the American team for an international six-day, 1,200-mile motorcycle endurance race in East Germany. He rode a Triumph Bonneville that his friend, mechanic, and sometime stunt man Bud Ekins had modified for speed.[3] During the race someone quipped that if Steve had ridden this cycle in *The Great Escape*, he would have made it to freedom.

Steve finished out of the money, but finished, something he was quite proud of. Then he and Neile packed their bags and reluctantly headed for the City of Lights, where the French premiere of *Love with the Proper Stranger* was scheduled for that September.

Steve was the superstar in Paris that he wasn't yet in America, primarily because *Wanted: Dead or Alive* had played repeatedly for years on French television. Steve, who liked expensive clothes and always wore custom-made suits, looked resplendent at the opening, his beach-blond hair offset by dark sunglasses. Neile dressed smartly, with an elegantly long scarf around her neck. To the French, they were the new inheritors of the throne of cool that Jean-Paul Belmondo and Jean Seberg had ascended to in 1960 as stars in Jean-Luc Godard's *Breathless*, a film that reinvigorated French cinema with its youthful combination of passion and insouciance.

After the opening there was a party at Maxim's, where crowds of young screaming girls stood outside the front door and backed up into the streets of Paris for blocks just to catch a glimpse of their blond American idol.

Steve loved the attention he received in Paris, so much so he began thinking about a return to the movies, but only if he could make meaningful movies like those Belmondo did in France—

---

[3] Steve rode a Triumph modified with a 1956 Triumph hub and 19-inch wheels to better distribute the weight. The forks were fitted with sidecar springs and the rake increased slightly by altering the frame at the steering crown. The rear frame hoop was bent upward with welded brackets for the Bates cross-country seats. The bars were Flanders, with leather hand guards, and the throttle cables ran over the tank, through alloy brackets to the twin carburetors. As for the engine itself, it was basically a stock Bonneville with the compression lowered from 12:1 to 8:12:1 for reliability, jumbo cams, and Lodge RL47 platinum-tip plugs.

more personal, less Hollywood, something that showed off the hipper, contemporary side of him.

Back in L.A., while waiting for that script to come along, Steve spent his days mostly at home working out to take off the weight that he tended to put on when he wasn't filming, and his nights drinking at the Whiskey, smoking pot, occasionally snorting the new "in" drug on the Strip, cocaine, and even, when the opportunity presented itself, tripping out on some sugar cubes laced with acid, which was rapidly becoming his drug of choice. While at the Whiskey with Sebring he met and became friendly with the actor and martial arts expert Bruce Lee, who was about to start work on *The Green Hornet* TV series and was desperate to become a big-screen action movie star. To him, Steve had real abilities as a fighter: "He was good in that department because that son-of-a-gun has the toughness in him. He would say [if a fight broke out], 'All right, baby, here I am.' And he would do it." Later on, Lee would help train Steve for some of his more physical roles.

Not long after, Steve received a script that interested him more than anything he had seen in a while, something called *The Sand Pebbles*, to which Robert Wise (*Somebody Up There Likes Me*) was attached as director at Fox. Steve had Stan Kamen begin discussions between Wise and Solar about the film. It wasn't exactly what he was looking for, but he loved the screenplay and especially the character of Jake Holman. However, when *The Sand Pebbles* stalled at Fox, Steve put his involvement on hold.

Anyway, he had more pressing issues at the moment, like Mamie Van Doren, a hot little starlet pressing against him every night at the Whiskey while they danced and slapping her sweaty blond hair in his face. Their affair began the same night the Beatles came to the club, bringing with them their own special brand of hysteria. Even the usually aloof celebrity Whiskey crowd wanted a glimpse of the Fab Four, while Johnny Rivers, whom the Beatles had specifically come to see, cranked it from the club's small stage loud and fast, a dynamo on speed.

That same night, amidst the wet fog of the club's hot dance floor, a grinning Steve held up a couple of pharmaceutical Sandoz sunshine acid tabs and offered one to Van Doren, who in the 1950s had been a Universal contract player of the teen blond beauty type—tight sweaters, suggestive Monroe-style mouth moves. Her second career was her determination to sleep with every beautiful contract boy she could get her hands on—young Clint Eastwood was one of her conquests—and she had a real thing for Steve. Although she had told him many times she was afraid of acid, he promised her, screaming over the music, that making love on Sandoz would be something she would never forget. He was very convincing.

Later that evening, they retired to a guest bedroom at Sebring's mansion: "I could feel the crinkle and crush of the bedspread beneath us as we lay in a tangle of arms and legs, creating our special tempo, our own frantic rhythms," said Van Doren. "From the haze of our lovemaking I could hear music in the house, guitars mimicking the beat of our bodies. My own voice, as I cried out, sounded as though it was someone else's. We encouraged each other to longer, more desperate fulfillments after the tidal wave of our first climax. The moments were too short, too long. We were all time, all beginning, quick thrusting, widening, our bodies each other's receptacle, and death and life were at our side. We kept on and on through the psychedelic night." According to Van Doren, after that night she and Steve became frequent and intense lovers; often he needed an extra boost to finish and liked to crack open a vial of amyl nitrate just before he came. Soon Van Doren wanted to marry Steve, and began to push him to divorce Neile, which, of course, was out of the question. Sex, even great sex, even super-acid-amyl-nitrate-screw-your-brains-out sex, he maintained, would never make him leave Neile.

❧

AFTER MORE than a year of doing nothing and everything, Steve, via Solar, quietly came out of retirement and formed a one-film partnership with Filmways for a production to be distributed by MGM. Steve made little of MGM's role at the time—he still held a grudge against them—because they were to act strictly as distributors while putting up his $350,000 acting salary separate from Solar's future profits; in other words, his salary could not be used against the film's costs if the film was a flop, or against Solar's profits if it was a hit.

The script cast him as a card shark who gets in above his head going up against one of the greatest poker players of all time. If this plot has a vague familiarity to it, it is because *The Cincinnati Kid* is very similar to Robert Rossen's 1961 *The Hustler*, the film that made Paul Newman an A-list star. Steve believed this was the script that would do the same for him.

To direct the film, he and producer Martin Ransohoff agreed on Sam Peckinpah, a veteran TV screenwriter/director with two impressive feature westerns under his belt—1961's *The Deadly Companions* and 1962's *Ride the High Country*. The suggestion to hire Peckinpah had originated with Don Siegel, who told Steve he thought Peckinpah could do a great job. Siegel had mentored the director during the latter's heady days of scriptwriting for hit TV westerns, including ten episodes of *Gunsmoke*, one *Have Gun—Will Travel*, six episodes of *The Rifleman* (several of which he also directed), seventeen episodes of *Klondike* (all of which he directed), and *Dick Powell's Zane Grey Theatre*. Siegel was high on him, but Steve had serious misgivings, including Peckinpah's well-known alcoholism and fits of delusion, both of which had slowed his career. Also, *The Cincinnati Kid* had a contemporary setting and at the same time an Old West feel, while Peckinpah's two westerns had an Old West setting and a contemporary feel. Yet Steve trusted Siegel enough to agree to let him hire Peckinpah to direct *The Cincinnati Kid*, a script by Richard Jessup adapted from his own novel.

Production began in November 1964 and after only four days was shut down when Ransohoff discovered that Peckinpah had already shot a couple of unauthorized nude scenes with an unnamed African American actress and actor Rip Torn. Peckinpah later claimed he thought the film needed a sex scene or two to get foreign audiences interested in it; never mind that he had the most popular American star in the world in the title role.[4]

Another problem was the casting of aspiring actress Sharon Tate in the small but sexy part of Christian Rudd, the Kid's (Steve's) girlfriend in the film. It was well known in Hollywood at the time (but never confirmed by any of the three) that Jay Sebring and Steve were both physically into Tate and had, on more than one occasion, shared her sexual favors at the same time and in the same bed while at Sebring's pad, fueled by alcohol, cocaine, grass, acid, and amyl nitrate.

Steve had all but assured her she was going to play Christian, but Peckinpah decided she was wrong for the part and, over Steve's and Ransohoff's vehement objections (it appeared he too had something going with Tate, referring to her on this film as his "protégée"), insisted the part should go to Tuesday Weld (another Ransohoff "protégée"). Steve, as it happened, also liked Weld for the part, having worked with her on *Soldier in the Rain*. Knowing what she could do on-screen and despite his personal involvement with Tate, he knew Peckinpah was right. Weld was better for the part, and, despite his other misgivings, he supported his director's preference this time.

---

[4] Although it has been reported elsewhere, Tate did not do those nude scenes. They were done by an African American actress whose name has long since vanished from the memories of those involved.

But when Peckinpah hired three hundred extras to film a riot scene that had little to do with the film, Ransohoff had had enough: he fired him and shut down the production until a new director could be found. To keep Steve from walking, MGM gave him a free trip to Las Vegas, along with $25,000 to play poker. The studio wrote it off as "acting preparation" for the role. According to Dave Resnick, one of Steve's posse, "Next thing I know I'm called in to Rogers & Cowan's office. MGM wants to hire me out to go with Steve to Las Vegas for two weeks. Now they paid me $1,500 a day . . . we bought a lot of coke . . . We went to Vegas and partied for two weeks."

With Steve safely on ice, wholesale changes were made to the production, beginning with Stan Kamen pushing one of his director clients, Norman Jewison, on Ransohoff. Jewison was a veteran of 1950s Canadian Broadcasting Corporation live TV, comedies and musicals. His direction of the 1961 Judy Garland comeback special, done in America for CBS in Hollywood with co-stars Frank Sinatra and Dean Martin, was attended by Tony Curtis, a friend of the Rat Pack, who at the time was looking for someone to direct him in a new Hollywood comedy. That night at the afterparty, he offered Jewison his first big-screen directing opportunity, *Forty Pounds of Trouble* (another remake of *Little Miss Marker*, which had been done at least four times), a light-touch gambling comedy to star Curtis and Suzanne Pleshette. It was released in 1962 and did well, and its success led to Universal Studios signing Jewison to a contract to direct several lightweight feature comedies, including two with Doris Day, *The Thrill of It All* (1963, which co-starred James Garner) and *Send Me No Flowers* (1964, reuniting Day with her most popular co-star, Rock Hudson), and *The Art of Love* (1965, Garner again).

All three were huge commercial successes, but Jewison had tired of the genre and wanted to do something a little weightier. When Kamen told him about *The Cincinnati Kid* he jumped at it. Kamen then set about convincing Ransohoff that Jewison was the right man to take over, based mostly on his string of hits, and especially *Forty Pounds of Trouble*, with its gambling motif. Ransohoff, hearing the tick of the studio clock and watching the film's budget escalate, agreed on Jewison, and then promptly lost one of the film's biggest stars, Spencer Tracy, who blamed his departure on poor health. Tracy had been set to play Lancey Howard, "the Man" (the Gleason-equivalent role from *The Hustler*) opposite Steve's "Kid" Eric Stoner, and may really have been too ill to make the film, but he was also a big fan of Peckinpah and had not been pleased with his firing. Tracy had envisioned *The Cincinnati Kid* as something closer to a Sturges film than a Doris Day–type vehicle and counted himself out. He was quickly replaced by Edward G. Robinson, whose casting rounded out a talented group that now included Steve, Karl Malden, Ann-Margret (yet another Ransohoff "protégée"), Rip Torn, Tuesday Weld, and Joan Blondell.

The first thing Jewison did was to change the film from black and white to Metrocolor, to give the final, climactic card scene more clarity—he believed that color would allow the audience to more easily tell the suit of the cards. Everyone was happy with the move except Steve, who had envisioned the film as his artsy version of the black-and-white *The Hustler.* Now it was turning into the kind of film he had no interest in making, a big, glossy, star-studded mainstream motion picture.

At this point, Steve thought about leaving, as Tracy had, but Karl Malden convinced him to play it smart and treat *The Cincinnati Kid* as if it were his first big movie, which in some ways it was. This was a major studio production, with lots of top-name stars, Malden said, and if it was a success, it would help Steve gain all the future control of his movies he could ever want. Steve listened to Malden and stayed.

With the film's budget now expanded to $3.3 million (including the Vegas hiatus money), filming resumed on location, only for some reason in New Orleans rather than the St. Louis of the original novel, despite the "Cincinnati" title of both, and with yet another key change: Jessup was out as screenwriter, replaced by Paddy Chayefsky. This in itself is not all that unusual. In Hollywood, a novelist is often lured into selling the rights to his book, usually for not a lot of money, with the promise that he can also write the first version of the screenplay. Most of the time that deal lasts through one or two drafts and then a professional is brought in (Jessup had written the film version even before the book was published, but Jewison wanted no part of it). Chayefsky, a veteran writer from the golden age of TV, had taken home an Oscar for his big-screen version of Delbert Mann's 1955 TV drama *Marty*. However, little, if anything, remains of Chayefsky's screenplay in the final version of *The Cincinnati Kid*. Steve didn't like his take and had him replaced with Ring Lardner Jr., who shares the on-screen writer's credit with a young Terry Southern (Charles Eastman also worked on the script, but, like Chayefsky, went uncredited).

Southern and Eastman were brought in to satisfy Steve's specific demand that there had to be at least one fight scene somewhere in the script—he was, after all, still an action star and loved physical scenes—something Chayefsky refused to write. As it turned out, it became the film's opening, and one more stunt-laden action sequence was added that had Steve jumping onto a roundtable in a train yard in one of the film's few exteriors.

As for the story itself, it remained a far approximation of *The Hustler*, but without the hero's artistic pretensions or suicidal lovers, or even the slightest hint of any of the homoerotic implications of men competing with their sticks all night while ignoring their women. By contrast, *The Cincinnati Kid* is, quite literally, child's play, a contest between great poker players, with some gratuitous PG sex thrown in, courtesy of Ann-Margret, whom Steve did not especially like—possibly because she wouldn't bow down to his image or roll over for him—and Tuesday Weld, who of course did. Steve and Weld remained close during their second movie together, despite the fact they were both married to others, Steve to Neile and Weld to the British actor-comedian Dudley Moore.

Set in the Depression, the film builds to its climactic card game between the Kid and the Man, during which the Kid loses a very high-stakes and extremely unlikely final hand—a full house to a straight flush (professional gambler Anthony Holden estimates the chances of that happening as something like forty-five million to one). Still, long odds make big drama, and the scene plays to a satisfying conclusion, with the Kid walking outside and losing a penny pitch to a shoeshine boy before meeting up with Christian (Weld), leaving the audience with that old only-in-the-movies adage that poor is really rich and that love is always the best bet.

THE CINCINNATI KID opened on October 27, 1965, eight months after *Baby the Rain Must Fall*, and was scheduled as one of MGM's major fall films. It received mixed-to-good reviews, with almost every critic comparing it unfavorably to *The Hustler*.

In the *New York Times*, Howard Thompson wrote, "The film pales beside *The Hustler*, to which it bears a striking similarity of theme and characterization." Judith Crist, in the *New York Herald Tribune*, noted, "*The Cincinnati Kid* is quite literally *The Hustler* in spades. McQueen is at his *Great Escape* best, embodying the surface cool and high intensity of the man who'll go for broke but hasn't had to."

Time said, "Nearly everything about *The Cincinnati Kid* is reminiscent of *The Hustler*, but falls short in the comparison, in part because of the subject matter. . . . Director Jewison can put his cards on the table, let his camera cut suspensefully to the players' intent faces, but a pool shark sinking a tricky shot into a side pocket undoubtedly offers more range. . . . [B]y the time all the bets are in, *Cincinnati Kid* appears to hold a losing hand."

Andrew Sarris, in *The American Cinema*, ranked Jewison in the middle directorial category of "Strained Seriousness" and noted that "Jewison is reasonably good with good actors"; he acknowledged the film as the first notable one of Jewison's career.

The Cincinnati Kid earned $2.9 million in its initial domestic theatrical release, and nearly three times that in the year it took to travel through the world market. It was the fifteenth-biggest moneymaker of 1965 (Robert Wise's *The Sound of Music* was number one) and made a lot of money for MGM, Ransohoff, and Solar. It earned no Oscar nominations (it did win a Golden Globe nomination for Joan Blondell as Best Supporting Actress) and ultimately failed to do what Steve had hoped it would—move him up to Paul Newman–sized respect and superstardom.

During the nearly yearlong gap between filming and the opening of *The Cincinnati Kid*, Steve had begun work on a new movie, a co-production between Solar and Joseph E. Levine's Embassy Pictures called *Nevada Smith*, a "prequel" adaptation of one of the sections of Harold Robbins's bestselling novel *The Carpetbaggers* (and Edward Dmytryk's 1964 hit screen adaptation of the entire book, also produced by Embassy).

However, production didn't get very far before the film's Louisiana location site was obliterated by Hurricane Betsy and had to be shut down for several weeks. The storm hit just days before Steve was scheduled to return to Hollywood for the gala red carpet premiere of *The Cincinnati Kid*. He then insisted that the receipts of the October 15, 1965, premiere, scheduled twelve nights ahead of the film's general release, were to be donated to the hurricane's victims.

The morning of the premiere, just as he was preparing to leave for L.A., he received a phone call from Mount Zion Hospital in San Francisco informing him that his mother had suffered a cerebral hemorrhage from which she would not recover. Jullian, believing she had a bad headache, managed to put herself into a cab and get herself to the emergency room, where she was immediately put into intensive care.

Within hours of receiving the call, Steve and Neile were at Jullian's bedside canceling their appearance at the premiere benefit. Later that same day, Jullian lapsed into an irreversible coma and died.

Her passing hit Steve very hard with a combination of grief, guilt, unfulfilled longing, and unresolved issues of abandonment. Neile wrote that his mother's passing "produced heart-wrenching sobs and left him guilt-stricken and bereft. He had hoped she would recover if only to ask for her forgiveness for the unhappiness he had caused her. He was not able to unburden himself to her and he carried the pain around for a very long time."

Jullian was buried in Gardens of Ascension, Forest Lawn Memorial Park, in Glendale, California, in a plot under a tree that Steve had purchased for her. "[Steve] cried at the funeral," recalled David Foster, who had attended the services with his wife. Also present were Neile, Stan Kamen, and Steve and Neile's two children, Terry and Chad. "He was a lost soul."

Chapter 9

I've done pretty well, considering I'm not the movie-star type.
I'm not pretty by any means, and I'm not that much of an
actor. I should have been a character actor, but somehow it
didn't turn out that way.

—STEVE McQUEEN

FTER THE FUNERAL, STEVE RETURNED DIRECTLY TO Louisiana and the set of *Nevada Smith*. If ever he had had an
opportunity to employ his Method skills, this was it. He was
playing half-breed Nevada Smith, a.k.a. Max Sand (half white, half
Kiowa Indian), an easy enough sense-memory association or "parallel," in Methodese, with his own childhood, where his parents'
brief encounter had left him feeling like an unwanted outsider,
incomplete, an emotional half-breed. The murder of Sand's parents, which serves as the impetus for his seeking revenge on those
who brutally killed them, perfectly dovetailed with the death of
Steve's own mother, an event that had both frustrated his desire
to reconcile with her and intensified his rage at not being able
to. Finally, the character of Nevada Smith is a manhunter, out to
avenge his parents' death, quite similar in nature to that of Josh
Randall, from *Wanted: Dead or Alive*, making the role in more ways
than one a familiar fit for Steve.

Nevada Smith was originally written by Robbins to be a teen-
ager, eighteen or nineteen years old. Steve was thirty-six at the
time of filming, but was able to project the image of someone

young and fit enough to make the film's essential story of a young man's murder, rage, and revenge plausible to moviegoers.

Harold Robbins had first bonded with Steve during the making of *Never Love a Stranger*, and when *Nevada Smith* was green-lighted, Robbins insisted Steve was the only actor who could play the title role. The author had sold the rights to *The Carpetbaggers* to Joseph E. Levine, envisioning a series of films of the extended backstories he had included for each of the novel's main characters. *Nevada Smith* was the first, and, as it turned out, the only one to be made into a movie. The character of Nevada Smith was said to be based on the combined early lives of two Hollywood cowboys, Tom Mix and William Boyd (the latter became identified in the movies and on TV as Hopalong Cassidy).

The cast of *Nevada Smith* included Suzanne Pleshette, Brian Keith, Arthur Kennedy, Janet Margolin, Howard Da Silva, Pat Hingle, Martin Landau, and, at Steve's insistence, Karl Malden to play the villainous Tom Fitch, who murdered Nevada's parents. The film was, to be sure, Method-heavy. Besides Steve and Malden, both Margolin and Pleshette were graduates of New York's High School of Performing Arts, a Method breeding ground for Broadway and live TV in the 1950s and '60s. Da Silva was an alumnus of the highly respected Method-teaching Carnegie Tech; Landau was a product of New York television, where almost every actor at one time or another had studied the Method. And Malden was a product of the Group Theater, where he had met Elia Kazan, who cast him in several key roles on stage and screen opposite Marlon Brando.

The screenplay for *Nevada Smith* was written by Robbins and Hitchcock favorite John Michael Hayes (1954's *Rear Window*, 1955's *To Catch a Thief*, 1955's *The Trouble with Harry*, 1956's *The Man Who Knew Too Much*). Hayes had also written several hit movies for other directors, but no westerns. Robbins was confident he could supply the action and authenticity the genre required and that Hayes could give it great dialogue. However, soon after casting was completed, Robbins distanced himself from the production, preferring to work on his next two novels and subsequent *Carpetbaggers* screenplays.

To direct, Levine chose Henry Hathaway, a veteran Hollywood journeyman whose career had begun in the early 1930s and for whom *Nevada Smith* was the thirty-first of his thirty-seven feature films, many of them westerns (*To the Last Man*, 1933; *The Trail of the Lonesome Pine*, 1936; *Rawhide*, 1951; *North to Alaska*, 1960; and *The Sons of Katie Elder*, 1965, to name a few). Hathaway was a straightforward, uncomplicated director able to spin a credible yarn. His unspectacular track record made him eager to direct one big movie before his career rode off into the sunset. Levine, always looking for ways to cut costs, liked Hathaway's price (or in this instance, what he was willing to take) and felt he could well handle the action of the story. To film it, Levine hired cinematographer Lucien Ballard, another Hollywood veteran whose career stretched back all the way to the silent era. Ballard had most recently been nominated for an Oscar for his work on Hall Bartlett's 1963 *The Caretakers*.

The actors drew their gritty against-the-wind inspiration from the horrible filming conditions left behind in the wake of Hurricane Betsy. There were no working bathrooms on location, causing everyone who had to go to do so in the same swampy stream where the film's climax was shot. Pleshette wore rubber panties throughout the shoot to protect her private parts from getting infected. Steve took to eating whole chickens cooked especially for him by his own private chef in his trailer, refusing to share them with any of the other cast members, fearing his food might get contaminated.

Steve and Pleshette became close friends but not lovers. They had known each other from their stage days back in New York, and

Pleshette was a good friend of Neile's as well. Whenever Neile did come to visit the set, which was not that often because of the poor weather conditions, the three always hung out together. Pleshette was seriously involved at the time with another man (who was married to someone else). When Neile left, Steve happily took off for New Orleans whenever his shooting schedule would permit, to feast on the large number of available and willing young women always there waiting like ripe cherries to be picked by him.

BY FEBRUARY 1966, Steve was already on-set filming his next picture, *The Sand Pebbles*. He'd joined the production late in 1965 after he was no longer needed on *Nevada Smith*. He'd received a call from Robert Wise, who told him *Sand Pebbles* was finally ready to go into production. Wise, who had provided Steve his entrée into movies, was somebody to whom Steve could never say no even though he had been seriously considering two other projects.

One came from Joe Levine, who wanted to do a second picture with him. He had what he believed was the perfect next Steve McQueen film, an adaptation of Romain Gary's novel *The Ski Bum*. Steve liked the book and Levine had had the rights for a long time but couldn't make it because he had been unable to find the right actor to play the sexy, athletic lead.

The second project was one Steve was still trying to develop with John Sturges. *Day of the Champion* would convey the drama and tautness of auto racing through real time, by shooting an actual race, start to finish, and capturing the characters' reactions to the various situations that come up. Although no one had yet made a film about auto racing that was a hit in America, the sport was much bigger at the time in Europe, there was talk that Paul Newman was trying to develop a similar project based on the

Indianapolis 500—but Steve wanted to be first. It was the film for which he had created Solar, and he'd already invested Solar seed money in it.

But after reading the revised Robert Anderson screenplay (or, more accurately, after Neile read it and summarized it for Steve), he reluctantly put aside *Day of the Champion* and *The Ski Bum* as well and signed on to play *The Sand Pebbles*'s lead protagonist, Jake Holman, for $250,000 and a hefty percentage of the profits.[1]

Anderson, a well-known Broadway playwright (*Tea and Sympathy*, 1953), had made the transition to Hollywood with his Oscar-nominated adaptation of the Kathryn Hulme novel *The Nun's Story*. He was hired by Wise, who was also *The Sand Pebbles*'s producer, to write the screen version of Richard McKenna's ambitious, bestselling novel, which had spent half a year on the *New York Times* bestseller list. The story was based on his own experiences as an enlisted navy man stationed in China between the world wars.

The specific action of the film takes place in 1926, in the early years of the Chinese civil war. The Kuomintang, the Nationalist military, was perceived by the outside world as no different from its Communist enemies, especially by England, France, and the United States, all of whom had benefited from China's natural resources for decades before the Qing dynasty was overturned and, under Sun Yat-sen, the Chinese Republic was born. Sun's death in 1925 upset the fragile government, and Chiang Kai-shek, the head of the new military Sun had created, declared war against the Communist insurgents. Following Sun Yat-sen's three principles—nationalism, democracy, and equalization—Chiang also encouraged the expulsion of all foreign nationals.

---

[1] To make the film, Fox agreed to let Solar Productions co-produce. The deal brought Steve's initial combined fees closer to $650,000.

While Western governments remained officially neutral, waiting to see which side would win the Chinese civil war, Western navies patrolled the Taiwan Strait and the strategically crucial Yangtze River with warships and gunboats, with orders not to intervene or commit any acts of aggression unless directly attacked.

The *San Pueblo*, known to the Chinese as the "Sand Pebbles," was an aging gunboat, typical of 1920s American naval patrol vessels, that was assigned to the area. The story of what happens to its captain, crew, and chief engineer is the heart of both the book and the film.[2] The captain, played to paranoid perfection by Richard Crenna in a performance that owes much to Bogart's Captain Queeg in Edward Dmytryk's 1954 *The Caine Mutiny*, eventually draws his men into a brutal confrontation with a small group of Chinese Nationalists in a show of strength intended to ignite his crew's war lust (and enhance the reputation he hoped to build as the man who brought America into and helped end the Chinese civil war). To do so, he orders his ship to head up the Yangtze to the China Light Mission to save the lives of several stranded American missionaries.

Here the film foreshadows Francis Ford Coppola's adaptation

---

[2] The film is historically inaccurate in both place and time, and its two main incidents of violence, the attempt to rescue the missionaries and the battle on the Yangtze, play fast and loose with the facts. The movie takes place ten years earlier than the novel. McKenna served in the Far East in the thirties and the book version of *The Sand Pebbles* is set in 1926. The only battle involving the U.S. Navy and Asians was the Yanay incident, which took place in 1937 between the Americans and the Japanese, not the Chinese. The attack on the USS *Panay* is likely what the attack on the *San Pueblo* is based on. One possible reason for the change of nationalities by the attackers is that, at the time the film was made, America was at peace with the Japanese but not the mainland Chinese, who actively supported the North Vietnamese. McKenna likely based the killing of the missionaries in the film on the murders of John and Betty Stam, which took place nearly eight years later than it does in the film, in 1934.

of Joseph Conrad's *Heart of Darkness*, 1979's *Apocalypse Now*.[3] In both films, a ship's attempt to go upstream—against the physical, cultural, emotional, and historical tide—affects each of the men aboard, none more than Jake Holman (Steve), the quintessential career sailor who by the film's end becomes not merely a gallant hero but a sacrificial savior, giving up his own life to let others live. During the film, Holman learns to respect the lives of the Chinese coolies who work without pay in his engine room and of the Chinese women exploited by the sailors on leave, and he comes to see the hypocrisy of fighting a war nobody except the captain wants— "the insanity of killing for flags," as he puts it, and the futility of trying to drop out of the system rather than continuing to fight for it.

In the novel, and even more so in the film, the relevance or "heat" of the story has little if anything to do directly with the Chinese civil war. However, as a clear and powerful allegory to what was happening in Vietnam and the feeling among many Americans that the country was being drawn by its leaders into a war in Asia that had nothing to do with America, the novel became a huge bestseller and the subsequent film one of the most powerful antiwar movies ever to come out of mainstream Hollywood. (Holman's—whole man's?—final words are "I was home, how did this happen?") The studio system was in its last throes, and the Production Code, which dictated the sociological and moral content of film, would soon be replaced by the less restrictive ratings system, but the fact that *The Sand Pebbles*, one of the most progressive and therefore subversive mainstream American films, was made at all is a remarkable achievement.

The film's Holman was a perfect fictional counterpart for Steve.

---

[3] Interestingly, when Coppola ran into problems filming *Apocalypse Now* (a film McQueen turned down, not wanting to return to the Far East to make another movie; his part was eventually played by Martin Sheen), Coppola screened *The Sand Pebbles* for his cast and crew as inspiration for what their film should look like.

According to Fox studio head Tom Rothman, "Look at the parallels between Jake Holman and Steve McQueen. Both were in the military; Holman is in the navy, Steve was in the marines, and both used the military as a form of escape from a troubled life. Both loved machinery. Both were loners, and in one lucid moment, Holman tells beautiful missionary Shirley Eckert [Candice Bergen] about his mother, saying his mother didn't count for much but was a good dame."

Holman is a man of few words; McQueen, too, was someone whose words in real life were few and precise. On-screen, reaching back to his Method training, Steve practiced the mantra "Acting is doing," not saying, as a way to avoid having to recite what he felt were a lot of unnecessary lines. Throughout the filming, Steve was constantly pushing Anderson (indirectly, through Wise), to reduce his lines and to let the camera tell the story.

Holman finds comfort in machinery; so did Steve. Holman treats the ship's engine room he is assigned to maintain as if he were a doctor on a lifesaving mission. He believes that anything can be fixed if the mechanic is good enough—an offbeat but nevertheless strong link to one of the film's essential themes of redemption: that a great "fixer" can save the lives of every man on his ship, as well as the ship itself.

Holman is detached; we learn this from the very beginning when he is punished for his nonconformity by being transferred from a glamorous navy warship to a small, decidedly unglamorous gunboat. At the start of the film, then, Holman is physically separated from the mainstream and emotionally detached from authority.

This detachment is amplified when the other sailors on the ship take their leave at a local whorehouse. Holman chooses not to partake in any physical pleasures. He keeps himself apart from the action. Then his shipmate Frenchy (Richard Attenborough, with whom Steve had become friendly during the making of *The Great Escape*) falls in love with a beautiful Chinese prostitute (advertised as a virgin) and learns that if he can raise $200, he can buy her freedom and marry her. Holman decides to help Frenchy free the girl, a decision that begins Holman's spiritual awakening. He soon befriends a Chinese coolie, an underdog with whom he identifies and whom he winds up mercy-killing, an act that haunts Holman throughout the rest of the film.

At the same time he meets one of the young missionaries, a beautiful white American girl named Shirley (Candice Bergen), and falls for her. He wants her, but doesn't know how to have her. She is cold to his earthly advances because her commitment to God is unshakable. Soon enough, Holman begins to consider the possibility of joining her missionary work in China as a way of being with this beautiful but unattainable woman. Peace, to him, begins to make sense, while war becomes ever more meaningless.

Perhaps the most jarring element of all is the specter of death that hangs over Holman throughout the entire film. He is the Jonas of the ship, as his men call him. He is unpopular, and not long after his arrival, several deaths take place. Two coolies die; Frenchy dies when he attempts to desert to be with his bride; the captain dies trying to save the missionaries (who, ironically, don't want to be saved); and finally, in a powerful final moment of bravery (and commitment), Holman sacrifices his life to save Shirley and the others from certain death at the hands of a murder squad sent by the Nationalists to kill the outsiders.

There was much meat on the bones of the character of Jake Holman, and Steve bit into it until, as the ancient belief goes, he ate the cow and inhaled its soul. Indeed, in this movie, more than any other, Steve became the character he was playing.

Or it became him. Either way, it was one of those memorable Method-actor performances where what is visible on-screen becomes the window to interior emotion, what is going on both inside the actor's head and in the character's world, rather than merely the reflection of an actor's exterior.

After *The Sand Pebbles* and Steve McQueen's hauntingly beautiful performance in it, his cinematic persona would never be the same. In this, his sixteenth picture, he would find his on-screen signature: a powerful, attractive, strong, unsmiling antihero. To this point, Hollywood had defined what a Steve McQueen hero should be like. After *The Sand Pebbles*, Steve McQueen defined what a Hollywood hero was.

And all because of a performance in a film that almost didn't get made.

IN 1962 McKenna had been paid a hefty $300,000 for the film rights by Mirisch/UA, who intended to use it as a star vehicle for Paul Newman. However, not long after, UA, in yet another bout of financial disarray that had become business as usual for the production/distribution house, put the project in turnaround, where it was picked up by 20th Century Fox. Wise, who was the original director, remained with the project and still wanted to reteam with Newman, who almost said yes when he thought the film was going to be shot entirely in San Francisco. However, when he realized Wise was going to shoot on location in Taiwan and Hong Kong (both substitutes for mainland China), Newman turned it down, not wanting to shoot it in the Far East.

Wise's second choice was Steve, although he too was hesitant about going to the Far East, but because it was Wise, Steve said yes. Fox, however, rejected Steve because they (wrongly) felt he was not enough of a mainstream star to carry such a big film—they saw him as, in a sense, a glorified cowboy. Wise then angrily withdrew, partly because of their treatment of Steve and partly because he now believed that Fox would not let him make the movie the way he thought it should be made. The project went instead to veteran director William Wyler.

In the interim, Wise made *The Sound of Music* for Fox. He had been given that project because of the success of his 1960 film version of the Broadway musical *West Side Story*. Budgeted at $8.5 million, *The Sound of Music* was presented as a road show, screened two times a day in only the biggest theaters, with an intermission and reserved seats (and higher prices) to duplicate the experience for audiences of watching a live Broadway musical. *The Sound of Music* grossed $100 million in its first two years, and literally saved the studio from bankruptcy following its 1963 production of Joseph L. Mankiewicz's *Cleopatra*.

According to Tom Rothman, "At the time Fox was drowning in cost overruns from [Joseph L. Mankiewicz's] *Cleopatra*, and couldn't afford to make *The Sand Pebbles* until *The Sound of Music* went on to become one of the most successful movies of all time, and won Wise a 1965 Academy Award for Best Director."

But then Wyler, for his own reasons, left *The Sand Pebbles*, and Fox quickly rehired the now highly coveted Wise, approving the same $8.5 million budget for *The Sand Pebbles* they had given him for *The Sound of Music*. This time he had no trouble from the studio casting Steve in the lead. Also, as a favor to Steve he asked that Solar be allowed to co-produce the film. Fox agreed. Fox also agreed to pay for Steve's family to accompany him for the entire shoot, relocation of the equipment from his home gym to Taiwan, and his entourage of six personal ex-marine stuntmen.

PRODUCTION ON *The Sand Pebbles* began in Taiwan on November 22, 1965, with a crew of 111 (and 32 interpreters), and the most expensive location prop ever constructed for a Hollywood film to date: it cost $250,000 to re-create the *San Pueblo* in Taiwan from the original blueprints for the USS *Villalobos*, a Spanish ship that was seized by the United States during the Spanish-American War and then sent for duty to the Far East. The reconstructed ship was fully operational, although unable to actually move in the water due to drill holes for lights, cameras, and other shooting necessities, and the need to permanently stabilize it so as to avoid unnecessary swaying during scenes. (It would have cost ten times that much to build it in Hollywood and have it towed to Taiwan.)

However, early on there were problems. As soon as he was no longer needed on the set of *Nevada Smith* and upon Steve's arrival at Tokyo's Haneda Airport in late 1965, when he attempted to transfer to a Taiwan-bound plane, he was detained by Taiwanese customs for carrying a loaded .38 caliber revolver in his luggage. After several hours of interrogation, during which Steve jokingly referred to the gun as something he intended to use in his spare time for bear hunting, the airline officials conferred among themselves, and diplomatic officials from both the United States and Taiwan were brought in, the local customs officers were told to let Steve go. The order reportedly came directly from Chiang Kai-shek's office.

The Taiwanese ruler wanted nothing to interfere with the filming, which he knew would bring millions of much-needed American dollars with it. Before production even began, however, Chiang had insisted that Fox build a $100,000 building near the Keelung River, a structure that would, after filming was completed, remain a government outpost, the studio's "gift" to the people of Taiwan; Fox quickly agreed. With so much at stake, Chiang was not going to let a little thing like a gun force the cancellation of the film.

To pass the time between scenes, Steve raced his 150 mph Grand Prix motorcycle (which Fox had brought over for him) all over the Taiwanese countryside. The roadside officials were told never to stop him, no matter what speed he reached.

Back home, the McQueen publicity machine was hard at work keeping Steve's name in the American consciousness while he settled in for the long shoot. "I've got apples, bananas and nuts on the table," he told one interviewer. "I've got a great 'old lady' in Neile and two terrific children. It's pretty damn good, all of it!"

No one, including Steve, could foresee that the shoot, originally set for nine weeks, would stretch into seven months. It quickly became a nightmare for Steve, his wife, and the kids, all of whom came to intensely dislike living in Taiwan. As Neile later recalled, "Taiwan was the pits. There is no other way to describe it. It was dirty and malodorous and because the country was technically at war with Red China, it was also, for all intents and purposes, a virtual military base . . . the war in Vietnam had been escalating rapidly and Taiwan was being used by our troops for 'R and R.'"

Because of the location conditions, Robert Wise later described the film as "[t]he most difficult picture I ever made." The weather was unstable; it could be 86 degrees one day and 30 degrees the next. And it rained almost every day they were there. Nobody had figured on the rainy season being a factor, but it forced Wise to continually change exteriors to interiors, shoots that were originally scheduled for Hollywood, now done to fill time during the weather-wasted days.

Living in an undeclared war zone that was the focal point for two wars (Vietnam, and Chiang's ongoing dispute with the mainland), bad food, poor housing, and severely limited social opportunities all contributed to the harder-than-usual shoot. Most of the other male actors and crew had taken to living on the ship, where conditions were actually better than they were in Taiwan, and the construct quickly became something of a social scene, rumored to be the main hangout for American soldiers either going into or coming out of Vietnam. Steve was said to have slept over on several occasions to help him get into character.

Troubles of another sort began when Steve insisted he be able to sit in on the dailies, the footage shot the previous day and screened to make sure it was usable, and to help with the actors' continuity—clothes, hair, and so on. It is not all that common for actors to ask to watch dailies, as most don't want to sit through them, but Steve told Wise that he should be allowed to see his scenes every morning. Wise agreed but soon came to regret it when midway through Steve told Wise he didn't like the way he was being directed. Wise asked what he meant, and Steve said he didn't like his readings of lines and the way he was being lit. Wise tried to brush it off, but Steve wouldn't let him. Every day he complained to Wise that Holman would not say the things he was being forced to say in the script, that he (Steve or Holman) was not that verbal, that he didn't need to be the film's vehicle for so much of its exposition.

To keep peace, Wise allowed Steve to improvise some of his lines, and even agreed to Steve's suggestion that they shoot each scene he was in two ways, meaning Wise's way and Steve's way, despite the huge extra expense it created. Wise was able to comfort himself knowing, at least in part, that Steve was spending his own money.

He did not let up on his complaints about the script, and eventually, in an attempt to appease him, Wise let Anderson go, something the screenwriter was not at all upset about; he had had more than enough of Steve and his improvisations. (Although another writer was brought in, Anderson and McKenna are the officially credited screenwriters.)

Then Steve complained about wardrobe. He had wanted his blue jeans custom-tailored and pre-weathered, and when one time they weren't made exactly that way, he threw a fit in front of Wise, who then threw one back. In the middle of a complicated setup, Wise reacted the way any adult would in the middle of doing something important while a child tugged at his jacket to complain about not having any ice cream. "For Chrissakes . . . You don't need those jeans now! I'm in the middle of something; leave me alone. We'll talk about it tonight!"

They didn't, not that night, not the next night, not for the next two weeks' worth of tonights. Steve, in turn, simply stopped talking to Wise for that amount of time, and afterward engaged only in minimal, grunting agreements or disagreements for the remainder of the film. Interestingly, his revolt against Wise during production neatly dovetailed with his revolt to the captain of the *San Pueblo*.

In the midst of all this, Steve developed a flu he couldn't shake that continually shut down the production and made him look a little dissipated on-screen, something that helped his character but made him appear, for the first time in his career, less boyish and more wasted. He also had an abscessed tooth he refused to let anyone treat until he returned to California. Again, it may have been a Method blessing in disguise for Steve—his tooth may have either motivated him to want less dialogue or added to the character's inner pain.

But what bothered Steve the most during the making of *The Sand Pebbles* had nothing directly to do with Anderson, Wise, or the film itself. What pushed him over the edge was something he saw in a copy of an English-language Hong Kong newspaper: a photo of James Garner in a race car. That was when he learned for the first time that Garner and director John Frankenheimer had begun production on a new racetrack film called *Grand Prix*, already being shot on location in Monaco. According to publicist Rupert Allan, "Steve went wild. Just nuts."

He had always suspected that Garner envied him a little too much and that he had gotten into racing only because it was a Steve McQueen thing. When Steve had moved to Brentwood, Garner did the same thing, even moving onto the same block, although his house was at a lower elevation and nowhere near as fancy as Steve's. "That gave Steve the last laugh. His favorite thing to do was to go out on his patio and piss down on James Garner's house. He used to get the biggest kick out of that," one of Steve's friends later recalled.

Two days before Steve read about Garner's film, back in the

States, Bob Relyea, Sturges's assistant director and production partner, was set to formally announce *Day of the Champion* as Steve and Sturges's next picture. The day before the announcement, Sturges and Frankenheimer happened to be seated next to each other at a benefit dinner in Hollywood. As they ate, they talked about their latest projects, and Frankenheimer mentioned he was working on a car-racing film he was calling *Grand Prix*.

Sturges almost choked when Frankenheimer told him the film was going to be loosely based on a book of photographs called *The Cruel Sport*. It was the same book that Sturges was, he thought, still in negotiations for. As it turned out, while Sturges had begun dealing with the photographer's editor, Frankenheimer cut a separate deal with the photographer himself. Aside from the legalities, the practical bottom line was that whoever's film got out first was the only film that would do business.

An intense competition began where, among other things, according to Relyea, drivers from one production were being given obscene amounts of money to refuse to drive for the other one. Fortunes were being spent by Sturges to try to kill Frankenheimer's movie, and the same went for Frankenheimer. Sooner or later it all came back to Steve's participation. Sturges wanted him off *The Sand Pebbles* by the original date of his contract no matter what stage of production the film was in, so that he could begin working on *Day of the Champion*. When Wise understandably wouldn't let Steve go, Jack Warner called Relyea to tell him the studio, which had partnered with Solar on the production, was killing *Day of the Champion*. Relyea tried to argue, but Warner was adamant. He knew he couldn't beat Frankenheimer's picture and didn't want to throw good money after bad. When Relyea called to tell Sturges the news, he was surprised at Sturges's matter-of-fact reaction: he said he was going fishing. Relyea couldn't believe it. Both sides had spent millions fighting each other to make competing films, wasting everyone's time involved in *Day of the Champion*, and all Sturges could say was he was going fishing? Relyea immediately resigned from his partnership with Sturges.

BACK ON the *Sand Pebbles* set, Steve's visceral response to the newspaper article caused him to begin talking out loud to himself and to anyone close enough to hear. *The Sand Pebbles* was going to be his last movie, *and this time he meant it.*

In May 1966, two months after his thirty-sixth birthday and after seven months in Taiwan and Hong Kong making *The Sand Pebbles*, whose original $12 million budget had ballooned to $15 million, Steve, Neile, and the children returned to Los Angeles, where Steve stepped off the plane, bent down, and kissed the ground.

IT WAS the start of a bizarre love affair of sorts. Steve was elated to be back in America, in his lavish air-conditioned mansion stocked with steaks and scotch and big beds and American radio and television, but less than two weeks after his return, despite his declaration, since made public, that he was once again "retiring" from making movies, he began an intense campaign that was aimed at getting him an Oscar nomination for his portrayal of Jake Holman in *The Sand Pebbles*.

Steve, always in sympathy with the mood of the disenchanted young and their distrust of authority, believed that *The Sand Pebbles* was an important movie on several levels, not the least of which were social and political. The year 1966 saw an intense upswing in student protests against the Vietnam War, a movement that had grown out of the civil rights marches of the early sixties and now had expanded to a wider stage. As the students of America kept reminding everyone on the evening network news broadcasts, the whole world was watching.

In an extensive interview he gave to columnist Sheilah Graham not long after he returned from the Far East, Steve, sounding as if he still hadn't completely flushed Jake Holman and his contradictions out of his system, rambled on about the war in Vietnam, one minute sounding as if he supported it, the next like the biggest antiwar activist of all time. "If Vietnam falls, the gateway to Asia falls," he said—a statement that is almost word for word what the captain says referring to China when he turns upriver before a fierce battle with the Chinese rebels. He then told Graham that a victory in Vietnam was crucial to preventing the domino-like fall of other Asian nations. He then switched gears to personal reflection: "We made our picture sometimes only eight miles away from the Communists. Officers and GIs were continually passing through on the way to the front, and I learned a great deal of what was going on. I wanted to go to Vietnam myself—only four hours by plane from Hong Kong—but the insurance people would not allow it." He then said something that at the time caused quite a stir in the Hollywood community: "One thing is inexcusable for our country—these boys who are writing letters to parents and wives, saying your son or husband died for nothing . . . I think we'd better learn to live together. It isn't the atom bomb that is going to destroy us, it's the war of the races. . . . I think in this country, the white man should start making concessions to the Negro, and the Negro should to the white man because this is our country too. I'm not a politician. I'm only a layman, but as an American, I think very strongly about my country. It's a wonderful country and I don't want to see it go down that drain." He was one of the first of the major stars to come out in opposition to the war, and it did nothing to help his chances with the Academy.

Continuing his Oscar campaign, Steve, in an interview with syndicated columnist Bob Thomas, this time deemphasized Vietnam and talked instead about his level of exhaustion, brought about by the grueling shoot, indirectly continuing his threat to retire. "I don't mind telling you," he told Thomas, "I'm beat. The thing I'd like most to do now is go to sleep for 20 hours." In response to a question about considerable money he was making, Steve said, "I'm just working for the government now. Not that I mind paying taxes. This is a great country, and I'm proud to be part of it. But does Uncle Sam really need all that money? . . . I've also got agents to pay, press agents, a business office, etc. . . . I work on a salary, that's a 70-30 deal—70 percent for the government, 30 for me. . . . If I'm really lucky I'll be another Jimmy Stewart—last 20 years or more. But it isn't likely. Three bad pictures and they start giving me smaller dressing rooms."

After that interview, he wisely turned away from carping about not earning enough money and having to pay excessive taxes, never a good idea for millionaires who play populist heroes in the movies, and set about promoting *Nevada Smith*, which opened June 29, 1966, to okay reviews. To everyone's surprise, it went on to become one of the summer's biggest movies, grossing $13.5 million in America, just behind Mike Nichols's fiery debut, *Who's Afraid of Virginia Woolf?* (the Edward Albee play adapted for the screen by Ernest Lehman), which earned $14.5 million in its initial domestic release.

The *New York Times* critic Vincent Canby was not impressed with the film but favored Steve in his review: "It is just too long. It also is too episodic. . . . [But] Mr. McQueen is tight-lipped, craggy and believable."

Wanda Hale in the New York *Daily News* wrote: "You cannot connect the current Nevada with the one played by the late Alan Ladd [in *The Carpetbaggers*]. Everybody has missed the point, which could have stimulated curiosity: how Nevada Smith got to Hollywood and into the movies. A tedious Western with too little suspense and too much talk."

Overseas, it caused riots at the San Sebastian Film Festival in Spain when too many people showed up with not enough seats to accommodate them. In Trinidad police on horseback had to be called in to prevent violence from breaking out due to the same problem. In England, in Japan, and throughout Europe, it was regarded as the quintessential American movie, regularly outgrossing everything there except for one other western that would not open in the United States until the following year: Sergio Leone's *The Good, the Bad and the Ugly*, starring Clint Eastwood.

The outsize financial success of *Nevada Smith*, which received no Oscar nominations, did not hurt Steve's Oscar chances for *The Sand Pebbles*, and he went back to his unorthodox approach to winning an Oscar nomination for it.

And then he quietly decided he wasn't through making motion pictures after all.

One day Robert Relyea received a call from Stan Kamen about the possibility of Relyea joining Steve at Solar as the company's executive director, with a guarantee of getting to direct at least one movie (something that had been Relyea's primary goal while with Sturges). Relyea said yes just in time to be a part of a multimillion-dollar nonexclusive six-picture deal Solar made with Warner Bros. Given the blockbuster success of Paramount's *Nevada Smith* and the pre-release industry buzz for Fox's upcoming *The Sand Pebbles*, in October 1966, Jack L. Warner personally announced the details of the deal to the press—six films in five years, three of them to star Steve, and three his company would produce.[4] To welcome Solar to Warner's Burbank location, Jack

---

[4] Stan Kamen brokered the agreement. The William Morris Agency would never allow a deal for a star of McQueen's magnitude to include any exclusivity, and if they did, the cost would have been prohibitive, even for Warner. The six as-yet-unnamed films were budgeted at six to seven million dollars each when they starred McQueen, three to four million when they didn't.

L. had the studio's tennis courts replaced with a two-story office building that was to be Solar's new headquarters. The once-mighty studio was, along with the rest of old-school Hollywood, starting to fall apart, and its founder was desperate to find a dependable star moneymaker. He believed that Steve, with Relyea's help, could single-handedly save Warner Bros. from having to be sold off in pieces.

When asked about the Warner deal by *Variety* columnist Army Archerd, Steve said he was "looking toward the day when I, too, will be able to direct." It was the first time Steve had ever talked about wanting to move behind the camera.

So MUCH for retirement, student unrest, taxes, and the war in Vietnam. Steve would make no more public comments about any of it. In the end, making movies rather than statements was where the action was and he knew it. Now, as Hollywood's reigning blue-eyed, blond-haired golden boy, he also made it his business to catch up with some of the perks he had so dearly missed while away in Southeast Asia: namely, drugs, fast cars, faster women, and the resumption of his favored all-nighters at the Whiskey. Somehow, he always managed to wind up at Sebring's place, where there was never a shortage of hot, eager starlets looking to show off their best talents for Steve and his celebrity entourage. Sebring was a master at a lot of things, not the least of which was his ability to self-promote and maneuver around the gossip press so that only his hairstyling was of any interest to them. Sebring's not being an actor provided a great deal of latitude for Steve and the others.

And, of course, there was always the occasional public appearance for Steve with Neile thrown in for good measure, at David Foster's insistence.

However, it wasn't all play and no work. Less well known is the extensive charity work Steve did. He donated considerable sums of money to the Youth Studies Center at USC and became a member of its board, where he helped steer significant funds to Boys Republic. He also participated in several clothing and medicine drives for needy children and infants and on more than one occasion personally showed up to help distribute both.

And whenever he could, he indulged his latest hobby, fishing in Alaska with the family, where, unfortunately, his star power apparently did not have the kind of sway it did in Hollywood. Not long after they arrived in Alaska the first time, he was promptly arrested for drunk driving, booked, and eventually let off. None of which bothered him in the least. He actually enjoyed having his mug shot taken. The lighting was lousy but at least he didn't have to learn any dialogue.

Ten years from now? I guess I'll be all gray by then and playing Paul Newman's father.

—STEVE McQUEEN

ECEMBER 12, 1966, A WEEK BEFORE THEY EMBARKED ON A major cross-country publicity blitz for the December 20 opening of *The Sand Pebbles*, Steve and Neile threw *the* Hollywood Christmas party of the season, a self-described modest bash whose invitations read simply, "Come as you are. Very casual," which in Hollywood-speak meant, "This is a *big* party, so come dressed to the nines." The night of the big to-do, Steve wore leather motorcycle pants, Hollywood-hip rebel duds, and Neile had on a sexy, revealing mini-tunic with matching decorated stockings. According to Neile, "Set decorators from Twentieth Century Fox transformed the Castle into the Red Candle Inn of Happiness, right out of the movie. . . . [T]he entertainment was provided by Johnny Rivers, by now a big star, and a new rock group known as Buffalo Springfield."

Steve had returned from the family fishing trip in Alaska refreshed and rejuvenated, ready to take on the promotional tour orchestrated by David Foster that Steve hoped would lead to his being nominated for Best Actor and a big win Oscar night. The party was actually the kickoff to the campaign, a purposely ostentatious affair meant to add a fresh layer of glitter to Steve's image after his long absence from the scene.

Among the industry A-listers invited to the party were the ever-glamorous Zsa Zsa Gabor, in a dress Neile later referred to as a black-sequined tent; her sister Eva, in a multicolored creation that, according to Neile, "covered her from chin to instep and left everything to your imagination"; Joan Collins, in a red fishnet see-through dress (sans then-husband Anthony Newley); Jane Fonda, in a black vinyl miniskirt, with husband Roger Vadim; the Milton Berles, the Pat Boones, the David Janssens, the Ricardo Montalbans, the Peter Falks, the Warren Cowans, John Wayne, Ben Gazzara, Robert Culp, George Hamilton, the Kirk Douglases, Janet Leigh, Carroll Baker, Gena Rowlands and John Cassavetes, Eva Marie Saint, Howard Koch, Vince Edwards and Linda Foster, Inger Stevens and Frank McCarthy, Adam West (TV's Batman), Noel Harrison, Jim Coburn, the Bob Mitchums, Lee Marvin and Michelle Triola, Stefanie Powers, Richard Crenna, Polly Bergen "in a slick silver suit," Elke Sommer "in a periwinkle thing which fitted like another layer of epidermis," Joanne Woodward and Paul Newman, Robert Vaughn, and Robert Wise. It was a quiet little get-together that caused Lee Marvin to quip, "If the bomb hit tonight, the motion picture industry would be wiped out."

The next day Steve, Neile, and David Foster left for New York, where Foster had lined up key appearances on TV's hottest live programs, *The Ed Sullivan Show, What's My Line?* and *The Tonight Show* with Johnny Carson. Steve did both *Sullivan* and *What's My Line?* the same Sunday night, December 18, 1966, two days before *The Sand Pebbles*'s big Tuesday night premiere. Both shows were de rigueur viewing for every American family. Sullivan's end-of-the-weekend telecast was always filled with tension, due mostly to Sullivan's quirky, non-telegenic qualities that somehow made him and his all-star show a must-see. After his Elvis and Beatles landmark shows, he had gained something of a reputation as an anointer of stars. On this night, midway through the show, he pointed out Steve, who was sitting in the audience dressed in a dark suit, white shirt, and black tie, his hair freshly lightened and shaped by Sebring, and his smile on high wattage. He stood up in what appeared to be more of an extended crouch and waved to Sullivan.

About an hour later he was sequestered around the corner in a smaller studio used by CBS for several live daytime shows and, on Sunday nights, *What's My Line?* Steve was scheduled to be the mystery guest, and two-thirds of the way into the show, the host, John Daly, asked the panelists to blindfold themselves and asked the mystery guest to sign in please! At that point, the screen switched to the familiar blackboard, and a hand scrawled "Steve McQueen" across it as the live studio audience went crazy. Steve then walked the few feet to the guest chair next to Daly and the questioning began. It didn't take long for the panelists, all upscale New York celebrities in their own right—actress and television and radio personality Arlene Francis, TV star Steve Allen, Helen Gurley Brown (sitting in for panel regular Dorothy Kilgallen), and Random House publisher and bon vivant Bennett Cerf—to figure out who the mystery guest was. Four questions after Arlene began—each guest was allowed to ask one question in a rotating format—Cerf asked, "Are you about to star in a big, spectacular motion picture about to open?" Steve, looking relaxed while doing a spot-on impersonation of actor Walter Brennan, said, "Yeah, yeah, there's no question about it." Foster's promotional campaign had made sure that anyone still breathing in America knew that Steve McQueen was opening in a big movie that week. The questioning went back to Francis, who asked, "Are you Steve McQueen?" and the audience's cheers gave her the answer. After answering a few queries from John Daly about the "fifteen hundred extras" used and how dangerous it was to film so near the war zone of Vietnam, which apparently interested no one on the panel, Steve graciously stood up, crossed over to the four panelists, shook each hand, and left.

The next night Steve was on *The Tonight Show*. Johnny Carson's uptightness often increased in direct proportion to the star quality of a guest he did not personally know. On this show, Carson did a quick, stiff interview and showed a clip from the film.[1]

Tuesday night, Midtown Manhattan was lit up like Coney Island, the streets filled with people trying to catch just a glimpse of Steve McQueen. The lavish New York premiere of *The Sand Pebbles* took place at one of Manhattan's movie palace jewels, the historic Rivoli, which had the biggest screen in Manhattan at the time, due to its having been the original home of Cinerama (the 1950s version of IMAX) and then Todd-AO, which left it with a specially enhanced sound system, 70 mm screening facilities, and a Dimension 150 screen that allowed films to be shown in a larger and wider screen format. Darryl F. Zanuck, the head of Fox, specifically ordered the Rivoli for the prestigious road show presentation of *The Sand Pebbles*.[2]

Later that week, Steve and Neile were photographed attending the opera at the Met (Steve left after the first five minutes of the performance), in restaurants, entering and leaving their hotel—doing everything together except going to the bathroom and making love.

The reviews for the film were among the best Steve had ever received. While not every critic was enamored of its overlong length and somewhat cumbersome, complex plot, they all loved his performance in it. Bosley Crowther in the *New York Times* called it "the most restrained, honest, heartfelt acting he has ever done."

---

[1] When Johnny Carson congratulated Steve for his great motorcycle jump in *The Great Escape*, McQueen graciously said, "It wasn't me. That was Bud Ekins."

[2] Dimension 150 had been purchased and developed by Mike Todd, who then coined the term Todd-AO to describe the screen-and-sound processes he used for his epic production of Michael Anderson's *Around the World in 80 Days*, which opened at the Rivoli in October 1956.

Variety declared that "Steve McQueen delivers an outstanding performance and looks the part he plays so well. Wise's otherwise
expert direction is matched by meticulous production."

Foster now moved Steve into dozens of events designed to keep
his name in the newspapers and on everyone's lips, especially those
of Academy voters. The big push was on, and everybody involved
on Steve's side meant for him to win an Oscar. Steve did his share
of goodwill-building hospital visits and campus lecturing. On January 3, he appeared before film students at USC and participated
in a Q-and-A, amply covered by the entertainment press.

The Sand Pebbles was nominated for eight Oscars, including one
for Steve for Best Actor, an accolade he felt he was long overdue.[3]
On March 21, 1967, about three weeks before Oscar night and his
chance at glory, Steve, enthusiastically playing the PR game, agreed
to leave his handprints at Grauman's Chinese Theatre. He was the
153rd star to press his palms and fingers into cement and sign his
name with a stick in front of the most famous movie house in the
world (but he was the only one who put his handprints in upside
down).[4]

To get to the ceremony he drove from Brentwood to Hollywood Boulevard in a brand-new burgundy Ferrari he had bought
for himself as a reward for being nominated for an Oscar. Two
thousand screaming fans were eagerly awaiting his arrival. It was

---

[3] The other seven nominations were for Best Picture (Robert Wise, producer),
Best Supporting Actor (Mako), Best Color Art Direction—Set Decoration
(Boris Leven, Walter M. Scott, John Sturtevant, William Kiernan), Best Color
Cinematography (Joseph McDonald), Best Film Editing (William Reynolds),
Best Original Music Score (Jerry Goldsmith), and Best Sound (20th Century
Fox Sound Department).

[4] Grauman's cement ceremony is different from the Hollywood Walk of
Fame, also on Hollywood Boulevard. Steve's star, the ninety-third, was added
to the walk on June 12, 1986, just short of six years after his death. It is at
6878 Hollywood Boulevard, not far from Hollywood and Highland, a very
good location.

a uniquely L.A. event that was broadcast all over the city on local station KTLA.

The next day, to celebrate their ten years of marriage, Steve surprised Neile with a brand-new Excalibur S3 Roadster.

DURING ALL of this Oscar excitement, Steve was trying to find the first script for Solar's new six-film contract at Warner, but he was not having much luck. He had narrowed his choice to a few screenplays. One was *The Kremlin Letter,* the 103rd project he'd considered (and which Neile had actually read) since being barraged following the public announcement of the deal and the first he thought had real possibilites. What made Steve interested in *The Kremlin Letter* was the involvement of John Huston, a director he wanted very much to work with. What killed the deal was its projected $3 million budget, exceptionally high for a thriller, and its location. Even though this was the height of the Cold War years, Steve wanted to make the film in Moscow. When it became apparent to him that Warner was not going to let it happen, he lost interest.

Another project he liked was something called *Triple Cross,* a film that would co-star Yul Brynner, whose Hollywood career had faded and who was now living full-time in Europe. Despite having promised Brynner that he would do another movie with him when he bowed out of *Return of the Magnificent Seven,* Steve turned down *Triple Cross* because Brynner didn't want to shoot it in America and Steve didn't want to do it in Europe.

Another film that caught Steve's eye, even though it wouldn't be a Solar Production, was the screen version of Truman Capote's bestseller, *In Cold Blood.* Director Richard Brooks was putting together the cast and had approached both Steve and Paul Newman to play the two killers, something that set Steve into enthusiastic overdrive. However, early on, Brooks decided the film should be shot in neo-documentary fashion with the leading roles played by two relative unknowns, Robert Blake and Scott Wilson.

Two for the Road, directed by Stanley Donen, was a film Donen wanted Steve for, but before it could happen, Albert Finney was cast opposite Audrey Hepburn. It was one of those that got away, a letdown to Steve who had always wanted to work with Hepburn.

Solar then acquired the rights to *Man on a Nylon String*, a short story that had appeared in *Life*, about a man who dies in front of the entire population of a town while stuck on a mountain in the Swiss Alps. It was the kind of quirky, physical story that appealed to Steve. He got as far as attaching a director, George Roy Hill, and was set to go into production when Hill pulled out to do *Thoroughly Modern Millie* starring Julie Andrews, and the project then died.

The previous May, while filming *The Sand Pebbles*, Steve had sent director George Stevens, the director of such classic films as 1953's *Shane* and 1956's *Giant*, a telegram asking if he would like to do a western together. Two days later Stevens sent back a telegram saying the idea sounded good and asked Steve what he was thinking about. Steve said he would be home in two weeks and was looking forward to talking about it, but the meeting never took place and there was no further communication between the two.

APRIL 10, 1967, the night of the awards, finally arrived. The ceremonies were held at the Santa Monica Civic Auditorium, with the reliable and always funny Bob Hope officiating.

The red carpet wasn't yet the commercial TV pre-show phenomenon it is today, but the public still lined up by the hundreds to catch a glimpse of their favorite stars. Steve, looking radiant in a custom-fitted tuxedo and accompanied by Neile in a white gown, received one of the biggest crowd ovations, causing him to whisper to her, "Listen, in Taiwan most people don't know who Lyndon

Johnson is, but they sure as hell know who John Wayne is." One reporter shoved a microphone in Steve's face and asked him what he attributed his great success to. Steve turned to Neile, nodded, and said, "Right here."

The event was broadcast live over the ABC television network but very nearly wasn't televised at all because of a thirteen-day-old strike by the American Federation of Television and Radio Artists (AFTRA) that had sent the Academy into a panic. If the strike continued, virtually no actors could appear without crossing picket lines, something that did not happen very often in Hollywood. The strike was settled barely three hours before airtime, but the damage had been done, as dozens of those scheduled to appear were suddenly unavailable, having been "called out of town at the last minute." Among the two biggest stars absent from the proceedings were Elizabeth Taylor and Richard Burton, who had been nominated for Best Actor and Best Actress in Mike Nichols's groundbreaking adaptation of Edward Albee's sensational *Who's Afraid of Virginia Woolf?* Liz and Dick were in Paris and claimed they could not get away in time, she saying that Burton was afraid of flying and that he wouldn't allow her to fly alone (her third husband, Hollywood power player Michael Todd, had been killed in a plane crash eight years earlier). No one at Warner believed them, and Bob Hope quipped that night that if Liz left Richard alone in Paris it would be like leaving Jackie Gleason locked in a delicatessen, which brought a good-natured laugh from the audience.

Nonetheless, except for *Virginia Woolf,* the night was shaping up as a battle between the Brits, with Lewis Gilbert's *Alfie* and Fred Zinnemann's *A Man for All Seasons* (the former shot in London and the film that introduced Michael Caine, in his third major role, to the American mainstream; the latter shot in Hollywood but with a screenplay by British writer Robert Bolt adapted from his own stage play, and a cast led by Paul Scofield). The two films, their directors, and their stars were generally regarded as the night's front-runners. Also nominated were Norman Jewison's comedy *The Russians Are Coming, the Russians Are Coming*, which nobody cared about, and *The Sand Pebbles*, considered something of a dark horse without much of a chance of winning anything.

As the evening wore on, *The Sand Pebbles* kept losing every Oscar it was nominated for, as *Who's Afraid of Virginia Woolf?* and *A Man for All Seasons* battled it out. Then, near the end of the long evening, Julie Christie, in a polka-dot miniskirt, came out from behind the curtain to present the Best Actor award. In her breathy British-toned accent, she read the nominees: Alan Arkin, *The Russians Are Coming, the Russians Are Coming*; Richard Burton, *Who's Afraid of Virginia Woolf?*; Michael Caine, *Alfie*; Steve McQueen, *The Sand Pebbles*; Paul Scofield, *A Man for All Seasons*. After struggling for a bit with the envelope, she ripped it opened and read out loud the name of the winner: Paul Scofield.

The audience erupted in applause, even though Scofield was one of the many who did not show up. His co-star, Wendy Hiller, accepted for him. She stepped to the microphone and said, "There is something very special in being recognized in a country other than one's own!"

And for Steve, there was something very unspecial about not being recognized in his own. After the ceremonies, Neile told a reporter that she was happy her husband had lost. "If he'd won, he'd have been impossible to live with," she chirped. "Not because of a big head but because he'd be worrying how to top himself next. I prayed he wouldn't win."

Steve said nothing to anybody that night. Several years later he was still bitter about the loss of the only Oscar nomination he would ever receive and took a jab at Marlon Brando, who won an Oscar in 1973 for his role in *The Godfather*, who not only didn't show up but had warned the Academy he wouldn't accept the award if he won it. They gave it to him anyway (how could they not?) and, true to his word, he sent in his place a Native American woman who, instead of making a polite acceptance speech, spoke of widespread injustice to Native Americans. Not long after, Steve told Hollywood columnist Sidney Skolsky, "Perhaps if I had announced that I wouldn't accept the Oscar, I might have won."

AFTER THE awards, Steve spent most of his days working out in his home gym: "Lawyers sharpen up with law books, and astronauts train in pressure chambers, but an actor has to do it the way a prize-fighter does. . . . [I]n most pictures, actors have to take their shirts off, or even strip down to shorts. If you look like John Milquetoast, John Public says good-bye." He put himself on a regimen of three extended at-home workouts a week.

And he spent his nights drinking, drugging, and womanizing with Sebring, whom he met up with at the Whiskey. On weekends, usually by Saturday afternoon, the always charming Sebring would stop at the house to cut and style Steve's hair, carrying his ever-present soft black leather bag filled with scissors, combs, and drugs. According to Neile, more often than not, by early evening, both men were "high as kites."

On the days he didn't work out, he did very little. "He can sit at home for hours doing nothing," Neile told one interviewer. "He doesn't particularly like to read, and except for playing pool and his passion for cars and motorcycles . . . he really doesn't have other pastimes."

On one such afternoon Steve was relaxing when he was surprised by Paul Newman, who drove right up to the front door. Newman was greeted by Neile first before Steve came out of the garage smiling and shook Newman's hand. They had seen each other very often for a while right after *Somebody Up There Likes Me*, but when that bit of camaraderie faded away, their social interaction was limited mostly to public events at which they would exchange passing nods. Recently, though, Steve had introduced Newman and his brother Art to desert dirt-bike riding. Steve and Newman became friendly again, and that allowed for the unannounced drive-up that afternoon.

Newman, grinning, said he wanted to kick back and hang out. Steve invited him to have a beer at the pool. Soon enough Newman brought up a script by William Goldman, who had written *Soldier in the Rain*. He was now a bestselling novelist as well as a hot screenwriter and also happened to be a close friend of Newman's. Goldman, Newman told Steve, had written a killer western about two handsome, charming young antiheroes who rob banks. It was actually a very funny film, Newman emphasized, and he thought it would be perfect for the two of them. The working title was *The Sundance Kid and Butch Cassidy*. Newman wanted Steve to play the Sundance Kid.

Steve listened intently and said little except that he would think it over. Newman finished his beer, said goodbye, and left.

By the time Newman had come by Steve's house that afternoon, Steve was already well aware of the project and had, in fact, been offered it before, when it seemed Newman would be unable to do the film. Though the script had been written specifically for Newman by Goldman, for a preemptive bid made by the studio for $400,000, Newman was in the middle of filming Jack Smight's *Harper*. When the producers decided to move forward without him, Newman was deeply offended and felt that they should have waited for him to make the movie. At this point, according to David Foster, Steve was quietly offered the part of the Sundance Kid, but because the film couldn't be made by or at least with Solar, Steve turned it down.

The part remained uncast (perhaps uncastable) until Newman was finally free to make it and he immediately signed on to play

Sundance, with his good friend Jack Lemmon (whose production company made *Cool Hand Luke*) in the Butch Cassidy role. After meeting with the film's director, George Roy Hill, Newman realized he was far better suited than Lemmon to play Butch. Shortly thereafter, Lemmon left the project. That left the role of Sundance still to be cast. Warren Beatty read the script and expressed interest, but to play Butch, and thought he could get Marlon Brando to play Sundance, but nobody wanted Brando, least of all Newman, and Beatty passed.

That's when Newman stopped by Steve's place. Steve knew that Lemmon, Beatty, and Brando had been considered before him. Still, he didn't say no directly to Paul, but he knew that day he wouldn't make the film.

According to Richard Zanuck, who was then the head of Fox, "The original title of the film was *The Sundance Kid and Butch Cassidy*. That was when we were sure we had Paul Newman as Butch and Steve McQueen as Sundance. When Steve dropped out and a far less-known personality came in, Robert Redford, Paul, through his agent, wanted the title reversed to *Butch Cassidy and the Sundance Kid*.

"Steve dropped out over billing. He was hotter than Paul at the time, having recently made *The Great Escape*, but Paul had been a star for many more years. They came into my office several times, with their representatives, and talked very frankly about who was bigger and who was less important. I had a globe and offered to split the world in two, with each star getting top billing in one half."

Tom Rothman, the current head of Fox added, "Paul was Steve's particular obsession. He was driven to get top billing over him."

Zanuck continued, "Well, Steve was the bigger star, and when he wouldn't take second position, he just conked out."

The film opened with Newman and Redford in October 1969, made Redford a superstar, kicked Newman's already hot career up ten notches, won several Oscars, grossed over $100 million in its initial domestic release, and remains one of the hundred top-grossing American movies of all time.

STEVE'S NEXT real project came from the William Morris Agency, via a script Stan Kamen sent to Steve directly and which Neile claimed to have discovered among another two hundred or so screenplays that she read while on the lookout for a suitable project for her husband. After she showed it to Steve, who glanced quickly through it, she told him it was the perfect follow-up to *The Sand Pebbles*—a 180-degree turn in which he would play an urbane, sophisticated, fashionable American James Bond—a real stretch for Steve, who had never before even worn a tie in a film. *The Thomas Crown Affair* was an offbeat caper film with a lot of twists and turns, something Neile believed audiences would love to see him in.[5]

Steve called Stan Kamen about the possibility of starring in the film and also making it one of the six he had to deliver to Warner, but Kamen told him to forget it—Norman Jewison had already put it in development with the Mirisch brothers at United Artists. No problem, Steve said; Norman and he could work out some kind of a deal with Solar. Not possible, Kamen replied, as Jewison already wanted Sean Connery or Jean-Paul Belmondo to play the lead.

It was true, Jewison thought Connery was the perfect Thomas Crown, but after much back-and-forth, Connery finally said no, fearing the role was too much like Bond—*and instead did another Bond film*, Lewis Gilbert's *You Only Live Twice*. (Years later Connery expressed regret at having turned down *The Thomas Crown Affair*, and in 1999 he did a not dissimilar film for Jon Amiel called *Entrapment*.) Belmondo eventually passed as well, preferring to

---

[5] It's possible that Steve first found out about the script from a friend, Steve Ferry, who may have read it while working on Norman Jewison's *The Russians Are Coming, the Russians Are Coming*. Jewison, at the time, was interested in the possibilities of turning it into a movie.

work with French filmmaker Louis Malle on *his* planned caper film, *The Thief of Paris*. Jewison next approached Rock Hudson, who wanted to do it but was already committed to John Sturges's *Ice Station Zebra*. At this point, Jewison considered using Steve, and invited him to come over and talk about it.

By the end of an afternoon spent standing and talking on Jewison's front lawn, Steve had agreed to play Thomas Crown in a joint venture between Solar and UA, for $750,000 in salary and Solar profit participation.

Everything was in place until the film's screenwriter, Alan R. Trustman, hit the ceiling. In his mind, Steve McQueen was the worst imaginable choice to play Thomas Crown. Trustman was an interesting case, a real-life reflection of the character he had dreamed up while sitting around bored in his law office in Boston, Massachusetts. One day he put some paper in a typewriter and banged out a fifty-nine-page script treatment about a suave, handsome, wealthy, and bored investment advisor who pulls off complicated capers just for the fun of it. Trustman sent his script over the transom to the William Morris office in New York, where it eventually fell into the hands of Stan Kamen, who thought it would make a great project for both Jewison and Steve, until Jewison optioned it and openly stated his intention to get Connery, casting that Trustman thought was perfect. When he learned about Steve, it didn't matter that he was one of the biggest stars in Hollywood, coming off a string of highly successful and profitable films and an Oscar nomination—Trustman insisted he could not be in the film.

Kamen and Jewison convinced Trustman to at least think it over. In typical lawyer fashion, Trustman asked for and was given every Steve McQueen film, and screened them over and over again until he began to see what it was about McQueen that was special—his cool demeanor, sly smile, and confident look. Then he set about tailoring his script to fit McQueen's specific range of emotions and strong physical presence. Crown thus became less suave, more mysterious, quieter, and more of a lover.

Jewison placed another jewel in his cast, the lovely Faye Dunaway, who had struck gold playing opposite Warren Beatty in her third film, Arthur Penn's *Bonnie and Clyde*, which had just been released. After a shaky start, and thanks to several second looks by major critics, it was making its way from cult status to commercial blockbuster. Dunaway's iconic portrait of the Depression-era Bonnie Parker initiated a new era of fashion and design for female leading ladies in Hollywood, and brought her an Oscar nomination.[6]

That June, Jewison began production of *The Thomas Crown Affair* on location in Boston. Early on, it became apparent that he had little interest in making a traditional caper movie in the style of John Huston's 1950 iconic *The Asphalt Jungle;* rather, he wanted to make a modish film in a wide-screen style, with split screens wherever he could fit them in. That way of telling a story was nothing so much as a distraction, and after Michael Wadleigh's documentary about the Woodstock festival, the style more or less faded away into the same bin where AromaRama and other such big-screen novelties are stored.

It would be a stretch and take something away from Jewison to say the film was saved by its cinematographer, but Haskell Wexler did a yeoman's job, giving the film a glistening look that perfectly matched the slippery personality of its lead character. And associate producer Hal Ashby, on his way to developing his own career as a director, managed to add an edginess, making a number of suggestions that helped move the plot along.

In the end, however, it was Steve's star wattage that made the

---

[6] She lost to Katharine Hepburn in Stanley Kramer's *Look Who's Coming to Dinner.*

film as good as it was, no matter what visual trickery Jewison tried with it. Steve looked resplendent in the kind of clothes he had never worn before in the movies and came off as a cross between James Bond and Bond Street, his white teeth shining and his all too infrequently seen smile here in ample supply. He gave a pin-point sharp portrayal of the wealthy, sly, bored criminal genius.

Unfortunately, Dunaway, whose own glamour was swathed in the film in no less than thirty-nine Theadora Van Runkle outfits, proved a poor fit to play the romantic lead; she was too cool a bird to play with an even cooler crow. Whereas she had sparkled opposite the dark, compulsive, narcissistic Warren Beatty, her innocent but eager sexuality a magnet for his boyish charm and smoldering appeal (even playing impotent, Beatty was hotter on the screen than most leading men and any woman who played opposite him came off hotter for it). With Steve, she came off cold and distant, look-at-me (to the audience) and aloof (to Steve), their relationship forced and noticeably lacking in heat. Later on, Jewison said of their pairing, "Faye Dunaway gave [Steve] a tough time, because I don't think she fell for his charm." (Neither, unfortunately, did audiences for Jewison's directorial style.)

Not that Jewison and Trustman didn't try to ignite the two; there were several set pieces intended to turn the audience on to the couple, but they just didn't work. One was a chess game that seemed lifted out of Tony Richardson's 1963 *Tom Jones*, substituting game pieces for food. Another was a polo match (Steve did his own riding) where Steve's physical prowess was meant to drive Dunaway crazy, but because of the split-screen work, she came off as distant and disconnected.

In the story, insurance agent Vicky Anderson (Dunaway) works closely with the FBI. Therefore, prior to the start of production, Jewison had written to the FBI to get their cooperation in the making of the film. As this was considered pro forma in mainstream Hollywood films, Jewison was surprised when the

FBI said no. The reasons, according to an FBI memorandum dated March 17 (that had J. Edgar Hoover's fingerprints, if not his name, all over it), was that the Bureau objected to the fact that Anderson "dominates" (their word) the FBI agents, making it seem as if a woman was able to tell an FBI agent what to do. Second, the Bureau found the sex between Crown and Anderson "too explicit," despite the fact they only kiss once in the film (Hoover, to say the least, was not a big fan of expressed hetero-sexual happiness).[7] And they also took exception to the fact that Crown gets away at the end, outsmarting the FBI, something Hoover would never condone.

However, it appeared the real target of the Bureau's refusal was Steve. The FBI by now had a thick and active file on him. Among their "observations" was a memo regarding his discipline problems and time spent in the brig while in the marines, and his presence at (or intention to go to) the 1963 March on Washington.[8] But what they objected to most vigorously was what they perceived were anti-American themes contained in *The Sand Pebbles* and several of the subsequent interviews he gave to promote the picture, which sounded to them suspiciously un-American in tone and content. Indeed, it is believed by many that that film was the reason Steve later showed up on President Nixon's notorious "enemies list," the existence of which was revealed in 1971.

The only thing that upset Steve about the report, which Jewi-son shared with him, was its sexual smear campaign, rumors that appeared to have been originated by the FBI itself. Despite the fact that Steve's career was based on his macho image as a strong, tough leading man who drove women crazy, and that if they had done

---

[7] It was, to be fair, quite a kiss. Long, erotic, and filmed up close, it took up fifty-five seconds of screen time.

[8] It remains unclear if Steve actually attended. Several sources offer contradic-tory versions, and none have definitive proof.

any real investigating they would have known about his consistent womanizing, rumors now began to leak that he was leading a secret gay life.[9] He and Neile received anonymous phone "tips" that Steve was on a list of "known homosexuals," and it proved unnerving to the both of them. These rumors never completely disappeared and remain today the basis for a subindustry of articles, books, and magazine articles looking to "reveal" the secret life of Steve McQueen without offering a single shred of credible evidence. In that sense, the campaign against him was quite successful.

DURING PRODUCTION, Steve was having trouble finding some way to physicalize his portrayal of the character of Thomas Crown. He tried dozens of standard Method exercises, including sense memory, improvisation, and searching for the moment in a scene that provided its motivation. Nothing worked for him until he began to rehearse in costume. Ironically, it was this external trigger that led him to an element of his character. Wearing the elegant clothes of Thomas Crown made him feel elegant. It was as if he were living inside Crown's skin rather than merely wearing his wardrobe. In this case, clothes did indeed make the man.

Still, Steve's idiosyncratic behavior on the set drove Jewison crazy, much the same way it had Robert Wise on *The Sand Pebbles*. Once again he demanded to see dailies, asked endless questions about why something was being shot the way it was, and argued against whatever Jewison offered by way of explanation. It was Steve's favored style of working, a manic sort of Stanislavsky-meets-Socrates coupled with his long-standing distrust of authority, but it certainly wasn't Jewison's.

---

[9] Thanks to the Freedom of Information Act and other sources, the author has seen parts of McQueen's FBI file, and has extensive experience working with Bureau files in connection with other published biographies.

One day, Oscar-winning cinematographer Haskell Wexler wanted to capture a certain outdoor light for a beach scene and had only a brief window of time to do it. They had to wait for hours, and just as they were about to shoot, Steve, who was in the scene, got in his dune buggy and drove away. Nearly half an hour later, when the light was long gone, Steve returned, hopped out, and asked with a big grin on his face, "What's everyone waiting for?"

"You know goddamn well what we're waiting for . . . we're waiting for you," Jewison snapped back. Many believe the rift that opened that day between the two never healed.

Another time when Steve disrupted filming and left the set in a huff, Jewison threw his hands up and screamed, "I don't care whether I ever finish this picture!"

Jewison eventually figured out a way to keep Steve out of everyone's hair. Nikita Knatz, a fifty-year-old Russian-born American war hero, was hired by Jewison ostensibly as an on-set sketch artist, but really to keep Steve distracted when he wasn't being filmed. Knatz kept Steve's attention by demonstrating to him the art of sword handling, and soon enough Steve began practicing along with him. Steve eventually introduced Knatz to Bruce Lee, and when the filming was completed all three began practicing martial arts Sunday afternoons at Lee's house. With his help, Steve eventually earned a black belt.

WHEN *THE THOMAS CROWN AFFAIR* completed production, Steve wasted no time moving on to *Bullitt*, the first Solar/Warner film project to actually get past the development phase and into production. Relyea had found a 1963 novel he liked called *Mute Witness* by Robert L. Pike (a pseudonym for author Robert L. Fish) and thought it would be perfect for Steve. *Mute Witness* follows the last days of an aging cop in New York's 52nd Precinct. The book had been optioned four times before, and each time it proved unmakeable for one reason or another. A film about an aging New York City cop was not a concept that especially turned anyone on in Hollywood.

Nonetheless, when former TV producer Phil D'Antoni read it, he took out an option and brought it to Warner, with Spencer Tracy in mind for the lead. Warner passed, mainly because of its uncertainty over the increasingly frail Spencer's ability to carry what was, essentially, an action film. The project lay dormant for several years until D'Antoni sent it to Relyea at Solar, who liked it and called Steve about it. "I received his approval without anything more than a five-minute conversation."

Relyea then hired Alan Trustman, who had written *The Thomas Crown Affair*, to write a new draft that shifted the locale to San Francisco, lowered the detective's age by at least two decades, and renamed him Frank L. Bullitt. Always reluctant to play any authority figure and especially a cop, Steve was nevertheless intrigued at the film's possibilities.

When Relyea received the revised script, he called in Harry Kleiner, a screenwriter he knew and liked (Kleiner had written the script for Richard Fleischer's highly successful 1966 *Fantastic Voyage*). Steve trusted Relyea's opinion and readily agreed that Kleiner should turn the screenplay completely inside out, eliminating most of the dialogue, emphasizing the action, and, because Steve always preferred location to studio settings, using the actual streets of San Francisco whenever and wherever possible. After reading Kleiner's version, Steve okayed it, even if the plot now seemed a bit muddled and confused.

According to Relyea, the script had problems that went back to the original novel and couldn't be solved. "With all due respect, Pike's novel will never be mistaken for a literary masterpiece, and our screenplay left holes in the story big enough for tanks to dance through. The fact that *Bullitt* had a weak script points out how, in filmmaking as in other art forms, it's possible for a silk purse to evolve out of a sow's ear."

Not to worry, Neile, ever the advisor, told Steve; the title alone would make it a blockbuster.

Steve now began screening films in search of a director. He was after new blood, someone he hadn't worked with before but who he felt could handle the film's showpiece, a nine-minute-and-forty-two-second car chase through the streets of San Francisco. After viewing dozens of films, none of which did anything for him, Steve and Relyea watched relative newcomer Peter Yates's little-seen *Robbery*, the British-born director's take on London's Great Train Robbery. The film is stark, fast-moving, and well detailed in police procedures, but the thing about it that really caught Steve's eye was its great car chase, shot on location through the crowded cobblestoned streets of London. Although the film was not a big hit in America, it was a smash in Great Britain and proved to be, after four good small features and several episodes of the highly popular ITC TV series *The Saint*, Yates's mainstream directorial breakthrough. Steve liked the film and loved the chase. He and Relyea sent Yates the script for *Bullitt*, and Relyea sat down to work out a budget with Warner.

In addition to the location shooting and car chase, with a wild climax at the San Francisco Airport, Steve also wanted Relyea to budget for an L.A. crew he wanted to bring with him, something that was not normally done by the studios mainly because it was too expensive. On-site shoots always used local pickup crews.

Relyea took the budget to Warner, which promptly turned him down. It wasn't that Jack Warner had lost faith in Steve; what he had lost was his own studio. In what was one of the signal shifts in the history of industrial Hollywood and the clearest indication yet that the dominant years of the studio era were all but over, in November 1966, Warner, the largest single stockholder in the namesake company he had helped found and which had borne his family name since 1905, sold the majority interest in the studio and all ancillary entertainment holdings to Seven Arts Productions, a Canadian-based conglomerate run by the entrepreneurial team of Elliot and Kenneth Hyman. Their first official act was to change the name of the studio to Warner–Seven Arts.

According to Relyea, "Jack Warner, the guy who built Warner Bros. from the ground up with his three siblings [was out]. . . . In came a Canadian corporation, Seven Arts, and an infusion of corporate attitude and practices. . . . [T]he difference . . . [was that] Jack Warner would ask, 'How are *you* going to make this picture?' The new management's style was closer to that of today's studios, who rhetorically ask: 'How are *we* going to make this picture?'"

The Hymans took over day-to-day control of the studio's operation, with Kenneth Hyman becoming the studio's executive vice president in charge of production. He was the one Relyea brought the budget to. After going over the cost of making *Bullitt*, and despite Steve's string of four consecutive big hits, Hyman felt it would be too expensive to shoot on location and would green-light the film only if it could be shot entirely on Warner's back lot, which by now was being used almost exclusively for television.

This led to an angry showdown in Burbank between Solar and Warner—more precisely, between Steve and Hyman. After Steve patiently explained to Hyman why he felt the film had to be shot on location, Hyman told Steve that if he wanted to make the picture on location, it was fine with him, as long as Solar put up all of the money.

End of meeting.

Steve immediately called Stan Kamen and told him to get Solar out of its six-picture deal with Warner. Kamen met with Hyman and soon, as had happened with MGM's three-picture deal after *The Honeymoon Machine*, the six-picture deal became a one-picture deal; Solar would produce *Bullitt* and Warner would distribute it, after which both sides would be free of any further obligations. The details of the separation were released to the press by Hyman, who called the split mutually agreed upon and amicable. However, Steve and Solar did not feel the same way. According to

Relyea, "After finishing our location work, I received a message from Ken Hyman's office through the William Morris agency. The studio wouldn't even communicate directly with us; once we delivered the answer [final] print of *Bullitt*, Solar must vacate the studio lot immediately. The majority of Hollywood break-ups are usually handled in such a way that the dismissed party can say they 'left.' Not this one. There was nothing subtle about it—we were fired. On the day we handed the studio our answer print, the security guys were changing the locks on our former offices and removing our name plates from the parking lot."

Relyea may have been offended by what was going down, but Steve was overjoyed. He had signed the six-picture deal before he became as hot as he was now, and yet he'd had trouble finding even one project for the deal with Warner until *Bullitt*. Now he knew he was once more free to produce independently, without a studio breathing down his neck. And as for *Bullitt*, he could make the film he wanted to make. He immediately set about tailoring the script to his exact specifications.

The first thing he did was to cut out almost all of Bullitt's dialogue and reduce most of the other characters' as well. He felt that the film was something to be seen, not heard. It was a subtle but radical decision, and it put the burden on Yates to deliver the plot—which, despite (or because of) its having been pared nearly to the bone, remained overly convoluted and nearly impossible to follow—in between the film's three major action sequences.

Working closely with Relyea and Yates, they came up with a budget of $5 million, and set a February 1, 1967, production start in San Francisco.

Steve, Relyea, and Yates now turned their attention to casting. Steve wanted Robert Vaughn for the role of Walter Chalmers, the supercilious politico, one of the key characters in the film. Since appearing in *The Magnificent Seven*, Vaughn had become an international television star playing the title role in *The Man from*

U.N.C.L.E. Now, eager to get back to the big screen, he quickly agreed to read the script, especially since it came from Steve and had a generous six-figure salary attached to it. One of the reasons Steve wanted Vaughn, besides their friendship, was that Steve saw *Bullitt* as a modern-day western, and he remembered how contemporary Vaughn's performance had been in *The Magnificent Seven.* That was the feel Steve wanted from Vaughn.

But after actually reading the script, where the three chases were merely indicated, Vaughn told Steve the story didn't make any sense, that it was "a mélange of mistaken identities, phony clues, double crosses and betrayals so confusing I became convinced several pages had gone missing during the photocopying process." Relyea concurred. Vaughn then suggested a female writer friend of his who he was sure could do wonders with it. Steve hired her to do some ghosting, or uncredited doctoring, but in the end it didn't help very much. Vaughn still had reservations but agreed to be in the movie. As he said later on, "I figured I would let critics and audiences figure out the entanglements."

The entanglements, of course, didn't bother Steve at all. He had customized the script the way he would a high-powered engine, to emphasize its speed and muscle. He was making *Bullitt* for the action, not the logic. Steve saw the character of Bullitt as a human projectile. Part of the appeal of the character was that he was a maverick, someone who bucked what he saw as a corrupt legal and political system, its participants in bed with each other for professional, political, and monetary gain.

Bullitt, on the other hand, is incorruptible and therefore unshakable in his mission to guard a valuable witness with unclear political connections for a weekend. What seems like a simple assignment quickly turns into something darker and more sinister than Bullitt can imagine (and the audience can understand), as it appears that someone wants the witness killed while others want him kept alive; intentionally or not, it is never made clear which side wants what.

At times it seems Chalmers desperately wants the witness kept alive, but at the very end of the film, when the witness is killed at the airport, Chalmers rides off in a limo, coldly satisfied reading the *Wall Street Journal*. As Steve knew he would, Vaughn played this ambitious if ambiguous character to perfection.

For his partner in the film, a role that in so many *policiers* serves as the verbalizer for the protagonist's inner thoughts, Steve chose Don Gordon, a character actor—a face without a name—who was a motorcycle buddy going back to the days of *Wanted: Dead or Alive*. Together, Steve and Gordon rode along for several nights with the San Francisco police to get a feel for what it was like to be behind the wheel of a squad car in this busy and beautiful West Coast city.

To play Cathy, Bullitt's girlfriend, Steve picked the gorgeous Jacqueline Bisset, an up-and-coming British actress. Because her part is small, and her character is the only one who actually talks about anything meaningful to the plot, it is therefore the weakest link in the film. Midway through, after she witnesses Bullitt react coldly to the murder of a woman in a hotel, she reads him the moral riot act, telling him that he is, in effect, incapable of feeling anything and therefore incapable of having a real relationship with her. The scene doesn't work. It's too verbal, too explanatory, superfluous. It almost turns this edgy film into a pedestrian treatise on male-female relationships. Other than her outburst, their relationship remained too vague and undefined to have any real meaning, and therefore did nothing to advance the central thrust of the film's single-minded notion of good versus evil. They are sleeping together, but that's about all we get to know—and, really, all we need to know. She doesn't put any restrictions on Bullitt, and understands that sometimes he has to get up in the middle of the night and go to a crime scene. He is the ultimate bachelor, which both attracts Cathy and repels her. What she doesn't say works much better than what she does. Her incredibly beautiful eyes tell us more in one close-up of her face than her pages and pages of argumentative dialogue.

On the set, Steve was all business, working with a seriousness and an edge that those who had been with him on other shoots quickly recognized as new and different. There were no moody, insecure Method-acting walk-offs, no driving Yates to distraction with endless questions. No all-night card games, motorcycle races, or drinking with the boys during the making of *Bullitt*. Some thought it was because Steve's company had such a significant financial stake in the film. Others thought it was the character of Bullitt itself that had taken hold of Steve. Still others attributed some of the tension to the fact that San Francisco was where his mother was buried.

About a month into filming, Steve, Relyea, and Yates were deep into preparing the three big chase scenes that hold the film together. The first takes place in a hospital, where an assassin has come to finish the job of killing the witness now being guarded by Bullitt (the assassin doesn't know that the witness is already dead—yet another turn in the film's twisty plot). What begins as the assassin's pursuit of the victim soon turns into something else, as Bullitt becomes aware that the killer is in the hospital. The pursuer becomes the pursued. Up and down staircases, through basements, around corners, and out windows, the chase builds to a suspenseful climax, when the killer finally eludes Bullitt and gets away.

The second chase scene, the one that the film is rightly remembered for and the reason Yates had been hired to direct, continues the pursuit/pursued theme, once again involving Bullitt and the assassin. For reasons not made clear by the script, although there is some hint that Chalmers may be behind it, Bullitt has been marked for death. Not long after the first chase, as he gets into his souped-up green Mustang GT 390, Bullitt notices he is being followed by the assassin's Dodge 440 Magnum. After letting the killer come up behind him, Bullitt slips away and comes up behind his pursuer—and the chase is on through the hilly streets of San Francisco, with cars flying off corners and dropping around bends.

To help coordinate the stunt, Steve brought in Carey Loftin, another friend from the old TV days, considered by many at the time to be the best stunt planner in the business. After Steve crashed and nearly broke his neck during one of the first shots of the sequence, Yates told Steve he wasn't going to be able to drive, except for close-up pickup shots. Loftin then hired Steve's old friend Bud Ekins, who had doubled for Steve in the motorcycle sequence in *The Great Escape*, to finish the chase.

Shooting began every day at 7:30 a.m. and went on until dark. Each move was carefully rehearsed several times at slow speeds until everyone felt they knew what they were doing, and then the cars shot up to, at times, 110 miles per hour. They sometimes become airborne, taking off only to slam down on the next hill and bounce off again, just as Steve had conceived it. As the chase continues, the two cars take on the character of their operators, at times reckless, daring, and single-minded in their relative missions of capture and escape. This merging of the personalities of the actors with their vehicles elevates the film to a level of unexpected kinetic beauty and is what the film is really about. It is the difference between being a good film with a complicated plot and a great film with no plot.

The personality of the landscape plays an important part as well. San Francisco has always been a favorite locale of filmmakers, each imparting their own vision on the city's unique streets. Hitchcock, in his 1958 meditation on lost love, *Vertigo*, used the hills and valleys as a way to express his protagonists' mood swings. Yates and McQueen emphasized the dangers of those unexpected hilly drops and steep elevations without thought or manipulative embellishment (Lalo Schifrin's crisp but spare soundtrack does not supply music during any of the chases).

The sequence comes to an apocalyptic end after nearly ten full minutes, when the villainous Dodge keeps its appointment with destiny by crashing into a gas station and exploding, its journey to hell complete. According to Relyea, "The chase between Bullitt and his adversaries wasn't in the original script. It evolved out of McQueen's love for racing and the potential we all saw in San Francisco's rollercoaster streets to provide an unusual twist. Our goal was to run the camera at normal speed, with the cars flying through the city at 115 miles per hour. We had two 1968 Ford Mustang GT fastbacks and two 1968 Dodge Chargers . . . one of each pair had to be used as a 'jumper' and the other as a 'runner.' . . . [T]he camera car had to be fast enough to stay with the Mustang and Charger. So Pat Houstis [one of the crew] picked up a convertible Corvette, stripped it and attached a special rig so it could function as the camera car." The sequence took three weeks to shoot, and a lot of it was improvised by the expert stunt drivers and by Steve. They only had two patrol cars to block off traffic, and everyone was amazed that no pedestrians or stunt doubles were hurt during the filming of this memorable sequence.

The third chase takes place at San Francisco International Airport. Bullitt now knows that the witness he was guarding, and who died, was not the witness at all but a double hired by the real witness to take his place, allowing for a quick exit out of the country. Bullitt also knows now the fake witness is also a killer, and traps him aboard a flight about to leave for Rome. The dramatic tension of the chases escalates—first feet, then cars, now planes.

The killer jumps out of a rear exit of the plane, and Bullitt follows. The killer runs across the tarmac as planes are taking off and landing; Bullitt is forced to duck under a rolling Pan Am 707 jet. The timing of the stunt, which took place at three in the morning in thirty-degree weather, was measured down to microseconds, and this time Steve insisted he do the shot himself, so that the camera could catch the whole breathtaking sequence in one unbroken take and audiences would know that it was actually him. Everyone on the shoot held their breath as the plane rolled out and Steve ran like a wide receiver, avoiding the plane's wheels and the blasts of hot air coming from the jet's engines. After the plane passed over him, its wing coming within two feet of the filming crew, Steve ran directly toward the camera, his face plainly visible. At the shot's completion, the crew broke out into applause. "Boy," Steve said at the top of his lungs and with a big grin on his face, "I love this business!" Later, a reporter on-set asked if they couldn't have used a dummy, to which Steve quipped, "They did."

When the killer gets to the edge of the strip, he hides near a ditch, takes out his gun, and fires at Bullitt. Once again, the pursued becomes the pursuer. Bullitt is relentless and keeps coming, chasing the killer back into the airport. Soon enough, gunshots ring out and the killer dies. Lurking nearby in the limo is Chalmers, whose reaction is either of anger and disappointment or of satisfaction and relief.

Bullitt goes home to his apartment. It is dawn. Cathy is in the bedroom, sleeping. He checks in on her, then takes off his gun and walks to the bathroom to wash up. The camera cuts to a close-up of the bullets on his gun belt as the film cuts to black and the credits roll.

In what would become a familiar stylistic touch for Yates, *Bullitt* dispenses with a traditional opening—no characters are introduced or established—and at the end the film offers no resolution other than the good guy getting the bad guy. The character of Bullitt actually appears to have lived a life before the film begins, and it continues after the movie ends. No unconvincing character changes help resolve anything (no bad guy becomes good, and there are no miraculous rescues that convince someone to change his or her ways, no mended broken hearts). Cathy is still there, sleeping. Bullitt has taken off his gun belt but, presumably, still has his gun fully loaded and ready for action. The audience gets it—he is what he shoots.

Neile, worried about Steve's safety during the filming of the three sequences, and knowing that Steve would want to do as much of his own stunt work as the insurance company would allow, decided during filming of the car-chase sequence that she would surprise Steve on his thirty-eighth birthday, Monday, March 24, by showing up unannounced. She hadn't gone up the previous weekend, because for the first time, her being on-set had become something of an issue between the two of them. In the past, Steve had always taken her and the children with him on location; they served as his anchor and as his protectors from the fans, from the production, from the press, from everyone. For this shoot, however, Steve told her that she could only come to San Francisco on weekends because "this is gonna be a tough location, baby."

She went directly to the set. She had planned to stay the entire week. To her surprise (but nobody else's) Steve was less than thrilled to see her. He told her he didn't want any distractions. That afternoon, Neile watched Steve and Bisset do a scene together. She couldn't help notice how well they acted together, and she wondered if their acting was *that* good.

Her instincts were correct. The two had started an affair almost immediately, and everybody on the set knew it long before Neile arrived and figured it out. Steve was drawn to Bisset, with her silken-haired beauty, husky, sensual voice, and gorgeous body, and she returned the interest, with such obviousness and intensity that no one could miss what was going on, even always-look-the-other-way Neile.

While Steve continued working, Neile decided to go to his apartment and get cleaned up. In the bathroom, she found a lady's hairbrush. Infuriated, she picked up Steve's bathroom radio and threw it against the mirror, which it shattered. Then she waited for Steve to come home. When he did, she greeted him by throwing the hairbrush at his head and shouting, "Happy birthday, asshole!" With that, she stormed out of the apartment, caught a cab to the airport, and was on the next flight back to L.A.

Filming was completed two days later. Steve made his goodbyes to one and all, including Bisset, and returned to L.A. to prepare for the big June opening of *The Thomas Crown Affair* and face whatever strident marital music Neile was going to greet him with when he arrived home.

He felt ready for anything.

I feel very protective about Hollywood, and I wouldn't rap my town, but I'll rap the things I didn't have the sense to avoid— which was to get very involved. . . . I was working sixteen hours a day and I was the president of three corporations. And I was uh . . . not very happy.

— STEVE McQUEEN

THE *THOMAS CROWN AFFAIR* HAD ITS WORLD PREMIERE at Boston's Sack Music Hall on the evening of June 26, 1968, and began a nationwide summer run the next day. Steve and Neile went east together for the big opening, although at the last minute he had a change of heart and tried to get out of it, claiming his ears, especially the near-deaf one, were bothering him and he didn't want to fly. However, Neile, still upset about San Francisco, managed to convince him it was an important enough occasion that he should try to make it, and that they could both put on their best brave faces for it.

Steve agreed, and that night, when they showed up, they both looked stunning in their formal attire. Steve's black tux made it appear as if Thomas Crown himself had shown up for the premiere, and the two gave a passable performance as the perfect happily married couple.

The event had prompted a mayoral declaration of "Steve McQueen Day," and just to get into the theater Steve had to be shielded by policemen when it seemed the crowd outside might break down the wooden barriers and crush him to death. Parties went on all weekend in celebration of the big event and sports events were held in his honor. Whenever he was asked in any of the endless interviews he consented to that weekend, he always made a point of saying of how happy he was to be married to Neile.

Those interviews, Neile said later, "gave me hope." Even now, she wanted to believe that regardless of anything that had gone down before, even San Francisco, their love and marriage could somehow survive it. Now, however, she had to move all that to the back of her mind; this was Steve's night and she did not want anything, most of all herself, to interfere with it.

THE REVIEWS *The Thomas Crown Affair* received were among the best of Steve's career, for his performance more than for the film itself. The *New York Times*'s Renata Adler, a writer who was not really a film critic, did not easily surrender her imagination to romantic fantasy in the movies. But she allowed herself to be charmed by Steve: "There is a long, soon-to-be-famous kissing scene that is so mis-directed that one thinks of Edsels on a summer's night. . . . McQueen is always special, and although this role is too indoors and formal for him, he does get a chance to race across the desert, or fly a glider or lounge on a beach, in the casual-intense work he is best at."

The New York *Daily News*'s Kathleen Carroll wrote that "a polished McQueen, minus his motorcyclist's mumble, shows a whole new facet of his active personality. He is cast most successfully."

Archer Winsten, writing in the *New York Post*, liked Steve's performance as well but was less impressed with the film: "McQueen, dashing around with verve, unlimited energy and bright, inquiring eyes, makes you wonder if he knows he's hatching something almost akin to a turkey."

And a young Roger Ebert, writing for the *Chicago Sun-Times*, gave it only two and a half stars out of four, calling it "possibly the most under-plotted, underwritten, over-photographed film of the year. Which is not to say it isn't great to look at. It is."

Nonetheless, everywhere it played, people pushed each other out of the way to buy tickets. Made on what was then considered a hefty budget of approximately $5 million, *The Thomas Crown Affair* wound up grossing $14 million in its initial domestic release, a lot of money in 1968 dollars. It was enough to place Steve third on the list of the highest-drawing actors that year.[1]

Everyone was happy with the financial results, including Norman Jewison, who was thrilled by the film's success but in private told one associate, "I can't honestly say Steve was the most difficult person I ever worked with because the rewards were so great. But of all the actors I've worked with, he was the most alone."

STEVE NEVER liked to work in the summer, and this year was no exception. He spent more and more time alone in the Palm Springs house, using as an excuse his desire to help the Navajo Indians by giving them clothing, food, and medical supplies. He almost always left Neile behind during these trips, as if the Palm Springs residence was intended only for him, to unwind and relax in solitude, while she took care of the children and the house in Brentwood. Only he wasn't exactly alone out there, and it didn't take much time to accomplish his voluntary obligations. All of his L.A. friends knew what he was really doing when he went to Palm Springs. One described Steve's place as "an upscale whore-house for a permanent clientele of one." It was also the perfect place for him to indulge in his favorite drug, high-quality peyote, which he could easily get from his Navajo friends.

---

[1] According to cumulative box office receipts, the eight top-grossing actors/ actresses of 1968 were, in descending order, Dustin Hoffman, Faye Dunaway, Steve McQueen, Warren Beatty, Peter Fonda, Henry Fonda, Jane Fonda, and Natalie Wood.

The desert wasn't all fun and games for Steve, and occasionally he even paid some attention to his film career. That summer, while in Palm Springs, he had settled on his next film, a choice that would have been hard to predict after *The Thomas Crown Affair* and with *Bullitt* waiting in the wings. Perhaps he longed to do some real acting, rather than contributing to the kinetically driven performance in *Bullitt,* and on-screen romance with high-strung actresses didn't hold a candle to the real thing for him. Romance in front of a camera always made him feel a little uneasy, whether it was for a detective magazine in his youth or a big Hollywood movie. He was a Method actor; he wanted to Method-act.

After the box office success of *The Thomas Crown Affair* every studio except Warner Bros. wanted to get next to Steve. Money offers flew to him like metal filings to a magnet. Everywhere he turned, more and more of them came his way.

Steve was approached by Columbia Pictures to star in a film adaptation of William Faulkner's final novel, *The Reivers,* which had been awarded the Pulitzer Prize after Faulkner's death.[2] Looking to add to Solar's bank, Steve and Relyea agreed that he should make the film. However, before the film went into production the executive in charge of the product, Gordon Stulberg, left the studio. As part of his buyout package, he was allowed to take a number of projects with him. One of them was *The Reivers.*

Relyea struck a three-picture, $20 million deal for Solar with CBS's Cinema Center Films, the network's new branch devoted to feature films. The new deal called for Steve to star in all three of the films, the key project being the one Steve had originally created Solar for, *Le Mans* (the new title for *Day of the Champion*). The other two projects were an adaptation of Whit Masterson's novel *Man on a Nylon String,* which Steve had considered once before, renamed *Nylon,* and *The Reivers.* As it happened, Stulberg

---

[2] Faulkner died in 1962, a month after the novel's publication.

had landed at Cinema Center Films, and wanted Steve to honor his commitment to star in the film. After discussing it with Relyea, to keep their three-picture deal running smoothly, Steve agreed.

Meanwhile, Solar took over the old Republic Studios in Studio City, at the corner of Ventura and Radford, to house its twenty-five full-time employees. Steve wanted anyone with a good idea to be able to get it read by his people, and he intended to make sure he had enough staff to keep that pledge. Several employees had no other function than reading scripts.

One such script came from an aspiring musician who believed he could also write movies. Someone at Solar read it and returned it with a note that said simply, "Not interested." It was one step up from a form rejection letter. The recipient was not happy. His name was Charles Manson.

STEVE DECIDED to leave the preproduction of *The Reivers* in Relyea's hands and spent what was left of the summer in Europe with Neile and the kids, knocking about, seeing the sights, and visiting friends. Actress Claudia Cardinale, who had met Steve in Hollywood, had invited him and the family to visit her and her husband, Franco Cristaldi, in Italy. From there it was on to London to visit Richard Attenborough, one of Steve's favorite co-stars from *The Great Escape* and *The Sand Pebbles*.

According to Neile, Steve managed to slip away several times during the London part of the trip to go to the Playboy Club, which was, like the rest of London, "swinging" with young and beautiful "bunnies." The Playboy Club was manna for Steve, with no shortage of girls eager and willing to be with him.

After Steve and his family returned to Brentwood, he had only a few days at home before his departure for Carrollton, Mississippi, for the scheduled fourteen-week shoot for *The Reivers*, to be filmed entirely on location (except for the climactic horse race, which was to be shot at the Walt Disney Ranch in Southern California). To direct, Relyea had chosen Mark Rydell, whom Steve knew from his own days of live TV out of New York. Rydell had gone on to a big-screen career that before *The Reivers* totaled just one film, *The Fox*, a weird screen adaptation of D. H. Lawrence's novel of the same name that included scenes of masturbation, three-way sex, and lesbianism. Made in the immediate aftermath of the dissolution of the Production Code, it failed both commercially and artistically (the switching of its locale from England to Canada is an apt metaphor for Rydell's inability to transfer the heat of the novel to the screen).

Rydell was not Steve's first choice. Far from it. Recalled Relyea, "Steve didn't react much to the recommendation of Rydell, other than to give me his typical nod of the head. . . . I didn't know that McQueen and Rydell had a long history together. I didn't know they attended the Neighborhood Playhouse and Actors Studio together. . . . I didn't know McQueen had stolen Rydell's former girlfriend, Neile Adams, who eventually became Mrs. McQueen. I didn't know that Hilly Elkins, Steve's former agent, once advised Neile not to leave Rydell for a loser who, in his opinion, would never amount to anything—and that insult stuck with him forever."

Steve had really wanted William Wyler, but he turned down the project, as did John Huston. When Rydell's name came up—he was already set to direct *Nylon*, although that film had not as yet reached production—Steve reluctantly said yes, but privately he was already having serious second thoughts about the whole project and was talking doomsday about it to Relyea. "This is career suicide," he said. "My fans will walk out of the theater feeling betrayed, and that will be the end of it." Relyea said nothing, but he tended to agree with Steve over this radical shift in styles from *Thomas Crown* and the upcoming *Bullitt*. Audiences wanted Steve to be the king of cool, not a sweaty southern country boy.

To write the screenplay, Steve chose the team of Irving Ravetch and Harriet Frank Jr., who had successfully adapted Faulkner for Martin Ritt's 1958 *The Long, Hot Summer* and Ritt's 1959 *The Sound and the Fury*. *The Long, Hot Summer* proved a strong vehicle for Paul Newman, another actor unlikely to feel at home in Faulknerland. They had also written the screenplay for Paul Newman's highly successful *Hud* in 1963, again directed by Ritt.

. The plot of *The Reivers* concerns a group of four people—a boy (Mitch Vogel), a black man (played by newcomer Rupert Crosse, whom it was rumored on-set that Steve did not particularly like, thinking that at six foot five Crosse was too tall to play opposite him), a prostitute (Sharon Farrell), and a hired hand (Steve), who make a four-day journey down the fabled road of life at the turn of the twentieth century, all seen through the eyes of the boy and heard as his grown-up memories (voiced by Burgess Meredith).

It is not difficult to understand why Faulkner, who was facing his own mortality, wrote *The Reivers*, a story of the old South, or his old South, seen through the eyes of a little boy. What is difficult to understand is why, despite the business advantages, Steve allowed himself to play what was, in effect, a minor and completely forgettable supporting role in it. After a string of rough, tough leading men, he looked a bit puffy on-screen, with a shaggy top and cheap, baggy clothes. The film became a tour without the force, and the film's 111 minutes felt much longer.

During filming, Steve fought, at times bitterly, with his director. Most on-set didn't know about the history between the two, and some thought the bad feelings were because Rydell had unknowingly made a pass at one of Steve's many starlet girlfriends who populated the set, but more likely it was an overall expression of frustration with how difficult it was for Steve to be playing an utterly wrong character in an utterly wrong film.

If Steve had initially tried to convince himself that he could use *The Reivers* to show that he was a "real," or Method, actor, not just a type or a personality, the film proved that, in fact, he couldn't.

Boon Hogganbeck is completely superfluous in the canon of Steve's career characters. Steve's money shot was always a combination of his sexual intensity and virile manliness. Both were wasted here on an affable character who wasn't too bright, very strong, or at all sexual, in a film that resembled nothing so much as an episode of the future TV series *The Waltons* (so much so that Will Geer, who played the patriarch in the film, would go on to do the same in that series in 1972 about small-town life seen through the eyes of a young boy, itself adapted from a different movie).

Things came to a head between Rydell and Steve when, during a break in filming due to an injury to Mitch Vogel while filming the horse race, Steve asked, as had now become his habit, that he see the dailies. Rydell objected, Steve insisted, they were run, and Steve exploded. He wanted Rydell fired, blaming him for the shortcomings in what he saw as his own meandering performance. Steve went so far as to call Bill Paley, the head of CBS, which owned Cinema Center, to have Rydell fired. Steve wanted some loyalty displayed by Paley, for whose network *Wanted: Dead or Alive* had made a lot of money.

Paley, though, had known and liked Rydell from the live TV days, and Rydell had made a lot of money for the network. Paley believed in his talent and refused to let him go. That did it for Steve, who often would not leave his trailer to shoot a scene when Rydell wanted him and who finished the picture holding a grudge against both Paley and Rydell that he never let go. Steve and Rydell would never work together on another picture, which suited the director just fine. In truth, they were a bad mix: Rydell's style of moviemaking was not compatible with Steve's Method intensity, turning Steve bland instead of keeping him cool.

Later on, Rydell put the blame for the film's commercial failure squarely on Steve's acting. Recalling an incident when Steve wouldn't leave the trailer and come to the set, Rydell said, "He wanted to feel that nothing could happen without him. He needed to feel that. . . . He was an entirely instinctive actor. He never learned his lines and after one, or at the most two, takes, he wasn't any good. . . . I eventually solved the problem by leaving McQueen in his dressing room and standing in for him for about nine takes and then I'd bring him out, if he'd come, then we'd get the take of them together we wanted."

Even as word began to spread in the industry that *The Reivers* was going to be a bomb, on October 17, 1968, *Bullitt* had its star-studded world premiere at New York's Radio City Musical Hall. It received across-the-board ecstatic reviews. Renata Adler, writing in the *New York Times,* called it "a terrific movie, just right for Steve McQueen—fast, well-acted, written the way people talk. McQueen simply gets better all the time."

Archer Winsten, in the *New York Post,* said: "McQueen keeps his cool as only he can, now that Bogart is long gone. . . . [The film has] the best, most exciting car chase the movies have ever put on film. . . . McQueen, motorcycle and auto racer, knew what he was doing and what had to be done."

Ann Guarino, in the New York *Daily News,* raved that "McQueen joins the ranks of top movie detectives. His portrayal is cool, calm, casual, and convincing."

Tom Milne, the *Sunday Observer:* "A curiously exhilarating mixture of reality and fantasy, so actual that at times one could almost swear that the fictional adventures must have been shot with concealed cameras."

Variety: "An extremely well-made crime melodrama, highlighted by one of the most exciting auto chase sequences in years."

And Roger Ebert, in the *Chicago Sun-Times:* "Steve McQueen is sometimes criticized for only playing 'himself' in the movies. This misses the boat, I think. Stars like McQueen, Bogart, Wayne or Newman aren't primarily actors, but presences. They have a myth, a personal legend they've built up in our minds during many movies, and when they try to play against that image it usually looks phony. . . . McQueen is great in *Bullitt* and the movie is great, because director Peter Yates understands the McQueen image and works within it. He winds up with about the best action movie of recent years. . . . *Bullitt*, as everybody has heard by now, also includes a brilliant chase scene. McQueen (doing his own driving) is chased by, and chases, a couple of gangsters up and down San Francisco's hills. They slam into intersections, bounce halfway down the next hill, scrape by half a dozen near-misses, sideswipe each other, and leave your stomach somewhere in the basement for about 11 minutes."

The film proved a smash, and in the wake of its enormous profits, the Hymans clammed up about that $200,000 location override and wished they had left McQueen alone. Official studio estimates put the cost of making the movie at $5.5 million, against $18 million earned in its initial domestic run (some estimates put the domestic gross as high as $35 million, and Alan Trustman, who had a percentage of the profits, estimated that *Bullitt* grossed nearly $80 million in its first year of domestic release).

It was, without question, the biggest, most memorable, and most influential film of Steve's career, the one that placed him finally and firmly in the pantheon of international superstars. Steve was named by trade magazine *Film Daily* as one of its "Famous Five" box office stars of the year. *Boxoffice*, another widely read industry rag, ranked Steve sixth (Paul Newman was first on both lists). Although Steve was not nominated for an Oscar for *Bullitt*, the film did receive two nominations and won one (Frank P. Keller won for Best Editing; John Kean was nominated for Best Sound).

It also proved a major influence on how future *policiers* would be made. Without *Bullitt* there would be no *The French Connection* three years later directed by William Friedkin, and Don Siegel's *Dirty Harry* owes more than a little to the character, style, and feel of *Bullitt*, right down to shooting locations on the streets of San Francisco and especially in Clint Eastwood's characterization of Harry Callahan, a carbon copy of Frank Bullitt. Even Steven Spielberg's 1971 *Duel*, his feature directorial debut, with its spare dialogue and feature-length chase, is more than a little indebted to *Bullitt*.

Several supporting actors who appeared in the film also owe a lot to it. Vic Tayback, Norman Fell, Robert Duvall, and Georg Stanford Brown all had their careers either started or kick-started by *Bullitt*. Jacqueline Bisset went on to a decade of major stardom. Peter Yates directed a series of successful movies, including *The Hot Rock* (1972, with a script by William Goldman), *The Friends of Eddie Coyle* (1973), *Mother, Jugs and Speed* (1976), *Breaking Away* (1979; Yates was nominated for an Oscar for Best Director and the film for Best Picture), *The Deep* (1977), *The Dresser* (1983, with Yates also as producer; it was nominated for an Oscar for Best Picture and Best Director), and *Suspect* (1987), among many others.

After the film opened, sales of green Mustangs jumped tenfold.

WITH *THE REIVERS*'s scheduled Christmas 1969 release still seven months away, Steve decided to take it easy before he plunged back into making his long-awaited *Le Mans*. He continued to run around L.A. with Sebring or shoot out to Palm Springs, where a new crop of eager blondes was always waiting for him. As the summer approached, and the planning got more intense for his racing film, so did his penchant for women, not caring whether or not Neile found out about them. While the family was visiting Palm Springs for Easter, an electrician asked her when she had dyed her hair dark.

ON THE afternoon of Thursday, August 7, Sebring went to Steve's house to give him a trim. Afterward, they went for some Mexican food at El Coyote in Hollywood. While they ate, Sebring told him there was a little soiree planned for the next night at Sharon Tate's rented house up at Cielo Drive and that Steve should come. Tate had since married filmmaker Roman Polanski but kept Jay and others from her single days close at hand. Polanski didn't seem to mind; he wasn't a very jealous man and believed that he and Sharon were so in love that nobody could possibly pose a threat. Nonetheless, everyone who knew Sebring and Tate believed they were still in love and still carrying on.

Tate's acting career was moving along nicely. Polanski had used her in 1967's *The Fearless Vampire Killers* and married her a year later, and her career as a magazine model was equally hot until her pregnancy began to show. She was in her eighth month, which kept her more housebound than she would have liked. While Polanski was off in England scouting locations for what he thought would be his next movie, *Day of the Dolphin* (which Mike Nichols would eventually take over), with his friends Warren Beatty and production designer Richard Sylbert and the woman Polanski was having an affair with, Michelle Phillips of the Mamas and the Papas, Tate held regular soirees at her home. The next one was scheduled for that Friday night.

Steve told Sebring he'd be there. The next day Steve happened to run into Robert Vaughn. The two chatted for a while and Steve invited him to come along that night, to Tate's place up on Cielo Drive. Vaughn politely declined; he had other business he needed to take care of.

Still later, Steve received a call from a young and beautiful blonde he had been seeing. He invited her as well, but she told him she had a better idea for just the two of them.

⌄

EARLY SATURDAY morning inside the house the mutilated bodies of Sharon Tate, coffee heiress Abigail Folger, Voytek Frykowski, and Jay Sebring were discovered by the housekeeper. Sebring had been stabbed seven times and shot in the head.

The news spread through Los Angeles like a firestorm. When Steve heard about it, he immediately arranged to have someone go to Sebring's house and clean out all the drugs, sexual paraphernalia, and anything else he knew his friend would not have wanted anyone to find (or that could possibly tie Steve to Sebring's lifestyle). Sebring was known as something of an S&M freak around town, and Steve did not want any of that turned into fodder for the gossipmongers; it was bad enough that coke and pot had already been found in Sebring's Porsche by the police at Cielo Drive that morning.

Two months later the Manson gang was arrested and charged with the Tate murders and others that had taken place during their spree. Part of the evidence the police found was a "hit list" that Manson had made of celebrities he wanted to kill. At the top of it was Frank Sinatra (he was going to have him seduced by one of the pretty young Manson girls and killed while having sex with her), Elizabeth Taylor and Richard Burton (they were going to be tied together and boiled alive), and Steve McQueen, whose death was to be made to look like suicide. Presumably he made the list because Solar had rejected his manuscript.

To be on Nixon's enemies list was one thing; to make Manson's death list quite another. Steve was freaked out and rightly so. He had every one of his homes completely wired and burglar-proofed with all the latest security equipment. He was not alone. All over town, celebrities were imprisoning themselves in their homes. Overnight, the peaceful, easy feeling that had permeated Hollywood, Beverly Hills, Brentwood, and Malibu was gone, replaced by an edgy paranoia that made it feel like one giant war zone.

Steve began carrying a loaded Magnum with him at all times.

However, no matter how safe and secure he made himself and his family, he could not shake the dark feeling of having come so close to death. A simple decision to get laid had saved his life. He would never again go out in public without a weapon, or let himself be as easily accessible as he had been during the wild nights at the Whiskey. No more screaming fans surrounding him like in France that time. His new phalanx of armed bodyguards were instructed to shoot first and ask questions later.

PART FOUR

Bedeviled Winds of Change

Chapter 12

Marriage is really difficult when you're in the public eye.
You're exposed to so many rumors about other women. . . .
[M]ost marriages in the industry crack up fast, mainly due
to this kind of pressure. But me, I'm no party stud. I'm with
one woman at a time, and she's my lady and that's it until the
ball game's over and we decide to walk in different directions.

— STEVE McQUEEN

THE MEMORIAL FOR THE VICTIMS OF THE MANSON MASSA-
cre took place on a warm sunny day, with the strong, dry
Santa Ana winds blowing across Southern California. It was a
beautiful day to be alive.

Steve attended the mass service for all the victims, and was
seated behind his wife, Neile, who sat next to Warren Beatty.
Steve was packing, and likely half the other attendees were as well;
none of the murderers had yet been apprehended. The FBI was
also there in force, as well as uniformed LAPD officers, who stood
unsmiling and stiff, white motorcycle helmets held between their
forearms and rib cages, weapons loaded, ready for anything.

Toward the end of the service, a male stranger leaped to his
feet and threw himself on Sebring's coffin, screaming, sobbing,
spewing incoherent gibberish. Steve and about thirty others drew
their guns, ready to pounce. The police grabbed the man and he
was gone. A few minutes later, so were the remains of Manson's
victims.

THE REIVERS opened Christmas Day 1969. Cinema Center and its distribution wing, National General, had been divided about *The Reivers*. Neither knew what to do with it, and they finally agreed if it was anything, it was a good Christmas Day film, despite its many subplots filled with prostitutes, gambling, theft, and racism. They put their money on the climactic horse-race sequence, filmed at Disney, hoping that might be the big draw.

The reviews for the film were for the most part positive, but not for Steve. The *New York Times* wrote that the film was "a decent adaptation, with a lot of conventional good humor taken almost word-for-word from the book. However, casting McQueen as Boon automatically gives the character an inappropriate tool and shifts the film's attention from its nominal protagonist, young Lucius." Ultimately, most critics found the performance too far afield from the Steve McQueen of *Bullitt,* and *The Thomas Crown Affair.*

This was not the Steve McQueen audiences wanted to see. Although the film went on to gross a healthy $20 million in its initial domestic release, McQueen fans who had lined up to revisit Frank Bullitt were disappointed by Steve's performance. Overseas, the film's Americana was completely lost on audiences, and it did nothing.

Nonetheless, the domestic take was good enough that Cinema Center agreed to partner with Solar to go ahead and make *Le Mans*, with a $6 million advance to seal the deal. It was the biggest advance budget for any Steve McQueen film.

As 1969 came to a close, Steve was hit with some bad financial news. At a Christmas week meeting, Steve's auditor sat him down and gave him the hard news that he was personally bankrupt and that Solar was the culprit. He had personally guaranteed all the company's operating expenses and because studios did what they always do, configured the books so that there was never anything that came close to a net return.

The corporate bottom line was that Steve was tapped out. He was facing 1970 the same way he had faced 1960: broke.

The only difference was, he was a big star now, but a forty-year-old one, up there with Clint Eastwood (also forty), Paul Newman (forty-five), and Brando (forty-six), all of them surrounded by a gang of hot new and younger leading men who had either made their big breakthrough or were about to and would become the major American movie stars of the 1970s. The list included Jack Nicholson (thirty-three), Robert De Niro (twenty-seven), Dustin Hoffman (twenty-six), Al Pacino (thirty), Richard Dreyfuss (twenty-three), James Caan (thirty), Ryan O'Neal (twenty-nine), and Harvey Keitel (thirty-one), all of them at home in the new era of independent films. Each was working or about to work with a new and exciting crop of directors that included Mike Nichols, Martin Scorsese, Steven Spielberg, George Lucas, Francis Ford Coppola, Milos Forman, William Friedkin, Hal Ashby, Warren Beatty (as director), and others who, for the most part, were not hampered by the usual conventions of mainstream studio moviemaking.

A February 1970 survey by Reuters, the international news bureau, conducted in forty-one countries in conjunction with that season's upcoming Golden Globe Awards, ranked Steve as the number one box office star in the world (based mostly on the spectacular success of *Bullitt*), with Barbra Streisand his female counterpart. But, like most acknowledgments and awards, the Reuters survey was based on the past. The future of Hollywood lay with the new kids in town. Steve would make only ten more movies, just three of which would find sufficient room alongside the avalanche of product coming out of the new Hollywood.

AFTER A series of discussions and consultations, it was decided, at Cinema Center's urging, that the only way Steve could save Solar was to cut staff, reduce the size of its office space, and go public.

Steve agreed to all of it, realizing it was the only way he could keep his company alive and not go even deeper into personal debt.

About four hundred thousand shares of common stock were offered at $9 a share. Out of it, Steve received about $1.5 million, in addition to his ongoing $500,000-a-year salary and his $1 million guarantee for each film he starred in, money that could not be cross-collateralized. He remained the sole owner of the company and its principal stockholder. The remaining profits from the offering were put into reserve for future film budgets. There was also a $5 million insurance policy taken out on Steve's life, paid by Solar, to cover injuries he might receive that would shut down production on any film he was starring in for the company.[1]

And what film did Steve want to do first under the banner of the revamped Solar? Still *Le Mans*. Cinema Center urged him instead to do something closer to *Bullitt*, even a sequel, if possible. They wanted to turn the film into a franchise (as Clint Eastwood would do a few years later with *Dirty Harry*, a role that Steve had originally turned down). Steve said no. William Friedkin offered him the starring role in *The French Connection*. Steve said no. (The part went instead to Gene Hackman, who would go on to win a Best Actor Oscar for his performance.)

Cinema Center's concerns about *Le Mans* were real; at the time, sports movies, with the exception of the occasional boxing

---

[1] According to public documents surrounding the 1970 offering, Steve and Cinema Center were in an ongoing dispute over how much *The Reivers* had actually made. According to Solar's records, the only other Steve McQueen/Solar productions that made any money at all were *The Cincinnati Kid*, which went into the black via TV, and *Bullitt*, whose world rentals were reported to be $23 million prior to its sale to television. At the time, all Solar/McQueen films were subject to a five-year delay before they could be sold to television. The thinking was not to hurt the popularity and profits of their theatrical releases. All of that changed later on with the advent of cable and video rentals and sales; now the future rights to a film are routinely sold prior to production to help with financing.

biography, like *Somebody Up There Likes Me*, rarely made money at the box office. They depended too much upon the drama of the real-time outcome of the game, or the fight, or the race. Film almost always destroyed that dramatic device.

In the end, though, Cinema Center knew there was nothing they could do but keep their commitment and back the film or their association with one of the biggest movie stars in the world would end. They green-lighted *Le Mans*.

With the $6 million in place, Steve promptly started looking for a script and a director. He interviewed several candidates, including a young TV director by the name of Steven Spielberg who was looking to break into features (Steve rejected him, according to Bob Relyea, because he was "too young") and another one, George Lucas (whom Steve rejected for being "too small"). He then suggested that Relyea himself direct the film, and Relyea agreed. Soon enough, though, it became clear that Relyea was not cut out to direct. He had been too much of an authority figure over directors almost his entire career. He knew how to run things, not how to create images with a personal vision. Finally, after interviewing dozens of directors, Steve settled on the one man he knew could make the film, and do it the way he wanted: John Sturges.

The first thing Sturges wanted was for the next Le Mans race to be filmed and the footage used later on as part of Steve's film. Before leaving for France, Sturges tried to convince Steve that they needed to come up with a real story. Steve had said he wanted the film to be a semi-documentary, but Sturges argued for a full-blown conventional love story, even if it was shot semi-documentary-style, because audiences needed something besides fast cars to keep them in their seats for two hours. Steve said he would think about it.

IN MARCH 1970, to the surprise of many, including Steve, the Academy nominated *The Reivers* for two Oscars: one for Rupert

Crosse for Best Supporting Actor (the first black actor to be nominated in that category; he lost to Gig Young in Sydney Pollack's *They Shoot Horses, Don't They?*) and one for Musical Score for John Williams (who lost to Burt Bacharach for *Butch Cassidy and the Sundance Kid*). Steve had been passed over for a nomination for Best Actor but professed not to care anymore about Hollywood's self-congratulatory pomp and meaningless circumstance.[2]

Instead, he focused on his new movie. In a way that might best be described as "Method racing," he entered the twelve-hour endurance race held every March at Sebring, Florida. For his co-driver, who would alternate with Steve in ninety-minute stretches in his Porsche Spyder (owned and registered by Solar), Steve chose thirty-one-year-old Peter Revson, a ranked Formula One racer, New York socialite, and billionaire by virtue of his inherited cosmetics fortune. Like Steve, Revson fancied himself good enough to race at the professional level, and, like Steve, he was handsome, smooth, and a consummate ladies' man. Steve thought Revson was as good as he liked to boast he was. In 1968 he and co-driver Skip Scott had placed twelfth overall at Sebring and fifth in their class, an impressive finish for relative new-comers. Steve felt he could depend upon Revson on the track, and

---

[2] The winner for Best Actor went to John Wayne in Henry Hathaway's *True Grit*. Wayne was considered long overdue for the award, which was given to him for what was, decidedly, not his best performance or movie. The other nominees were Richard Burton, representing old, glamorous Hollywood, in Charles Jarrott's *Anne of the Thousand Days;* Dustin Hoffman, part of the new generation of actors, in John Schlesinger's *Midnight Cowboy;* Jon Voight, also part of the new wave, in *Midnight Cowboy;* and Peter O'Toole, also old Hollywood and, like Burton, foreign, something the Academy always revered, in Herbert Ross's *Goodbye Mr. Chips*. Interestingly, neither Newman nor Redford was nominated, despite the fact that *Butch Cassidy and the Sundance Kid* grossed $103 million in its initial domestic release ($500 million in 2010 dollars), a truly astonishing amount of money for 1969, when the average ticket price in America was $3.50.

that off it the two of them could have a really good time, which they most certainly did.[3]

Some reports had Steve and Revson winning the race—the *Hollywood Reporter* headlined, "Steve McQueen Takes a 1st Place in Sebring Race"—but in fact, as it was later determined, they came in second, 23.8 seconds behind a 5-liter Ferrari driven by Mario Andretti, despite Steve participating with his left foot broken in six places and in a cast up to his knee, the result of a motorcycle accident two weeks earlier. Afterward, he was voted the Hayden Williams Sportsmanship Trophy by the news media because of the great job he had done while under the handicap of his broken leg. How did he do it? He told one interviewer, "The foot hurt early in the race, after my first two-hour stint, but I didn't want to take any kind of drugs. The pain subsided as we went along."[4]

In the victory circle, Steve, hailed as racing's newest movie-star athlete, stood atop his car and gave the peace sign as the crowd cheered.

IF THERE was any cost-cutting taking place at Solar, it did not apply to *Le Mans*. Production and principal photography began June 7, 1970, in France. Steve acquired all the equipment he wanted for the shoot, including a new Porsche 917. A specialist mechanics crew headed by Haig Alltounian was brought over to personally maintain the Porsche. Alltounian was a friend from *Wanted: Dead*

---

[3] Peter Revson's father was Martin Revson, his uncle Charles Revson, the founder of Revlon, the family cosmetics empire. His brother, Douglas, was killed in a racing accident in Denmark, in 1968. Peter died in 1974 at the age of 35 in a racing accident in South Africa.

[4] The broken leg was not the only discomfort Steve endured to indulge his favorite sport. Steve suffered from acute hemorrhoids and had to wear two sanitary napkins to ease the pain of years of bouncing up and down on hard leather triangular riding seats.

or Alive. In keeping with the way he did things, Steve once more reached back to those he had known before he became a superstar, people whose loyalty would be unquestioned. Alltounian was one such friend.

As shooting began, Sturges became increasingly alarmed that he still did not have a script. The previous draft, which he did not like at all, had been completed more than seventeen months earlier. Sturges had some footage from an earlier Le Mans race, but none of that had proved usable because many of the drivers and sponsors had changed. Steve wanted Sturges to stage a fake race before the next real one, and use all of the real race footage to enhance the parts where Steve was seen in close-up driving his Porsche. All of this on-site planning, meanwhile, was costing Cinema Center and Solar $100,000 a week, still with no actual shooting script.

Finally, after Bob Relyea warned Steve that production costs were spiraling hopelessly out of control, Cinema Center decided to pull the plug. Steve blew a fuse, and Abe Lastfogel and Stan Kamen accompanied Steve to Los Angeles to meet with everybody and see if there was any way the project could be saved.[5]

A take-it-or-leave-it deal was negotiated between the William Morris agents and Cinema Center: Steve would have to forfeit his $1 million salary, Solar would no longer produce the film (meaning Steve would have to give up all creative control), and he would have to surrender his personal profit participation. Relyea had to take a salary reduction and give up his profit participation as well.

Steve agreed to everything; he had no choice if he wanted to get the film made. He asked for one last rewrite, and Cinema Center said no. Steve went back to the William Morris Agency hoping

---

[5] According to a source who wishes not to be identified here, at one point during production Cinema Center considered replacing Steve with Robert Redford and making a much less expensive film. Redford considered the idea but turned it down. Apparently Steve was unaware of Cinema Center's growing panic, or if he was, he did not care. It is unclear if he knew about the Redford offer.

they would support him on this one point, but there was no way he could get any changes to the deal.

The next day he fired Stan Kamen and the William Morris Agency.[6]

The production was shut down for two weeks so that everyone could regroup. Steve then hired agent Freddie Fields, who was also Paul Newman's agent. And at Fields's urging, as leverage against Cinema Center, Steve became a partner in First Artists, a production company created in 1969 by Sidney Poitier, Barbra Streisand, Paul Newman, and later on Dustin Hoffman. First Artists was modeled after and named for the original United Artists, created in 1919 by Douglas Fairbanks, Mary Pickford, Charlie Chaplin, and D. W. Griffith. In both instances, the intention of the performers was to have more control over their projects and to be able to play roles against type they wouldn't ordinarily get to do (eventually, First Artists was dissolved and has no relation to First Artists Management, a talent agency presently in operation in Hollywood).[7]

---

[6] There is some question as to why Steve really fired Kamen. According to industry sources, Steve had wanted to let him go for a while because Kamen had refused to take a cut in the industry-standard 10 percent agent commission. Even if he had wanted to, Kamen's employer, the William Morris Agency, had an ironclad policy about commission rates. Some believe this was the real reason Steve let Kamen and William Morris go, and used the dispute over the rewrite as the excuse to break his contract.

[7] Freddie Fields, a partner in First Artists, was also the founder of Creative Management Associates (CMA), one of the first serious rivals to William Morris's domination of Los Angeles–based talent. CMA later became International Creative Management (ICM). Because Fields also became Steve's manager, he was able to play fast and loose with his fees, and reportedly often waived his agent fee while collecting his management fee. Fields, who died in 2007, was also the longtime agent for Paul Newman, Robert Redford, and Barbra Streisand. He was known for his ability to handle "difficult" clients. Later on, he would help make stars out of Mel Gibson and Richard Gere. Steve McQueen originally joined First Artists in 1971, followed subsequently by Dustin Hoffman in 1976.

⌄

WHEN WORK on the film resumed, just before Steve left for France, Neile gave Steve a copy of a book she had read and liked called *Papillon*, about a French prison escape. She thought it might make a good movie; it had elements of *The Great Escape* that she thought fit right into Steve's comfort zone. He shrugged and threw the book into one of his suitcases.

Neile was rapidly losing whatever was left of her marriage to Steve. She had become increasingly bitter about his drug use and extramarital sex; he had never made a secret of either and she believed he was falling apart right in front of her eyes. What made it even worse for her was how pompous and self-congratulatory Steve had become whenever he granted the occasional interview, trying to sound like a thoughtful, careful, fiercely antidrug redeemer of lost youth. Every time she read one of these interviews, she realized he never mentioned her anymore or their "perfect" marriage. When he returned from Sebring, according to Neile in her memoir, Steve declared that he "can't breathe," that "half my life is over and I wanna fly! I wanna go!" A badly upset Neile asked him if he

---

Approximately two dozen films and television shows were produced by First Artists. First Artists was the brainchild of Creative Management Associates talent agent Freddie Fields. Stars would forgo significant up-front salaries in lieu of a percentage of their films' profits. In January 1975, when First Artists was operating as a subsidiary under the umbrella of Warner Bros., *New Times* magazine outlined the financial arrangement under which the company operated. "First Artists was a subsidiary of Warner Bros., a company controlled by the 'artists' Dustin Hoffman, Paul Newman, Sidney Poitier, Steve McQueen and Barbra Streisand. In return for making three pictures without the million-dollar 'front money' that any other studio would have to pay them, the stars could make whatever movies they wanted, so long as the budget was under $3 million for a dramatic film, $5 million for a musical. Warner got the distribution rights, reimbursing First Artists for two-thirds of the film's negative cost upon delivery of a finished film. And the artists received twenty-five percent of the gross—a quarter for every dollar the theater owners returned to Warners—right off the top."

wanted a divorce; he shouted no. Then he calmed down and acted as if nothing ever happened.

Neile had kept scrapbooks of their relationship from the time they first met. As she remembered, it was not long after that confrontation about their marriage that she abruptly stopped and never went back to them again.[8]

Back in France, Steve began taking his anger and frustration out on John Sturges, the director who, more than any other, had helped make him a superstar. He began the familiar pattern of difficult behavior, criticizing how Sturges set up a shot, refusing to show up on time, insisting again on seeing dailies, and rejecting every attempt that Sturges made to film the shooting script. As it finally came together, the story, slight as it was, focuses on the day of the race and one driver, Michael Delaney (Steve), shot semi-documentary style, with less than a dozen lines of dialogue spoken by Delaney in the entire film.

When Neile arrived at Le Mans with the kids, Steve showed up at the airport to pick her up with a pretty young girl by his side. What else was new. But the worst of it came at the Château Lornay, about forty-five minutes away from where everyone else was staying for the duration of the shoot. Steve's eyes were dilated and unfocused, and she became alarmed at his deteriorating physical condition. She also realized that he had separated himself from the rest of the cast and crew so he could indulge his use of drugs.

When Neile visited the set, she couldn't help but notice all the young girls who seemed to follow Steve's every move. When she confronted him about it, his answer was chilling. "Look, ah, I should tell you. There'll be women coming from all over the world to visit me this summer." After a pause, he said, "Well, we are kinda separated, right?"

And with that, he walked away. That night, back at the chateau,

---

[8] She later donated the scrapbooks to the Academy of Motion Picture Arts and Sciences Library.

Steve seemed to have come down enough to try to apologize to Neile, or so it appeared, but things soon took an even uglier turn. In bed that night, Steve asked Neile if she had ever had an affair. She denied it and said she was outraged by the question, but Steve persisted. He said he couldn't understand how she could not have; she was young and beautiful, and he had obviously not been monogamous in their relationship. The more she denied it, the more he pushed her. Steve then suddenly got out of bed, went over to the bureau, rummaged through a drawer, and found some cocaine. He took a toot, and then offered it to Neile. She told him she didn't like that sort of thing, but he pushed her, and to keep the peace between them, she did a little bit. Now Steve lit up a joint. They both got back in bed, and once again, Steve brought up infidelity. Only this time, after the coke and the pot smoke hanging in the air, Neile's resistance broke down, as Steve had to have known it would, and she confessed she had—with a famous actor who had won an Academy Award.

Silence followed as Steve got up and went into the other room. A few seconds later he returned with a pistol and pointed it at Neile's head, insisting she tell him who the actor was. When she didn't answer he cocked the trigger and pressed the tip of the barrel hard against her temple. Again he asked her who it was. Again she didn't tell him. Steve, twitching and red-faced, shouted at the top of his lungs that he wanted to know who it was.

This time she told him.[9]

Steve then sat her in a hard wood chair and gave her his version of the third degree—where it had happened, who had spoken first, who had picked whom up, who had wanted it. And then, while admonishing her, he began to hit her, punching and jabbing and

---

[9] Neile never mentions his name in her memoir, but Terrill, in his biography, quotes David Foster as saying that one day over dinner Steve told him it was Maximilian Schell, who had won a Best Actor Oscar for Stanley Kramer's 1961 *Judgment at Nuremberg.*

smacking her in the face, until she confessed that she had liked sleeping with the other man.

When he was finally finished, he left her in that chair, beaten up, bloody, and sobbing. He ran out of the house, got into his Porsche, and shot out of the driveway. He returned at six that morning, contrite and apologetic, with tears running down his face. The drugs had apparently worn off and he'd realized what he had done.

According to Neile, in her memoir, this scene was repeated several nights in a row: Steve would get high, grill her, hit her, leave, and come back with his tail between his legs. Not long after, Steve went to Bob Relyea and calmly asked him if he could hire the actor Neile had named. As it happened, he was unavailable, which probably saved his life.

BACK ON the set, Sturges was becoming increasingly fed up with Steve's behavior. He was not a documentary-style filmmaker, and hadn't bargained for having to make something that was uncomfortably close to that style of moviemaking. He kept asking an increasingly surly and sullen Steve where the human element was in the film.

Soon enough, Relyea, Bob Rosen, who was Cinema Center's man on-set, and Sturges got together and decided to shut the film down again until they could all settle on a plot. Steve abruptly took off with Neile and the kids to Morocco. Sturges then quit the film. The next day Cinema Center hired TV director Lee H. Katzin to finish it, without consulting either Relyea, Fields, or Steve.

When Steve finally returned to the set to resume production it was already August, and the cost overruns had reached the $6 million limit; any additional costs would, by agreement, have to come out of Solar, which meant Steve's personal money. Bill Maher, who had already once saved the company from bankruptcy with his idea to take it public, was waiting for Steve. This time the news was worse than before. Solar could not be saved. To prevent total financial disaster for both the company and for Steve personally, it had to be dismantled. Steve agreed, said nothing to anybody, and quietly finished the movie.

After, that, he blamed almost everything that had gone wrong on Bob Relyea, accused Relyea of betraying him, and told him they were finished. They would never work together or speak again.

In August 1970, Neile found out that she was pregnant.

Steve didn't believe it was his.

The next week she flew to London and had an abortion.

Upon her return to Los Angeles she decided to get some help. She went to a marriage counselor, who immediately suggested they get separate psychiatrists, which they did, but Steve's physical violence toward her and the emotional battering continued. Finally, she decided they had to separate, but when she tried to discuss it with Steve, he just moved out, finding a small guesthouse in the Pacific Palisades. It had none of the accoutrements of the Castle, but it did serve to at least get him out of there and away from his wife and kids.

No sooner had he unpacked his things than he called Neile. Not long after, they were dating again, three times a week.

Le Mans had taken a year and a half to make and cost $10 million (more than $50 million in today's dollars). Steve did not participate in the postproduction, and when he saw a screening of the film in its finished form, he knew that Sturges had been right all along: it had desperately needed a real story to tie all the racing sequences together. In a moment of rare humility, Steve personally apologized to Bob Rosen, Cinema Center's man, for all that had gone wrong with the film—but to no one else.

The premiere was held June 23, 1971, in Indianapolis, home

of the Indy 500. Not surprisingly, the movie was not well received by the critics. In the *New York Times*, Howard Thompson wrote, "Racing-car buffs will probably flip over *Le Mans*. . . . But the star's exchange of monosyllabic utterances and long, meaningful stares with other drivers, and especially with Elga Andersen, a sensitive-faced blonde, add up to tepid, monotonous drama during the two-day race intervals. Dramatically, the picture is a bore." Kathleen Carroll, in the New York *Daily News*, wrote, "There was no attempt at characterization. *Le Mans* may be the most famous auto race in the world, but from a theater seat it just looks like a big drag." Worst of all, comparing it to John Frankenheimer's *Grand Prix*, *Newsweek*'s Jay Cocks called it *Petit Prix*.

THE FILM died a quick and merciful death, grossing about $6 million in its initial domestic release, not nearly enough to cover the cost of making it or pay back what was left of Solar (on paper) or Steve himself, let alone turn a profit.[10]

However, the real costs to Steve were much higher and more personal. During the making of the film he had ruined his relationship with John Sturges, with whom he never reconciled. He had lost his longtime agent, Stan Kamen, and the William Morris Agency, which had been so vital in setting up deals for him and finding money partners to fund his projects. He had lost his company, Solar (although it did continue to exist in name only as a tax shelter). And he had lost Bob Relyea.

The second director, Lee Katzin, wanted nothing more to do with Steve, or the movies. After making one more feature, he returned to the more familiar confines of the TV lots, where he continued to grind out small-screen fare.

---

[10] In 1979 Inter-Planetary Pictures offered to fund a sequel if it starred Steve. He turned it down.

Not long after, Steve was hit with a $2 million lien from the IRS for unpaid back taxes. The government wanted everything. As part of the deal, the racing overalls he wore during the race were given up and sold off to a British newspaper that used them for a circulation-boosting contest that was won by a local schoolboy.

But the worst loss of all for Steve was the end of his marriage to Neile. In one last attempt to salvage it, Steve vowed to Neile that he would give up drugs and try to get himself back to the man she had married when she was a big star and he was a struggling actor. On Memorial Day 1971, they arranged to go out on a date. That evening he came to the Castle, spent a little time with the children, Terry and Chad, and then escorted Neile to the car. On the way to the restaurant, Steve reached into the glove compartment and took out a vial of cocaine.

They ate at Chez Jay, a popular Venice Beach seafood restaurant. Very little was said between them. On the way home he took more coke. He told her not to worry about it. Before they arrived at the Castle, Steve was higher than a kite and began asking questions about the man with whom Neile had had the affair, including where she had met him. Neile, frozen with fear, said nothing. When Steve pulled up to the driveway of the Castle, he ran around to the passenger side, even as Neile was desperately trying to get out and run to the house. He kicked her from behind, and she went flying onto the cobblestones of the courtyard. Steve screamed, "Why did you do it, you whore?" and began slapping her on the head. As she crawled to the house, Steve began saying softly, "I'm sorry, so sorry."

NEILE OFFICIALLY filed for divorce in October 1971. Steve was shocked when he was served with the papers, believing up until the very end of the process that she could not actually go through with it. He was sure no matter how hard he pushed her away, no matter how crazy he got, no matter how he tested her limits, she would never leave. But he'd pushed too hard, and she did.

Two weeks after Neile filed papers in a Santa Monica court to end their marriage, Steve signed on to star in *Junior Bonner*. While the lawyers fought over the division of their considerable property—and that would take more time than either party expected—Steve sought to lose himself in this new project about a talented but over-the-hill rodeo cowboy who tries to reconcile with his difficult family. Not a lot of Method research was needed by Steve for this one.

Junior Bonner was not Steve's first choice for his next project. When David Foster bought the rights to the novel *The Presbyterian Church Wager*, Steve assumed the lead would go to him. Instead, Foster offered it to Warren Beatty, who took it. The film opened that same year with a new title, *McCabe and Mrs. Miller*, and was directed by Robert Altman, hot off his 1970 smash hit *M*A*S*H*. Steve's next pick was *American Flag*, based on a novel by Elmore Leonard, who was also writing the western *Joe Kidd* for John Sturges (who had managed to bounce back from the debacle of *Le Mans* and, despite threats from Steve that he would never work again, quickly landed at Clint Eastwood's Malpaso production company, directing Eastwood in the title role).

Steve hoped that First Artists would produce *American Flag*, but the company had stumbled out of the gate with a series of flops, including Streisand's *Up the Sandbox*, directed by Irvin Kershner, which eventually opened in 1972 and did little at the box office; Newman's *Pocket Money*, directed by Stuart Rosenberg, same story; and Sidney Poitier's *Buck and the Preacher*, ditto again. After these three, First Artists' board of directors decided to cool it for a while, which ended Steve's hopes that he could get them to fund *American Flag*.

Just as he was contemplating which way to go, Sam Peckinpah, the director who had been fired in 1965 from *The Cincinnati Kid*, struck career gold in 1967 with *The Wild Bunch*. Originally called *The Diamond Story*, it was meant to be an ensemble western, to star George Peppard, Charles Bronson, James Brown, Alex Cord, Robert Culp, Sammy Davis Jr., and Steve. Peckinpah had taken it to Warner Bros. and they liked it, except they thought it was too close to *Butch Cassidy and the Sundance Kid*. When it became clear the film couldn't be released before *Butch Cassidy*, the studio reconceived it as a group of last-roundup cowboys whose world ends with a bang, not a whimper, and with a new cast that included Edmond O'Brien, William Holden, Robert Ryan, Warren Oates, Ben Johnson, Strother Martin, and, in the role Peckinpah had originally envisioned for Steve, Ernest Borgnine. Released in 1969, *The Wild Bunch* was a huge hit and brought Peckinpah back in from the cold. He followed it in 1970 with *The Ballad of Cable Hogue*, which didn't do nearly as well, and then rebounded once again with the violent and highly successful 1971 release *Straw Dogs*, which starred Dustin Hoffman.

After the failure of Peckinpah's 1970s nonviolent *The Ballad of Cable Hogue* and the success of *Straw Dogs*, Peckinpah was hoping to combine elements of the two films into a nonviolent film capable of attracting a wide audience. *Junior Bonner* was the project, and he wanted Steve to play the title role. With nothing else on the table, Steve took it, grateful that Peckinpah had remembered how Steve had tried to save *The Cincinnati Kid* for him.

Peckinpah also wanted Gene Hackman to play Steve's younger brother, but when he couldn't meet Hackman's price, Peckinpah hired a far less well-known actor, Joe Don Baker, a year before his star-making turn in Phil Karlson's *Walking Tall*, to play Curly, the more practical (and successful) of the two boys. For the role of Ace, Steve's father, from whom he has been estranged, Peckinpah hired aging stage actor Robert Preston. Steve was concerned about the disparity in their sizes. Preston was a strapping six-footer, and Steve insisted he wear sandals during the scenes they had together. The only significant female role in the film, Junior's mother, Elvira, estranged from Ace, was played by Ida Lupino. Steve also insisted on doing all his own stunts, and because the budget was so small, no one from ABC Pictures chose to notice.

"Sam Peckinpah, boy," Steve told Joyce Haber of the *Los Angeles Times* when the picture was announced. "He and I will be some combination. They say ABC just bought a lot of aspirin!"

The film took seven weeks to shoot on location in Prescott, Arizona, and when it was over, Steve returned to Los Angeles to face an increasingly uncertain future.

Look, I'm an actor, not a racer. I love bikes for the fun they give me, not the money they might have given me. You can't earn more than $80,000 a year racing bikes, and you work your tail off doing even that, races every weekend for seven months of the year and from coast to coast. I think if I started young enough in motorcycle racing, I could have been ranked.

— STEVE MCQUEEN

MOST PEOPLE DIDN'T UNDERSTAND WHY, AFTER FINALLY finding the perfect movie formula for himself with *Bullitt*, Steve had thrown it away and made one oddball film, one semi-documentary, and now one real documentary that had nearly succeeded in turning his golden-boy Hollywood career to lead.

On Any Sunday was released in 1971, which Steve agreed to finance for $300,000 in exchange for a brief appearance in it. The film was directed by Bruce Brown and used twelve cinematographers. Brown had also directed 1967's groundbreaking documentary about surfing, *Endless Summer*. Steve appeared in the motocross and cow-trailing sequences. Ironically, *On Any Sunday*, a glorified vanity film, went on to make more than $10 million, which helped keep Steve solvent. He has no lines in the film and plays no character other than himself.

His goal with *On Any Sunday* was to elevate his reputation as a serious bike rider, and biker movies themselves. "Brando's movie *The Wild One* set motorcycle racing back about 200 years," Steve told *Sports Illustrated* in 1971. "Most bike flicks in the past concentrated on the outlaw crap, Hell's Angels and all of that stuff, which is about as far away from the real world of motor-cycle racing as I am from Lionel Barrymore."

It was not all that unusual in transitional Hollywood for actors to shift professional direction. Brando had simply turned his back on the industry; and Beatty and Newman tried to find ways to grow older gracefully on-screen and extend their acting careers. But Steve, after his brief and slightly bizarre campaign to elevate the stature of motorcycle movies, wanted to distance himself from everything—his career, his racing, his wife. The aloofness that had always been there on the surface, the celebrated cool, had turned into a chill after Sebring's murder and the utter failure of *Le Mans*. Steve became an even more mistrustful loner, unwilling to commit to anyone or any-thing. His professional and social withdrawal had begun.

The small house Steve rented on top of Topanga Canyon became his private sanctuary where he enjoyed getting up late, popping open a couple of cold ones, and spending his afternoons alone watching soap operas and game shows. He couldn't find any-thing else worthwhile to do, and none of the scripts sent to him were interesting enough to make him turn off *The Guiding Light* and get up from the sofa until David Foster personally visited him one day with a script sent to him by Neile called *The Getaway* under his arm.[1]

Steve told Foster he would read it. When he did, he was sur-prised at how good it was, especially the complexity of the main character's tough-but-tender nature, which could shift from prison victim to sociopath to passionate lover to generous and sympa-thetic robber without missing a beat.

And the deal was good, too. Foster, who was producing, could

---

[1] One of the many scripts he turned down during this interim was *Play Misty for Me*, yet another Clint Eastwood film that came to Steve first. He didn't like it, a friend said, because the woman had a stronger role in it than the man. The script then went to Eastwood, who in 1971 starred in and directed it for Malpaso. It became one of the biggest films of the year.

offer nothing up front but a full 15 percent of the gross. The more money the film made, the more he made, and because his share was based on the gross there could be very little industry "tinkering."

Carter "Doc" McCoy was an outlaw, tough, rangy, and vulnerable, the type of antihero Steve felt at ease playing. McCoy especially reminded him of the charismatic killers done to perfection by his two favorite film actors, James Cagney and Humphrey Bogart; no matter how dark the characters these tough guys played, their roots were always in the working class and there was an ever-present element of self-righteous social outrage in them. Because of it, they always managed to hold the audience's sympathy and compassion in the palms of their fight-scarred hands. Audiences empathized with their plight. The closest he had come to playing a character like McCoy was the rootless and rebellious loner/victim Jake Holman in *The Sand Pebbles*.

When the project was first announced, Joyce Haber, a Hollywood columnist, was given the script to read and immediately saw the connection between Bogart and McCoy. "The role is a natural one for Steve," she wrote in her interview column. "It's that of a Bogart-type character who's involved in a heist." "He's bad, he really is bad," Steve told her with his tongue firmly behind the trigger of his mouth. "And being the Peter Perfect man that I am it's gonna be difficult for me."

David Foster's previous big-screen effort, *McCabe and Mrs. Miller*, which he had done with Beatty in the lead, was a critical success but a financial failure. For a brief period Foster retreated into episodic TV until he came across the 1958 "dime novel" paperback original *The Getaway*, by Jim Thompson. Thompson was then a struggling crime writer who would achieve lasting fame after his death, but at the time Foster had optioned his book, Thompson was sixty-six, frail, and severely alcoholic. Broke and without any income, Thompson had taken to making photocopies of all his old novels and handing them to any producer he could get close enough to, in the hopes that someone, anyone, would option one. Foster got a copy of *The Getaway* and immediately saw it as both his and Thompson's salvation.

Foster recognized in the script elements of *Bonnie and Clyde*. In *The Getaway*, tough bank robber Carter "Doc" McCoy's beautiful and devoted wife, Carol, sleeps with corrupt local Texas politician Jack Benyon, with Doc's permission, to get him out of jail. In return for his freedom, Doc will rob a bank and split the take with Benyon. However, once Doc is freed, nothing goes as planned, and after some surprise turnabouts, a spectacular hotel shootout and fire, and some intense sexual scenes, Doc and Carol make a last desperate run for the Mexican border and freedom. (They make it—at least in the version of the film seen in the United States. When released abroad, several countries insisted on a different ending, wherein Doc goes back to jail).[2]

Foster optioned the rights to the book for $2,500, from Thompson's agent, Mike Medavoy (after Paul Newman had let his option on it lapse), which included an obligation from Thompson to write a first draft of the screenplay. Steve, meanwhile, began preparing for the role. As a model, he used the character of Roy Earle, as played by Humphrey Bogart in Raoul Walsh's 1941 film of W. R. Burnett's ex-con adventure novel *High Sierra*, adapted for the screen by Burnett and John Huston. Steve watched the film over and over again, studying every nuance of Bogart's performance, and even started wearing his hair like Bogie's in *High Sierra*, con style, buzzed on the sides. When production began he had wardrobe make him an exact replica of the suit Bogart wore in the film

---

[2] There are more, if less obvious, echoes of *Bonnie and Clyde*. In Arthur Penn's movie, there is an extended interlude with an innocent couple taken hostage in the midst of the action. The couple, played by Gene Wilder and Evans Evans, are vividly reprised by another innocent kidnapped couple in *The Getaway*, played by Sally Struthers and Jack Dodson.

when he leaves jail, a flea-bitten number with cuffed too-short pants. These became Steve's physical touchstones around which he built a fully detailed, powerfully nuanced performance.

For the role of Carol, Foster's short list included Dyan Cannon, Angie Dickinson, and Farrah Fawcett. To play Benyon, he wanted veteran cowboy character actor Ben Johnson. And for the role of the murderous and oversexed assassin out to kill Doc because he double-crossed Benyon, he wanted screen tough Jack Palance.

When Foster and Palance could not agree on price—Palance wanted more than the $65,000 Foster was able to offer—producer Al Ruddy, who was working at the time on Francis Ford Coppola's *The Godfather*, recommended a little-known nephew of a real-life mobster, a reputed East Coast hit man for the mob who also fancied himself a screenwriter and actor, Al Lettieri (Sollozzo in *The Godfather*). Foster offered Lettieri the same $65,000 plus three net points in the film, and Lettieri accepted.

Foster then set about to find a director. He first choice was Hollywood newcomer Peter Bogdanovich, whose not-yet-released debut film, *The Last Picture Show*, had terrific industry buzz. When Foster and Steve saw a screening of it, they both agreed Bogdanovich had to direct *The Getaway*. They offered him the job and he accepted. Foster then gave him Thompson's first draft, which Bogdanovich did not like at all, and Foster scrambled for a screenwriter who could better translate Thompson's grimy novel to the directorial tastes of Bogdanovich. Bogdanovich suggested Walter Hill for the job. As it happened, Hill had worked on both *The Thomas Crown Affair* and *Bullitt* as an uncredited second unit director, and had also written an unproduced screenplay, *Hickey and Boggs*, intended as a reunion vehicle for Bill Cosby and Robert Culp, who had starred together on TV in the sixties in *I Spy*. Steve liked Hill and urged Foster to hire him to rewrite the film. With Bogdanovich and Steve in place, and Hill's much-improved script,

Foster knew he would have no trouble getting a deal for the project with Bob Evans at Paramount.

And that's when the fun really began.

Evans, the vice president and head of production at Paramount, had led a life that sounded like a cross between an F. Scott Fitzgerald novel and the plot of one of Evans's better movies. Born in New York City, the young and extremely handsome Evans worked with his brother in the city's garment district, each eventually owning an interest in Evan Picone, a men's clothing manufacturer. Evans's head may have been on Seventh Avenue, but his heart was in Beverly Hills, where he frequently vacationed. On Election Day in 1958, while sitting by the fabled Beverly Hills Hotel's pool, he was spotted by Norma Shearer, the aging widow of MGM's legendary Irving Thalberg. She decided to mentor his acting career and pushed him for a major role in Joseph Pevney's upcoming 1959 film bio of Hollywood great Lon Chaney, *Man of a Thousand Faces*, which starred the equally great James Cagney. Evans got the role and never looked back.

After appearing in several movies, he decided acting didn't do it for him and declared himself a producer, purchasing the rights to Roderick Thorp's 1954 novel *The Detective*. He somehow persuaded Frank Sinatra to star in the title role, originally played by Alec Guinness in Robert Hamer's 1954 British film adaptation, *Father Brown*. Evans's version was a huge hit, one of the biggest box office successes of 1968, and led Charles Bluhdorn, the head of the Gulf + Western conglomerate, which now wholly owned Paramount Pictures, to offer Evans the position of executive head of worldwide production at the floundering studio.

Nobody in the business expected this onetime *garmento* to reverse the fortunes of Gulf + Western's newly acquired Paramount Pictures, which currently sat at the bottom of an industry of failing or fallen studios co-opted by mega non-Hollywood corporations.

Evans put together a string of hits that saved the studio from going under, and as a result, he became one of the newest and most powerful of the post-studio-era transitional players in the late 1960s and early 1970s.

The forty-year-old Evans had also gained a strong reputation as a ladies' man and already had two failed marriages under his belt when he first noticed the coltish thirty-two-year-old Wellesley-educated Ford model Ali MacGraw in her strong debut as the rich and spoiled Jewish princess Brenda Patimkin in Larry Peerce's 1969 surprise hit screen adaptation of Philip Roth's novella *Goodbye, Columbus.* Evans immediately cast her in the much-sought-after role of the beautiful but doomed Jennifer Cavalleri in Arthur Hiller's 1970 adaptation of the bestselling *Love Story* and at the same time asked her to marry him.[3] The picture both catapulted MacGraw into superstardom and trapped her in an unhappy marriage with Evans, something both would live to regret.

According to MacGraw, writing in her memoir, "Just before the actual filming of *Love Story* began in the autumn of 1969, Bob asked me to marry him. . . . [T]he overriding feeling of the early days of my marriage to Bob was that we were in love, two highly successful people in a business that idolizes winners. . . . We apparently looked good enough together that people in Hollywood seemed to love the idea of us as a couple, part of the ultimate fantasy of the dream machine."

Evans saw their marriage a little differently: "I had a great sex life with Ali until I married her, and I couldn't fuck her once after our marriage. Couldn't get it up."

---

[3] It was Evans's third marriage and MacGraw's second (she had already been married to and divorced from Robin Hoen). Evans had been previously married to Sharon Hugueny (1961–62) and Camilla Sparv (1963–65). He would be married a total of seven times.

According to writer Peter Biskind, "Evans evinced a peculiar mixture of treacly Hallmark Card sentimentality that would flower in his romance with Ali MacGraw, and a self-destructive darkness that would lead him into murky waters way over his head."

BY THE time Foster formally presented *The Getaway* to Paramount and Evans agreed to do it, several major and unexpected changes had already taken place with the project. First, Bogdanovich opted to exercise the escape clause in his contract in favor of writing and directing *What's Up, Doc?* for Barbra Streisand at Warner Bros., a move that did not sit well with Foster. According to screenwriter Walter Hill: "Peter Bogdanovich and I were going to co-write a new draft, then Peter and Steve didn't see eye-to-eye and suddenly Peter was no longer doing *The Getaway*. . . . I'd known Steve for a number of years. I'd worked with him on *The Thomas Crown Affair* and *Bullitt* and known him slightly socially. He seemed to lose his equilibrium after he and Neile split up."

With Bogdanovich out, Steve and Foster turned to Peckinpah to direct. Peckinpah always needed money, especially now that he had just gotten married, for the third time, and wanted to move to Mexico as soon as possible (perhaps because of the tenuous legal status of his latest marriage). Steve and Foster offered him $225,000 and 10 percent of the film's net profits to direct the film, with an extra 25 percent up front to do a rewrite. He agreed on the spot.[4]

---

[4] Thompson later filed a grievance with the Writers Guild of America, demanding equal screen credit as co-writer. The WGA rejected his claim and Walter Hill received sole credit, although everyone involved with the making of the film agrees that Peckinpah and Steve deserved co-credit for the amount of changes they made to Hill's original script.

Peckinpah was familiar with the Thompson novel and had wanted to get his hands on it for a long time. He hated Hill's and Bogdanovich's draft. The problem with their version, according to Peckinpah, was that Hill was too young to "get it," and had "scrubbed away all the shadows and polished the story into a slick action vehicle."

According to Hill, "Evans began pushing for his wife to play the lead opposite Steve, as a way of expanding her range."[5] Foster and Steve loved the idea of using MacGraw as well, not so much for her acting talent or to stretch her screen persona, but for her golden marquee value—"McQueen and MacGraw heat up the screen in *The Getaway.*"

However, Peckinpah, the film's new director, preferred Stella Stevens, a barely known movie actress whose best previous role had been in Peckinpah's 1970 flop western *The Ballad of Cable Hogue.* MacGraw, Foster argued, was the hottest actress in Hollywood. The only reason anyone could figure for Peckinpah's wanting Stevens was that, like Steve, he had a penchant for blondes.

After much persuasion, Peckinpah finally gave in and agreed to MacGraw starring in the picture. All they had to do now was get her to be in it.

Evans invited Foster and Steve over to his mansion to help them push for MacGraw, who was apprehensive about meeting Steve in person. They had never met, but MacGraw had seen him in *Bullitt* and hadn't forgotten the effect he had had on her.

According to MacGraw, "It was one of the very rare times in my life, especially in my grown-up years, when I left the movie theater with my knees knocking for the star. Whatever it is that Star is about, Steve had it onscreen. And, I was later to find out,

---

[5] It remains unclear whose idea it really was to cast MacGraw. MacGraw claims that it was Steve's idea. Peckinpah's biographer says it was Foster who wanted to put her in the movie. Foster says he's not sure where the idea came from.

in [that] room, I knew [if I made *The Getaway*] I was going to get in some serious trouble with Steve. There would be no avoiding it. He was recently separated and free, and I was scared of my own overwhelming attraction to him." By the end of the night, Foster officially offered Ali the role of Carol, and she accepted.

Ali was perhaps the best Method actress of all. She had had an affair with Ryan O'Neal during *Love Story* and had a reputation of having slept with every leading man she played opposite, maybe to help her find the romantic reality of her characters. She was a woman attracted to wealth and power, mostly men like Evans, while at the same time a woman in need of what they couldn't give her. Working with Steve, Ali knew, was going to be a sexual time bomb waiting to explode.

During the last days of postproduction on *The Godfather*, Paramount's big gamble on period gangsterism that Evans was sure was not going to do anything at the box office (a feeling not helped by early negative audience reaction), he was stuck in New York City with the film, while his wife was jumping into bed with Steve McQueen every chance she got.

HOWEVER, before filming even began, Evans put *The Getaway* into turnaround. He may have begun to suspect his wife's heated attraction to Steve, or perhaps he was unhappy over the loss of Bogdanovich as director. Whatever the reason, it relieved Paramount of any further obligation to make the film.

To Foster and Steve, losing Paramount was a setback but not a disaster. Evans, who had signed MacGraw to an exclusive three-picture deal with Paramount, of which *Love Story* was the first, let her stay with the project no matter where it landed—*if* it landed—in return for her agreed-upon $300,000 salary (to be paid to Paramount as part of a loan-out deal) plus all of the film's net earnings in Germany, where Steve was a huge star.

Steve, meanwhile, still owed First Artists three pictures. With Foster's okay, he decided to take *The Getaway* there.

Their offer was not what Foster had hoped for but he accepted it. There was a ceiling on what any of its founding members could spend for a First Artists film, which was $3 million, and all the profits were shared among them. Because of these budget restrictions, the actors only brought films to First Artists that every other studio had already turned down. Obviously, if they could get a better deal elsewhere, they would (only one other First Artists film ever made any money—Sidney Poitier's *Uptown Saturday Night* [1974], after which the company folded. Had *The Getaway* been made today, Steve would have walked away with at least $25 million, in star-salary and percentages alone, even without also producing the film).

Just before Steve arrived in Texas to begin shooting, he had to take care of some difficult and unfinished personal business, signing the papers that finalized his divorce. When it had become painfully clear to him that there was no way he could salvage his marriage, on March 14, 1972, he gave in and signed all the necessary papers, ending his fifteen-and-a-half-year marriage to Neile.

She signed off on it two weeks later, on April 26, 1972, for a $1 million settlement and $500,000 alimony and child support every year for the next ten years. She received custody of both children with visitation rights for Steve. They divided all the other assets equally, including the beloved Brentwood castle that had represented so much to the both of them. It was quickly purchased by Mr. and Mrs. Zubin Mehta.

The press played up the divorce as the final, sad act of what had once been one of Hollywood's brightest fairy-tale couples. A sympathetic Joyce Haber wrote in her syndicated column, "If you ask me, the other party wasn't a woman, but rather one of Steve's bikes or racing cars!"

At a party at Richard Chamberlain's house shortly after the

divorce, Neile told April Ferry, the wife of Steve Ferry and one of her oldest friends, reaching all the way back to when they were both on Broadway in *Kismet*, "I got a million dollars from that son of a bitch." To which Ferry replied, "You deserve more."

Neile's brave face and catty words could not hide the pain of the truth that she and Steve were finished, their fifteen-plus-year marriage over for good.

THE SHOOTING schedule for *The Getaway* was set at sixty-two days, with a budget of $2,826,954, which fit just under the First Artists budget allowance. (When the film ran $300,000 over budget— the negative cost came to $3,352,254—with Evans's permission Ali graciously forfeited her salary, but Paramount still kept Germany).[6] Production began February 28, 1972, on location, first at Huntsville for a few days, then in San Antonio for the last five weeks.

Steve wasted no time making his move on Ali, who was more than receptive to him. Almost immediately, they began a blazing, we-don't-care-who-knows-it love affair while still in Huntsville. (Foster, one of Steve's best friends, and who was with them for virtually the entire on-location shoot, claims he was oblivious to any of it until he read about it in the tabloids.) According to Ali, "I was obsessed with Steve from the moment he stepped into my world, and there was never enough air for me to breathe to change that feeling. He was very taken with me, too, although I wasn't necessarily his dream lady, physically. . . . [F]or the next three months

---

[6] MacGraw agreed to defer her salary in exchange for 7.5 percent of the picture's net profits. "MacGraw made the right move, since with advanced bookings of more than double its negative cost *The Getaway* made money before it even opened." David Weddle, *If They Move . . . Kill 'Em!* (New York: Grove Press, 2001), p. 441.

of filming I walked the nasty razor's edge between occasional moments of sanity and remorse on the one side and, on the other, feverish excitement."

Even from the earliest days, when the two lovers were in their deepest mutual heat, Steve—as always, fueled by coke, pot, and beer—could not resist his desire, or need, to have sex with as many groupies lingering on-set as he could manage, and he made no attempt to conceal any of these liaisons from Ali.

"One night [in San Antonio] we went together to a small local party," Ali later recalled. "Halfway through the evening, sufficiently loaded, he began carrying on with two local beauties right in front of me. I was livid, and left the party. Later that night Steve returned, and I could hear him in his apartment next door with the two girls. It was excruciating. The next morning he sauntered out onto his front step and casually asked if I wanted to come and make him breakfast. And the amazing thing is, I went in and cooked it. He had a kind of spell over me, with all of his macho swaggering . . . for a while I found it sexy. Here I was, out in the wilds of Texas with the man's man of all time."

The film proved a difficult shoot for all the principals, both on and off the screen. MacGraw, for instance, could not drive a car, which made the scenes in which she had to be the getaway car driver extremely challenging. In another scene, Steve, as Doc, insanely jealous despite Carol's having followed his instructions to get him sprung by sleeping with Benyon, improvised his fury by slapping Ali around, on her face and across her body. The scene was eerily reminiscent of Steve's violent attacks on Neile. The set went silent when Peckinpah finally called cut and then everyone broke out in applause. The take made it into the final cut.

Peckinpah and Steve, meanwhile, despite their loyalty and camaraderie, were increasingly at odds over the amount of violence in the film (Steve was upset at how much violent screen time Lettieri was getting)[7] and how the film should be edited. The more Steve tried to rein in Peckinpah, the more violence the director wanted. According to Hill, "Steve and Sam had several fights. I mean real fights. I saw one that was a rough one. And I saw one where Steve threw a big magnum of champagne at Sam and almost killed him. Sam just ducked in time. I came in next day and there was a big hole in the wall where this giant bottle had gone half-assed into it like a cannonball."

As filming drew to a close, Steve remained unsatisfied with the way the dailies looked and decided he had to take over from Peckinpah and put together the final negative cut himself. As one of the producers, he had the contractual right to do so, but it did not endear him to Peckinpah. "McQueen's playing it safe," Peckinpah later said. "He chose all these playboy, pretty boy shots of himself."

Steve also decided he didn't like the music of Peckinpah's favorite composer, Jerry Fielding. He fired Fielding and replaced him with Quincy Jones, further enraging Peckinpah.

Tension during the last days of shooting was high enough, but it was about to increase with the arrival of Bob Evans, who by now had read all the stories in the tabloids about his wife's steamy romance with Steve, the biggest illicit Hollywood affair since Elizabeth Taylor and Richard Burton. "He had to know," Foster said later. "Every day there were helicopters filled with paparazzi flying

---

[7] Peckinpah was a friend and drinking buddy of Lettieri's. Throughout the shooting of *The Getaway*, Peckinpah and Lettieri were often drunk on tequila by eight in the morning. During the course of production, Peckinpah kept enlarging Lettieri's role in the film, especially his sex scenes. Several members of the cast and crew resented Lettieri's bullish manner and his expanded role, believing it took away from the singular focus of what was essentially a crime-and-escape film. However, when Lettieri saw Steve's final cut of the film, Lettieri threatened to have his kids killed, according to Foster. Lettieri's promising movie villain career was cut short when he died of a heart attack in 1975 at the age of forty-seven.

above us, and I began to dread getting that call from a furious Bob Evans." Sure enough, Evans, finally able to free himself from the long hours of postproduction on *The Godfather*, called to tell Foster he was coming down to get Ali and bring her back home, finished picture or no finished picture. Foster told Steve, who wanted no part of facing Evans, and he asked Foster to break the news to Evans about what was going on between him and Ali. Foster refused, and it was left to Ali to be the one to tell her husband that everything he'd read was true.

At the hotel near the Mexican border where Evans was staying, he and Ali had it out. She broke down in tears and confessed to Evans that she was in love with McQueen. Evans then went to Foster, who pleaded for just twenty-four more hours to wrap the film, which Evans agreed to let him have before he pulled his leading lady for good even if the production still needed her. Evans then assigned a chaperone to stick close to his wife every minute she was off-set those last hours. For the entire time of Evans's visit, whenever Steve finished a take, he disappeared and was nowhere to be found.

Not everyone sympathized with Evans's playing the cuckold. Frank Yablans, the head of Paramount distribution and someone who was very close personally to Evans, had this take on the McQueen-MacGraw affair: "Evans pushed them together. He created the breakup with Ali, the public cuckolding. 'Bob, you're gonna lose your wife. These two are going at it hot and heavy,' to which he said, 'It's just a passing thing.' He didn't give a shit. It didn't matter to him. He's a very strange man. He couldn't be married, couldn't live a normal sane life. He drove her out." Evans's version was a little different: "My wife was fucking another guy, and I had no idea. She has as much interest in being with me as being with a leper. She was looking at me and thinking of Steve McQueen's cock."

Before he left, Evans had a talk with Peckinpah, whom he had never liked for the film, and that also did not go well. Peckinpah, already fed up with everyone involved in the project, failed to commiserate with Evans, who, already frustrated at not being able to get his hands on Steve, blew his stack on Peckinpah. "Fuck you, Sam," he said. "McQueen is fucking me in the ass. Well, the fuckin' is over. If there was going to be any fuckin' it's gonna be me doin' it."[8]

The next day, exactly twenty-four hours after he set the deadline, which Foster managed to meet, Evans sent a car for Ali that took her to Murrieta Hot Springs in California. Evans had arranged a two-week vacation for her to get away from everyone, including himself. He also leased her a brand-new Mercedes.

Nothing helped. She was hopelessly in love with McQueen and intended to divorce Evans so she could be with him.

AN ON-SET affair is one thing; leaving one's husband for another man at film's completion is quite another. Production romances almost always end when the film shuts down (Steve McQueen and Jacqueline Bisset, for example) and people return to their "real" lives. With Steve and Ali, however, it was different. They got even hotter and heavier after the picture was finished, and when they returned to L.A., they were inseparable.

Still, no one in the Hollywood community could quite figure why this lovely, educated, elegant woman would be attracted to a rough cut like Steve. The consensus among her friends was a resounding "Don't do it." According to Sue Mengers, her agent at the time, "Ali was a saint, Steve was a prick."

---

[8] There were nearly as many real-life twists and double-crosses connected to *The Getaway* as there were in the movie. As part of her exclusive deal, MacGraw had wanted to make a movie out of F. Scott Fitzgerald's *The Great Gatsby* with Evans producing and Steve starring as Gatsby opposite her Daisy. That did not happen. The film was made in 1974 at Paramount, directed by Jack Clayton, starring Mia Farrow and Robert Redford.

According to writer Sheila Weller, it was the very nature of their opposite upbringings that made Steve and Ali love each other so intensely. "She was the biggest female star of the year: he was the biggest movie star in the world. She was a Wellesley-educated aesthete who fantasized about living in Paris . . . he was a motorcycle-racing reform-school kid who had worked as a towel boy in a brothel and had spent 41 days in the brig as a marine and generally had the kind of street cred Jack Kerouac would have killed for. Theirs was one of the great love affairs of the past century."

Perhaps the most revealing explanation came from Ali herself: "It was very, very passionate, and dramatic, and hurtful and ecstatic. . . . It happened at a time when psychoanalysis and therapy were considered self-indulgent, he had no way to deal with [his lifelong] pain but to drink . . . all the pain and loneliness festering inside while his pride kept him from revealing his vulnerability . . . On the one hand there was the angry, physically violent authority figure, and on the other there was a gentle, elegant loner, a kind of mysterious genius, the romantic genius with troubled eyes, capable of equal amounts of unpredictable rage and tenderness at a moment's notice."

Only that was not about Steve. It was about her father.

Me a legend? You wanna know what a legend is, look at Duke Wayne. Me? I'm just a dirty old man who can't wait to get out of here and go play in the dirt.

— STEVE MCQUEEN

*T*HE *GETAWAY* WAS SO FULL OF OFFSCREEN DRAMA THAT nobody made much of one incident buried among the others. Midway through the shoot, Steve developed a hoarseness in his throat that turned into a regular cough he could not get rid of. He was talking to Neile every day on the phone, mostly about the children, and she noticed something different in the sound of his voice. She advised him to stop smoking cigarettes and grass, to which he replied that he had to have some way of winding down at night. And he couldn't stop production to go to a doctor, he said, but he assured her he had seen the production nurse, who'd given him a packet of aspirin and told him to drink some hot tea with honey as often as he could.

When the hoarseness and cough persisted, Steve called his regular doctor in Beverly Hills, who gave him the name of a top ear, nose, and throat man at the University of Texas Medical Center. Steve never liked missing a day's shoot, for reasons of pride on someone else's film and pocketbook on his own. Not wanting to do so now, he reluctantly called the doctor and got him to agree to stay late at the hospital. After shooting for a full day, Steve, Ali, and David Foster drove the hour and a half from San Marcos to the medical center in Austin.

During the examination, the doctor found a small nodule on Steve's vocal cords and told him he should have it removed as soon as filming ended. Steve, by now thoroughly immersed in his role, replied as if he were Doc McCoy: "Give it to me straight, Doc. Do I have the Big C?" The doctor smiled and told him no, he did not have the Big C, but that he should give up smoking. It was 1972 and Steve was forty-two years old.

Two days after he finished shooting *The Getaway*, Steve returned to Los Angeles and underwent surgery for the removal of several polyps in his throat. Ali was not there; Freddie Fields was present, and so was Neile, both of whom waited nervously in the hospital coffee shop during the entire operation.

JUNIOR BONNER opened August 2, 1972, after all the major summer releases, and grossed a paltry $2,306,120 in its first year of worldwide release. It was not a complete disaster because it had cost so little to make, but in no way could it be considered a hit. Coming after the mild box office receipts for *The Reivers* and the disastrous *Le Mans*, it was clear that Steve's career had cooled off considerably since *Bullitt*.[1] He and Foster were both hoping *The Getaway* would turn things around and restore Steve's box office popularity.

Archer Winsten, writing for the *New York Post*, said that "McQueen has a chance to do a lot of what he does so well; nothing much while he thinks about some action that has happened or will. He keeps it all in focus with those steady blue eyes of his. A hero from the past, McQueen, as always, makes you believe it."

The *Los Angeles Times* said, "Steve McQueen is explosive and forceful in one of his finest performances."

---

[1] Self-funded documentaries, like *On Any Sunday*, have never figured into the arc of stars. They are considered vanity productions whose numbers, good or bad, don't really measure into a star's true box office worth.

But perhaps it was Sam Peckinpah who summed it up best: "I made a film where nobody got shot and nobody went to see it."[2]

Despite the movie's box office failure, Steve loved *Junior Bonner* and often referred to it as his favorite of all the films he'd made. During its production he had told one reporter, "There's a rare quality in my town, y'know?" He went on to explain, "People in Hollywood will hem and haw and fuck around playing all kinds of cute little games, and then you'll finally realize they want something from you. Sam's not like that." Peckinpah had felt the same way about Steve. He told the same interviewer, "If you really want to learn about acting for the screen, watch McQueen's eyes." Their mutual admiration, combined with the emotional disarray in both their lives, their battles during *The Getaway*, and their insatiable desire for women (and their endless troubles with them), made them a pair of crazy kindred souls.

The Getaway opened December 13 to good reviews. It grossed $18 million in its initial domestic release, enough to make it the seventh highest-grossing film of the year. It made an additional $35 million overseas.[3]

THAT SEPTEMBER 1972, Ali's divorce from Evans became final. She found an empty house for rent next to Steve's up in Topanga

---

[2] *Junior Bonner* was the only Steve McQueen film that actually lost money; by ABC-Cinerama's tally, the film lost $4 million. According to box office returns as listed by *Variety*, the top five films of 1971 were William Friedkin's *The French Connection*, Sam Peckinpah's *Straw Dogs*, Don Siegel's *Dirty Harry*, Stanley Kubrick's *A Clockwork Orange, and* Peter Bogdanovich's *The Last Picture Show*. *Junior Bonner* finished out of the top one hundred.

[3] The top ten highest-grossing movies of the year were *The Godfather,* Irwin Allen and Ronald Neame's *The Poseidon Adventure*, Bob Fosse's *Cabaret*, John Boorman's *Deliverance*, Peter Bogdanovich's *What's Up, Doc?*, Sydney Pollack's *Jeremiah Johnson, The Getaway,* Sidney J. Furie's *Lady Sings the Blues*, Woody Allen's *Everything You Always Wanted to Know About Sex but Were Afraid to Ask*, and Martin Ritt's *Sounder.*

Canyon. Because of the eccentric layout of the homes to ensure privacy, her driveway was almost four miles away from his, though the actual houses were separated only by a large field. It was not exactly an intimate setup, but Ali didn't care. She wanted to be as close to Steve as she could get.

They were not together in the canyon for very long. Steve had decided to star in an adaptation of the worldwide bestseller *Papillon* (the book Neile had given to him, via Foster, while they were still married), Henri Charrière's account of his true-life escape from Devil's Island. The film was scheduled to be shot on location in Jamaica and later in Spain as a substitute for French Guiana, off the coast of which the notorious Devil's Island was situated.

What had made the book so compelling was that no one had ever escaped from Devil's Island. Charrière had always claimed he was innocent of the crime of murder (of a pimp) and unjustly convicted. Sentenced to Devil's Island for life, he served seven years in solitary confinement and nearly that much again in limited general population. The atrocities he witnessed and the cruelty he endured for all that time drove him to attempt his daring, "impossible" escape. These were the perfect ingredients for a great action-adventure film with a deep emotional sensibility.

Steve may have been impressed with the story and its cinematic possibilities, but because of his divorce, the failure of Solar, and his string of less-than-successful films, he owed some more back taxes and needed cash; he suggested to one interviewer that that was the real reason he had agreed to make *Papillon*. "I may be doing the film version of the famous French bestseller," he told Liz Smith. "And then again I may not if we don't see a good script. I owe the government a little bit of money, so I'll have to work a little."

Steve was offered $2 million by Allied Artists to star in the film. (It would not be part of his First Artists deal and came with no producing responsibilities; it was strictly an acting job for pay. Allied Artists' foreign partner was Columbia, which did not invest in the film but handled worldwide distribution.) Dustin Hoffman, cast as Charrière's prison mate Louis Dega, accepted $1.25 million for his work in the film. Despite his sensational debut in Mike Nichols's 1967 *The Graduate*, Hoffman had no problem accepting the lesser figure. He was not as big a star as Steve, and it had become increasingly difficult to find commercially viable roles for him. Audiences went to see Steve McQueen in this film, not Dustin Hoffman.

The director and co-producer was Franklin Schaffner (*The Best Man*, 1964; *Planet of the Apes*, 1968; and *Patton*, 1970, for which he won an Oscar for Best Director, were among his biggest hits). The other producer was Robert Dorfman, who had originally purchased the rights to the novel from Charrière for $600,000. Dorfman had a hard time getting Charrière to sell the book to him, and to help persuade Charrière to make the deal, he had promised that the film would be a French production starring France's biggest native star at the time, Jean-Paul Belmondo. However, even as he tried to sign Belmondo, it struck Dorfman that the film would be much bigger if it were made in America, and if he could get America's and France's biggest foreign star (Steve was always huge in France) to play the title role of Papillon.[4] With Charrière's reluctant approval, Dorfman went after Steve.

Steve knew Schaffner from way back, from when they both worked on the TV show "The Defender." He felt comfortable around him and knew he wouldn't be challenged every step of the way, as he had been with Peckinpah. And with no producing responsibilities, he could concentrate on developing what he knew would be his most complicated character.

Production began in February 1973, without a completed shooting script. Schaffner had hired the writing team of Robert

---

[4] Charrière's nickname was Papillon, which means "butterfly" in English, and refers to his reputation in prison to be able to escape confinement by simply "flying away."

Benton and David Newton, who'd won Oscars for *Bonnie and Clyde*, to convert the ponderous novel—it had no in-depth character development, no action, inadequate descriptions, and a certain flair for the dramatic that played fast and easy with some of the facts of the story—into a mainstream entertainment film. Their price for a first draft was $500,000, and as far as Schaffner was concerned, what they produced was worthless. He tossed it out just days before the entire cast and crew were to arrive in Jamaica.

Schaffner then turned to William Goldman, who did several script revisions before he was replaced by Dalton Trumbo, who had to travel with the production to Jamaica to keep writing pages ahead of filming. Because of the unusual way the script was written, and for practical purposes, *Papillon* had to be shot in sequence. That made everything far more expensive because of the nature of film economics, which dictates that all scenes using the same setup of lights and scenery be shot together, and which includes daylight and other factors. Soon enough, not surprisingly, the film quickly ran into serious money problems. Per diems had to be suspended, along with "voluntary" weekly paychecks for those members of the production on salary. When Steve heard about this, he refused to work until every penny owed to the cast and crew was paid. After a five-day work stoppage led by Steve, Allied Artists coughed up $250,000 to get the cameras rolling again.

Into all of this came Ali MacGraw. She had decided to fly down to Jamaica to be with Steve, who was understandably distracted by the film's financial troubles and his increasingly frustrating attempts to try to explain to fellow Method neurotic Dustin Hoffman how to play a believable Frenchman. Steve, always looking for something physical he could use to build his character, remembered Eli Wallach's gold tooth in *The Magnificent Seven* and had one made for himself to wear. His struggle to let it shine through his smile paralleled his quest to find the interior jewel in the roughness of his portrayal of Papillon.

Moreover, since being in Jamaica, he had gained some visible weight and his ego was bruised by it (though not enough to stop him from drinking a dozen bottles of beer a day and staying constantly stoned on Jamaican ganja), especially when he was forced to wear oversized prison garb to hide his girth while playing a man who was being starved to death by his captors. Hoffman, on the other hand, lived on half a coconut a day during the entire shoot.

Hoffman and Steve did not get along especially well. In the scenes they had together each was concerned the other was stealing it. During the course of the production they fought verbally over some relatively petty incidents that permanently damaged whatever friendship they had tried to forge. Above all, Steve objected to what he perceived as the steady stream of invited guests who came to see the always affable Hoffman, most of whom brought cameras and shot dozens of pictures while Steve was trying to act. Steve eventually banned all outside visitors, something that infuriated Hoffman.

With all that was going on and the difficulty of the shoot, it took some time for Steve to warm up to Ali, which she did not especially appreciate. However, she played the good soldier and did whatever she thought she needed to do to help Steve get through.

That May, somehow a week ahead of schedule, the film's final scene was shot; Papillon hugs Dega goodbye and makes his suicide leap into the ocean and his miracle escape on his homemade coconut-shell raft. The production needed the time that had been saved, as it faced a difficult postproduction schedule to make its December 1973 release date.

THAT OCTOBER, Ali and Steve moved together into a house that David Foster had found for them in Trancas, a quiet little beach community just beyond Malibu. At the time, it had two gas stations, one supermarket, and a honky-tonk bar. Along its main stretch of sand, Broad Beach, the houses are a little funky and a bit farther apart than the ones further south, and surfboarders regularly roamed the shore waters. Trancas provided just the kind of out-of-the-way privacy that Steve wanted. They could walk, unrecognized and undisturbed, along the beach together every afternoon. Steve liked to call it living in domestic bliss.

They had one phone line in the house, with one receiver, and Steve appointed himself the official voice of the household. He was serious about wanting to get away from making movies, from Hollywood, from everyone and everything except Ali. He still felt the emotional burn from *Le Mans* and the physical exhaustion from *The Getaway.*

Ali, who went along with all of this eagerly at first, had no intention of retiring, but she did tell her agent, Sue Mengers, to maybe cool it for a while until they were settled in. Mengers, for whom Steve had no love, nonetheless called almost every day, and one time heard Steve's voice on the other end: "[Ali] works only with *me* on a project I'll choose for both of us." After that, he angrily slammed down the phone. He didn't want Hollywood intruding on Trancas. Steve intended to keep a promise he had made to himself about not making any more worthless movies, and made Ali promise that she wouldn't do any either.[5] The only exception was if they found something of real quality that they wanted to make together. Ali agreed, to keep the peace, but she never intended to stop working. To both her amusement and annoyance, this was Steve's version of being a husband, except they weren't living in the year of the Pilgrims. Surely, she believed, the first good film that came along for either would put this fantasy to rest.

They had no live-in help, except for a Frenchwoman Ali hired to help her with Steve's two children whenever they visited and with her son, Josh, whom she had had with Evans in 1971. She

---

[5] Steve did sign a $1 million deal to star in a series of commercials for Honda, with the stipulation they only be shown in Japan and stress safety. They were never shown in America.

had custody of Josh, and he lived with Steve and Ali. They did the everyday household chores themselves. Steve canceled all mail deliveries, threw the mailbox that was outside the house into the Pacific, and canceled his post office box. Ali decorated the small house with homegrown flowers and candles and filled makeshift wooden shelves with her favorite books. She liked to listen to classical music on a small sound system in her part of the house while Steve watched television in his. They let their dogs run free, and kicked back. It was a lifestyle that, for Ali especially, couldn't have been further away from the privileged princess role she had lived while married to Evans. For Steve it was a split from the rat race that he'd previously never been able to get ahead of. After the failure of *Le Mans*, he had found himself back in mainstream moviemaking like *Papillon*, but to him, that had little really to do with acting and everything to do with money, something that, after all the financial debacles, didn't interest him all that much. He wanted to withdraw from the whole scene and revert to a simple life, to think about what his next step might be.

Meanwhile, Steve enrolled Terry and Chad in a local school, and Neile was very easygoing about it. Steve wanted to keep all the kids, including Ali's son, Josh, whom he treated like one of his own, as far away from Beverly Hills as possible. He often took Chad motorcycling on weekends in Palm Springs. "I tried to raise him as a real kid," Steve said later. "He likes to ride in the desert and he bought his own bike, a Yamaha 60-cc Mini Enduro, out of his own pocket money. . . . I grounded him for eight weeks earlier this year when his grades got sloppy. He's shaped up nice since then. Christ, riding has got to be good for a kid. I was stealing cars at his age."

As David Foster remembered, "He never wanted Ali to work, no matter what. Barefoot and pregnant, as the expression goes, was how he wanted to keep her, a glorious housewife all to himself hidden away from the world." To ensure they never found that perfect script, Steve told Freddie Fields he wouldn't even look at

272 ✦ Marc Eliot

one unless there was a half-million-dollar "reading fee" paid to him directly and in advance.[6]

He took to calling Ali his "old lady." "They lived a simple life," according to Foster. "She put meat and potatoes in front of him every night at six. He didn't want her to work so she didn't"—all of which made her agent, Sue Mengers, even more furious, as Ali was the number one female star in America and a huge earner for Mengers.

Not surprisingly, after a while, listening to Bach, breathing salt air, peeling vegetables, and "living tranquil in Trancas," as the local expression went, morphed into a mild ennui for Ali, but whenever she brought up the idea that she might work again, Steve would blow a gasket and remind her of their pledge. Ali would counter with the fact that since they weren't married, she had no security, no assurances, nothing, and that she needed to work as a form of insurance, so she had some money in the bank in case they ever split up. One night in July 1973 "we had a terrific fight," Ali later recalled, "and Steve said, 'Okay, baby—if you want to get married, it's tomorrow or never. That's it.'"

She called his bluff, if that's what it was, and the next day, Steve packed Ali and the kids into a car, drove to a nearby airport, flew them all to Cheyenne, Wyoming, rented a truck, and drove the bunch to the nearest Holiday Inn. Steve chose Wyoming because to Steve the name sounded "very cowboy-romantic." According to Ali, "Steve and Chad slept in one bed, Terry, Steve's daughter, and I in the other. Josh in a crib in the middle."

On July 12, 1973, Steve and Ali were married in a public park by a local justice of the peace, the Honorable Arthur Garfield, whose name Steve had picked out of the local phone book. The ceremony was witnessed by Steve's son, Chad, thirteen, his daughter, Terry, fourteen, and Ali's son Josh, two and a half years old.

---

[6] Some sources report the "reading fee" was as high as a million dollars.

But not before Steve at the last minute produced a prenuptial document he made Ali sign right then and there. It said, in effect, that if they divorced, she waived any claim to his money. When he made it clear to Ali that he would not go ahead with the marriage unless she signed, she shrugged, put pen to paper, and gave the document back to him. Then they exchanged their vows in front of Judge Garfield. That same day they flew back to Trancas.

Now they played the happily married couple for a while. She cooked and took care of the kids; they all hiked together around Trancas and occasionally planned hikes up at Big Sur, during which Steve wanted to have a picnic, serving only army rations. On some weekends Steve liked to go for rides with the Hell's Angels and hang out with them afterward. One night while Ali and Steve were alone in Big Sur, Steve invited a bunch of Hell's Angels and their "old ladies" over to where they were staying, and one of the "old ladies" stole Ali's bathing suit.

Another time the two invited the Reagans to dinner in the Santa Monica Mountains. Ronald Reagan, no longer governor, loved it; Nancy less so.

According to Ali, there were "blocks and blocks of time from my marriage to Steve that I cannot remember in any detail. My sense of it today is that we would go along peacefully for days on end, and then suddenly find ourselves in a horrible fight. . . . [O]ur worst fight resulted in Steve inadvertently backhanding me on the forehead, breaking open the skin next to my eyebrow. . . . After the encounter Steve was so upset that he decided that every time we had an argument it would be 'safer' for him to go into town to spend the night."

Not long after their marriage, Steve rented a pied-à-terre for himself at the Beverly Wilshire Hotel similar to the one that Warren Beatty had there, and put $50,000 worth of redecoration into it to make it the perfect married man's bachelor pad. According to Ali, a friend reported there were models and starlets going up to his apartment every time he was there. News of this confirmed what Ali feared—that their marriage was already failing. "In spite of the fact that we loved each other enormously, the situation was doomed by the phantoms of the past. Love was not enough."

On December 16, 1973, a fully bearded and reluctant Steve, accompanied by a dazzling Ali, attended the Los Angeles premiere of *Papillon*. He hadn't wanted to go; she'd insisted. He thought he was physically out of shape and emotionally out of touch with the business. He did it just for Ali, who really wanted to go.

The next day the film received mixed-to-negative reviews, with most critics dismissing Steve's performance. Vincent Canby, in the *New York Times*, wrote that the film was "a big, brave, stouthearted, sometimes romantic, sometimes silly melodrama. As played by McQueen, Papillon is as all-American as a Rover Boy."

Pauline Kael, in the *New Yorker*, said: "A monument to the eternal desire of movie makers to impress people and win awards. To put McQueen in a role that requires intense audience identification with the hero's humanity is madness. McQueen is an amazing actor of considerable skill, but a reserved actor whose expressive resources are very small. If there ever was a wrong actor for a man of great spirit, it's McQueen."

Andrew Sarris and David Thomson stood nearly alone in their positive reviews of the film. Sarris, in the *Village Voice*, praised the director: "Schaffner has really made an exhilarating movie out of the most dangerously depressing material." Thomson, in his *Biographical Dictionary of Film*, wrote: "*Papillon* is not that good a film, but McQueen is very touching as the man who defies solitary confinement, madness and aging and becomes a wistful genius of survival. . . . [H]e has moments of inspired, heroic craziness."

The film did phenomenal box office; clearly, people wanted to see Steve McQueen. *Papillon* earned nearly $55 million in its initial domestic release, making it the third-highest-grossing film of the year.[7] Talk began that he was going to be nominated for and win his long-overdue Academy Award.

In early January, Steve was notified that he was nominated for a Best Actor Golden Globe. Steve replied that he would not attend the award ceremonies, and that if he won anything, they should mail it to him.

A few weeks later, the Golden Globe for Best Actor went to Robert Redford, for his performance in *The Sting*. Redford showed up in person, tanned and smiling and appreciative, to accept it.

Papillon was nominated for only one Oscar, for Best Original Score, which Jerry Goldsmith won.

Despite Ali's urging him to take her to the Oscars, this time Steve did not, nor did he attend himself.

NOT LONG after, Steve, still plagued with financial troubles, asked Freddie Fields to come up with a deal so big that it would be the last film Steve McQueen would ever have to make.[8] Fields quickly found several First Artists deals for Steve, among them one called *The Johnson County War* to be directed by newcomer Michael Cimino (who would not get the picture made until 1980, as *Heaven's Gate*, which became one of the biggest flops in film history that all but brought down United Artists and effectively ended Cimino's directing career).

---

[7] Billy Friedkin's *The Exorcist* was number one, earning an astonishing $204 million. George Lucas's *American Graffiti* came in second with $115 million. Robert Clouse's *Enter the Dragon*, starring the late Bruce Lee, came in fourth, with $25 million.

[8] For money. Steve had a "creative" project he wanted First Artists to make for his second of three films: a filmed version of Ibsen's *An Enemy of the People*. First Artists turned down the project, claiming it could not afford to make something with so little commercial potential. Steve put it aside and then decided to make his big blockbuster and use that money to self-finance *An Enemy of the People*. His first film for the company was *The Getaway*.

At the same time, Warner Bros. acquired the rights to a novel by Richard Martin Stern called *The Tower*, about a fire that destroys a commercial high-rise. It was based on a real-life disastrous fire that had taken place at One New York Plaza, a Manhattan high-rise. The book drew a $390,000 option price from Warner Bros. for its relatively unknown author because big-budget, star-studded disaster movies were in vogue after Irwin Allen's *The Poseidon Adventure*. The key elements were a big-name Oscar-winning ensemble, a horrifying disaster, the terrifying uncertainty of who was going to live and who was going to die that kept audiences on the edge of their seats, terrific special effects, an Oscar-winning song, and heroics by the dozen.[9] *The Poseidon Adventure* went on to become the second-highest-grossing film of 1972, taking in nearly $43 million in its initial domestic release, second only to *The Godfather*. *The Poseidon Adventure* eventually earned $160 million (including world and ancillary rights). Considering *The Poseidon Adventure* cost $5 million to make, every studio wanted its own big disaster movie.

Meanwhile, Irwin Allen had bought the rights to a similar novel, *The Glass Inferno* by Thomas N. Scortia and Frank M. Robinson, intending to make his own competing tragedy-in-a-tower for Fox.[10] Gordon Stulberg, having moved from Cinema Center to Fox, feared the two films would cancel each other out at the box office, and called Ted Ashley at Warner, who agreed. The two worked out a deal to co-finance one film that would be an amalgam of the two novels,

---

[9] *The Poseidon Adventure*'s star-studded cast of past Oscar winners included Shelley Winters, Gene Hackman, Red Buttons, and Ernest Borgnine, surrounded by a tier of second-level faces—Stella Stevens, Carol Lynley, Pamela Sue Anderson, Jack Albertson, and others. The fun of these movies is to figure out who dies first by calculating the stars' name value. The bigger the name, the longer the star lives.

[10] Both authors claimed their books were based on the construction of the World Trade Center towers in New York City and what would happen if a fire ever broke out in one of them.

to be called *The Towering Inferno*, with Irwin Allen to produce and direct. The cost of the film would be split between Warner and Fox; Fox would have the domestic release, Warner the rest of the world.

When Freddie Fields brought the script to Steve, he was at first interested in playing the architect, who is called in to help the fire-fighters figure out the interior of the brand-new building so they can rescue those trapped above and get themselves out safely. The other major role, the fire chief, was slated for Ernest Borgnine, one of the stars of *The Poseidon Adventure*. Although the fire chief only had about ten pages of dialogue and action in the film, Steve knew it was a key part and wondered if it wasn't in fact a better role than the dry, intellectual architect.

While he was trying to figure it out, he was caught up in a real-life fire that not only changed his mind about what part he wanted in the film but became a gift of Method preparation. In May 1974, while Steve was working with Los Angeles Battalion Chief Peter Lucarelli, the film's technical advisor, a fire broke out at the Goldwyn Studios in Hollywood. Lucarelli allowed Steve to go along on the call. Ali was with him that day, and she too went to the fire site. When they arrived, the soundstage, where endless movies and TV shows had been filmed, was engulfed in flames. Several people who happened to be working that day, actors, actresses, and technicians, were all trapped inside as two hundred firefighters tried desperately to rescue them. Steve put on a hel-met, jacket, and boots and followed Lucarelli into the inferno. He stayed inside for the better part of an hour before emerging cov-ered with soot, his eyes red from smoke, and fell into Ali's arms.

At home that night, as he recovered Steve became convinced that the up-from-the-streets battalion commander of the San Francisco Fire Department really was the better of the two lead roles in the film, the architect being a little too sophisticated and well-educated for him. He decided to call Neile and run it by her. She fell quickly and comfortably into her familiar role as Steve's advisor and reassured him that it didn't matter which role he played, as long as he was there at the end for the film's exciting climax. That made sense to Steve, who decided he'd choose the role of the character that had the final line in the film, the fire chief.

Screenwriter Stirling Silliphant was hired to combine the two books' stories into one workable screenplay. Silliphant had written some of the best screenplays of his era and had won an Oscar for *In the Heat of the Night*. Allen, intrigued with the idea of two books made into one film, wanted Silliphant to write two stories that overlapped into a single movie. One was essentially the action parts, which Allen would direct; the other was all the dialogue scenes, which Allen hired British director John Guillermin to direct, believing the British excelled at wordy, plot-heavy stories. Guillermin's most recent film had been 1972's *Skyjacked* (an American film shot at Metro, starring Charlton Heston and Yvette Mimieux), which got him the job co-directing *The Towering Inferno*.

Expensive sets were built for the interiors, designed inside a five-floor high-rise mock-up at Fox's Malibu ranch, with existing high-rises in San Francisco, the Bank of America Plaza entrance in Los Angeles, and the façade of L.A.'s Hyatt Regency used for the exterior shots. The Hyatt's indoor glass elevators were also utilized. All of it was edited into a single locale.

While the script was being written and the sets designed and built, Allen continued to put together the rest of his ensemble cast, using his tried-and-true method of choosing famous sports figures and Hollywood legends, most of them long past their professional primes. Robert Wagner, Robert Vaughn (his third film with Steve), O. J. Simpson, Fred Astaire, Jennifer Jones, Richard Chamberlain, William Holden, Susan Blakely, and Faye Dunaway, who was Steve's co-star in *The Thomas Crown Affair*, and who made Roman Polanski's *Chinatown* the same year, rounded out the cast.

The key role of the architect, the part Steve turned down in favor of the fire chief, went to Paul Newman.

Unlike the debacle that had gone on with *Butch Cassidy*, this time the question of billing was far easier to solve, as Freddie Fields offered the same proposition he had offered both actors for *Butch Cassidy and the Sundance Kid*—equal billing, the name on the left lower than the name on the right in America and the names reversed in Europe. This time there was no problem with it from either side. Announcing the arrangement, *Variety*'s headline ran: "Bit Player of 1956 Now Co-Equal with Paul Newman."[11]

Newman said, "It didn't make any difference to me. Any way anybody likes it is all right by me." Steve agreed, except he also wanted Silliphant and Guillermin to make sure that both his character and Newman's had the same exact number of words in the script, and that the final shot and sentence spoken in the film would belong to him. Everyone agreed, including Irwin Allen, who had the final say.[12]

These were the final hurdles, after which *The Towering Inferno* went into production that spring. There were some bruised feelings from some of the other actors at the kid-glove treatment Steve and Newman received during the making of the film and the fact that they received 90 percent of all the close-ups in the action sequences. William Holden, who had been one of the biggest American male stars of the 1950s, complained bitterly, accord-

---

[11] Steve McQueen came first, Paul Newman second but higher, William Holden and Faye Dunaway were third and fourth, each one successively lower than Paul Newman.

[12] The film ends with the fire chief (McQueen) telling the architect (Newman), "You know, they'll keep building them higher and higher. And I'll keep eatin' smoke until one of you guys asks us how to build 'em." The architect replies, "Okay, I'm asking." The fire chief replies, in close-up, "You know where to find me. So long, architect." The scene also gave audiences the chance to finally see whose eyes were bluer.

ing to someone on-set, that he had nothing to do in the film but answer the phone and sound grim.

DESPITE THE difficulties of filming the many special-effects sequences, for the most part production went smoothly. Steve and Newman had almost no scenes together, and they were cordial to each other, even friendly by some accounts (including Robert Vaughn's in his memoir), whenever they encountered each other on-set. Dunaway, Steve, and Newman even sometimes got together between scenes, often caught up in laughter and the general bonhomie that permeated Irwin's set. Dunaway was content with her smaller role as long as the money was good and arrived on time (and she knew *Chinatown* was going to put her back on top). Steve had a few complaints—when he didn't like the helmet he had to wear, costumes found him another one—but for the most part, it was a very professional set where the potential for danger kept everyone attentive and cooperative.

Filming was completed September 11, 1974. Postproduction went smoothly and *The Towering Inferno* opened three months later, on December 18, 1974, perfectly timed for Christmas. It received ho-hum reviews for its script but raves for its production. Vincent Canby's *New York Times* review called it a "suspense film for arsonists, firemen, movie-technology buffs, building inspectors, worry warts," and went on to conclude that it appeared "to have been less directed than physically constructed. . . . [It] is overwrought and silly in its personal drama, but the visual spectacle is first rate . . . a vivid, completely safe nightmare." Russell Davies, writing in the *Observer*, correctly identified the real incendiary aspect of the film: "It all boils down to the moment when Newman and McQueen face each other over a packet of plastic explosive."

The combined star power of McQueen and Newman proved irresistible, and the critic-proof film grossed more than $116 million in 1974 dollars ($500 million today) in its initial domestic release, enough to make it the top-grossing film of the year.[13]

The Towering Inferno won three Academy Awards—Best Cinematography (Fred Koenekamp and Joseph F. Biroc), Best Film Editing (Carl Kress and Harold F. Kress), and Best Song ("We May Never Love Like This Again," written by Al Kasha and Joel Hirschhorn, sung by Maureen McGovern). It was nominated for Best Picture but lost to Francis Ford Coppola's *The Godfather, Part Two*.

After the film's gala premiere, which they attended, Steve and Ali retreated to the privacy and solitude of Trancas. Steve believed he had done it—found the picture that would financially allow him never to have to work again. As far as he was concerned, he had gone out on top and was finished with making any more films. Of course that meant Ali had to be too.

Only Ali didn't see it that way at all.

---

[13] Second was Mel Brooks's *Blazing Saddles* ($100 million), followed by Brooks's *Young Frankenstein* ($86 million), Mark Robson's *Earthquake* ($79 million), and Roman Polanski's *Chinatown* ($29 million), the last produced by Bob Evans.

Cut to Black

Ali MacGraw is a good wife for me. We're both actors, but neither of us is a great, big, fat talent, and she's not all wild-eyed about her career, which suits me fine.

— STEVE MCQUEEN

THREE YEARS PASSED, WITH STEVE AND ALI DOING LITTLE together that took them outside of the confines of the Trancas bunker or the house in Palm Springs. Except for occasional errands and Steve's forays alone to his bachelor pad at the Beverly Wilshire, which he explained to Ali was his "much-needed office" to keep business out of their home, they lived the lives of rich beach hippies. Steve loved it but Ali didn't, and she grew increasingly disenchanted with both it and Steve, who imposed it on her and kept his thumb tightly pressed down on any career offers that came her way.

And there were many. She was, after all, still one of the biggest movie stars in the world, and even though she hadn't made a film since 1973, the last three films she had starred in—*Goodbye, Columbus; Love Story;* and *The Getaway*—had grossed more than $200 million, a very impressive figure.

She was, in fact, a bigger star than Steve. In 1975, he had benefited enough from *The Towering Inferno*'s popularity to place ninth on the list of the top ten most popular movie stars as determined by theater exhibitors, but it would be his last time on it.[1] Ali no longer listed because she had not had any new product in the theaters, but everybody in the business still wanted her and scripts arrived by messenger to the house all the time. At first, immediately following *The Towering Inferno*, she didn't even look at any of them. However, as time passed and the children no longer needed her constant attention, she began to feel even more stifled in her environment, and thought about returning to films as a way to escape this sandbox life with a husband who was increasingly domineering, distant, and nonverbal. It was as if the two were living together separately.

When Steve sensed there was a problem between them, he suggested they have a baby together. It almost happened, but during the making of *The Towering Inferno*, while sitting with Steve between takes, Ali had found herself suddenly sitting in a pool of blood. She was miscarrying. "I never even knew I was pregnant. It was very disturbing, and Steve in particular was upset. He always felt that if we had a child, we could save our marriage. Alas, I didn't think so. We were headed for a terrible collision and having a baby would only have created one more child whose foundation would be severely rocked, as our children's had been."

Ali's agent, Sue Mengers, kept urging her to come back to work, telling her that the marriage was no good for her, and that while she was still getting offers, they weren't going to keep coming forever. Plus, with that lousy prenup Steve had made her sign, Mengers reminded her, she had no real security if their marriage ended. Mengers had a script she insisted Ali at least read, for a film called *Convoy*, starring Kris Kristofferson, who was red-hot after co-starring with Barbra Streisand in her 1976 remake of *A Star Is*

---

[1] He was topped by Robert Redford, Barbra Streisand, Al Pacino, Charles Bronson, Paul Newman, Clint Eastwood, Burt Reynolds, and Woody Allen. Then came Steve, followed by Gene Hackman. Also, McQueen netted 10 percent of *The Getaway*'s $35 million worldwide gross, making him the highest-paid American actor in 1973, the year following the film's Christmas 1972 opening.

Born (a role that both Neil Diamond and Elvis Presley had turned down). One of the sticking points for Ali was that Sam Peckinpah was slated to direct. Peckinpah and Steve hadn't talked to each other since their falling-out. She was afraid Steve might see that as some kind of betrayal and use it as an excuse to explode.

Steve, meanwhile, after finishing *The Towering Inferno*, had let himself go. He stopped working out and, with all the beer and junk food he was so fond of, quickly started putting on a lot of weight. For the first time in his life, he had a noticeable beer belly. Believing movies were no longer a part of his life, he saw no reason to keep himself in shape.

Film, to Steve, was a young man's game. He was rich again from *The Towering Inferno* and still famous, but what had seemed reasonable to him at twenty-seven seemed silly at forty-seven. He didn't want to or have the need to descend into the kind of roles that older, less wealthy actors in Hollywood had to settle for and humiliate themselves with, like William Holden in *The Towering Inferno*. Steve never liked to work that hard, and he wasn't narcissistic enough to want to work to hold on to his looks. To him fat *meant* rich. He just wanted to sleep, eat, ride his bike, take drugs, and have sex with girls; there wasn't a lot of room in there for anything as difficult as serious filmmaking. Besides, he'd gone to the top of his game; the only direction left was down.

The problems between Ali and Steve were many and complicated, not always obvious, and ultimately unfixable. Besides his distance, moodiness, and obsessive womanizing, the issues raised by their distinct career goals proved insurmountable. Ali was eight years younger than Steve, on the outskirts of her thirties, a time when most actresses and especially those who had begun as print models began to fall away from the Hollywood spotlight. But not Ali. She had aged beautifully; her face had gained a certain maturity that would allow her to play roles with more depth and believability than spoiled brats or lovesick college girls. At thirty-nine, she was still quite marketable as a film star. That's where the lines were finally drawn in the sands of their marriage. She could no longer bear this decidedly ungilded cage that she had allowed herself to be put into.

As she later put it, "The early warning that my marriage with Steve was going to have its rocky times was his insistence that I sign that prenuptial agreement, because, he said, his first wife, Neile, had taken an enormous amount of money from him when they divorced. Personally, I did not think that was true at all. She had given up a promising career as a dancer and spent sixteen years bringing up their two children and holding his hand through the early days of his career. . . . I was caught up in the fantasy that we were so much in love that divorce was not an issue."

Ali was no Neile; she wasn't willing to give up her career, and she grew increasingly eager to rejoin the living, as it were, to continue to make movies and enjoy the glamorous life of a movie star. Whether it was Evans in his wildly ornate Beverly Hills mansion or Steve's hiding-from-the-law glorified shack, she'd had enough of being the prisoner of a powerful man. She'd had enough of making sure Steve's dinner was on the table at six sharp, meat and potatoes every night, so that he could eat with the kids in front of the TV. She preferred eating later by candlelight, in "a pathetic attempt to be civilized," while Steve went off on a post-meal motorcycle ride around Trancas and Mulholland, and was in bed by eight, just as she was putting the finishing touches on her own dinner. Besides, Steve was, according to Ali, "somewhat stoned every day of our six-year relationship."

On the rare occasions when he did engage in meaningful conversation with Ali, it was more often than not some kind of put-down. "Baby," he said to her on one occasion, "you have a great ass, but you'd better start working out now, because I don't want to wake up one day with a woman who's got an ass like a 70-year-old Japanese soldier."

Although MacGraw signed up for exercise classes the next day to please her powerful husband, she was far more interested in becoming a powerful woman. For a long time, Ali later confessed, "I did the sullen holdback. I was tight. Judgmental. Simmering . . . inauthentic at the beginning. I didn't state my case, 'You know, even though I told you I'd rather be on a motorcycle opening a can of beer, the truth is I'd rather go to Paris.'"

For his part, from the beginning of their relationship Steve had no interest in her onetime world of glamour. According to writer Sheila Weller, "He resisted going to a formal party for his film *Papillon* because 'the intellectual heavyweights like Jonas Salk' would be there. 'But there isn't one person in the room who can't wait to meet you,' [Ali] implored him, forcing him into his tuxedo."

One of the few times during those years she did manage to book a modeling shoot—in the summer of 1976, for photographer Francesco Scavullo's book *Scavullo on Beauty: The World's Most Beautiful Women*—she flew to New York by herself and stayed at the house of a girlfriend who was away and left her the key.

She was thrilled to be back in "her" city. In the afternoon she was interviewed by the *Vogue* writer doing the captions for the book. At night she had a bowl of pasta with a friend, and afterward the two walked the streets of the city catching up on all that had happened. The next day she had just taken a long and soothing bath when the phone rang. It was Steve. He wanted to tell her how much he loved her. They spoke for a few minutes and she hung up. About an hour later there was a pounding at the front door. She went to open it, and there stood Steve, drunk and disheveled. He had flown in from L.A., certain she was having an affair with another man, and called her from the airport in New York after his plane had landed. That night he gave her the same kind of sit-down-in-this-chair grilling he had given Neile the night he'd made her confess her affair with Maximilian Schell. Ali was both furious and frightened, and she had nothing to confess, which kept Steve going for hours. Then he wanted to make love, after which he passed out on the bed, leaving a highly upset Ali to curl up with her cashmere shawl on the bathroom floor in front of the toilet.

The next morning, before Scavullo could shoot her, she had to have her eyes made up extra heavily to hide the black rings of sleeplessness.

BACK IN Trancas, Ali continued to think about *Convoy*, a project she really wanted to do. She decided to tell Steve she was returning to making films, and he hit the low ceiling of his hot temper. At first he offered to make another movie with her, which Ali thought might not be a bad idea, except nobody wanted them. Ali could have any film she wanted, but Steve, in his present condition and with his reputation for being difficult, was a hard sell. Then, when Ali told Steve she had decided to make *Convoy*, "he was sitting in a chair, nursing a beer. He turned to me and said, 'In that case we are filing for divorce.'"

Ali remained cool. She pointed out that she had no money and that if their troubled marriage did indeed fall apart, she would be left penniless: the film was a good way for her to make fast cash. Steve offered to match the deal she was offered out of his own pocket—in essence, paying her not to work.

She said no and took the film, even if it meant divorce.

Steve backed off from both his offer and his threat.

STEVE WAS approached about starring in *Sorcerer*, Billy Friedkin's bizarre remake of Henri-Georges Clouzot's 1953 masterpiece *The Wages of Fear*. He thought it was the best script he had ever read and wanted to do it, until Friedkin told him it was going to be shot in South America. When Steve asked if the locale could be changed, Friedkin said no. Steve then confessed he was worried about his marriage to Ali and that if he had to be away for any length of time, she would not be there waiting for him. Friedkin said he was sorry but there was nothing he could do. Steve asked if he would write a part for her. Friedkin said no. Steve asked if she could be an associate producer. Friedkin said no. Steve finally turned the project down. Eventually, Roy Scheider played the part. The film opened in 1977 and laid a gigantic bomb.

IN THE spring of 1977, Ali went to New Mexico to make *Convoy* and Steve stayed behind. He made a rare appearance beyond the confines of Trancas when he attended his daughter's eighteenth-birthday party, a black-tie affair thrown by Neile at her new house and attended by many of Steve's friends, including Jim Coburn, the David Fosters, and the George Peppards. When asked where Ali was, Steve just said she was in Albuquerque, scouting locations for a project.

Ali later described Peckinpah's location shoot as "a study in drugs, alcohol and insanity, and I was certainly a manic participant." Once again Steve showed up without warning, and this time Ali, feeling safe and creatively sparking, welcomed him with open arms. What she didn't know was that while she was away, Steve had started an affair with a twenty-eight-year-old dark-haired beauty he had "interviewed" at the Beverly Wilshire for a film that didn't exist. Her name was Barbara Minty, and she was a gorgeous Ford model with a resemblance to a young Jackie Onassis. He was already planning to move with her up north.

He made no secret of the affair. Liz Smith, writing in her syndicated column, had these observations about Steve, Ali, and Minty: "Steve McQueen and Ali MacGraw were just steeped in too much 'togetherness.' They had become virtual recluses. . . . [T]he story goes that Steve has taken an interest in a beautiful Ford model, Barbara Minty. You have seen her in the pages of *Vogue* or in the Cole of California [bathing suit] ads. . . . Steve likes dark-haired girls with bushy eyebrows . . . Steve is also being seen lately in the Beverly Wilshire bar with an unidentified redhead (he keeps sleep-in offices in that hotel)."

According to Minty: "I had no idea who he was when we met over lunch at the Beverly Wilshire Hotel. I thought I'd be meeting Paul Newman—that was the face I'd put on the name 'Steve McQueen' in my mind's eye. But with his beard and long hair, he seemed more like a beach bum than a movie star."

CONVOY OPENED in the summer of 1978 and took in the biggest box office gross of Peckinpah's career—nearly $50 million in its initial domestic release—and gave Ali her fourth hit movie in a row.

To celebrate the opening, Steve, Ali, and Chad went for a vacation to Paradise Valley, where they had a great time until Steve, who had been drinking a lot of beer, cornered Ali and relentlessly grilled her about what he thought he had just seen, her flirting with one of the other guests. He kept it up during the drive all the way back to Los Angeles until Ali could no longer take it and screamed at him that she wanted a divorce, scaring Chad with the force of her anger.

She meant it. Less than a month later, at her insistence, they formally separated. Steve did not try to persuade her to change her mind. Ali found a house nearby, so Josh's schooling wouldn't be interrupted. According to Ali, shortly after she moved into it, "I called Steve on an impulse to tell him that I thought we had made a terrible mistake. His reply sent a dagger through my heart: 'I am not in love with you anymore. I love you, but I am not in love.'"

That was it for her. As soon as she hung up the phone, she

alerted Mengers to get her another picture as soon as possible. She did one, then another, then some TV, and eventually mended fences with Evans.

And never married again.

Steve, meanwhile, was serious about moving north with Minty. Film offers continued to come in, and he continued to turn all of them down. He turned down $1.5 million to play Willard in Francis Ford Coppola's *Apocalypse Now*, he said, because of the seventeen-week shooting schedule in the Philippines. He still hadn't quite gotten over the Taiwan–Hong Kong nightmare of *The Sand Pebbles*. Besides, he didn't want to be away from Barbara or his children that long. After Al Pacino turned the part down, Harvey Keitel was fired, and James Caan, Robert Redford, and Jack Nicholson all said no, the role finally went to Martin Sheen. Coppola then came back to Steve and asked if he would consider the smaller, less exacting role of Colonel Kurtz. Steve said he would— for $3.5 million for what amounted to a three-week shoot. When Coppola balked, Steve stood firm and turned the film down again.[2]

Steve also turned down Sir Richard Attenborough's *A Bridge Too Far*, a World War II battle epic. Despite the fact that he and Attenborough had remained good friends since *The Sand Pebbles* and the role was only a cameo (part of an ensemble all-star cast), Steve asked for $3 million. Attenborough had to say no; the film had too many stars and not enough budget. There was, perhaps, an extra incentive for Steve not to want to make this film: Maximilian Schell was in it.

There was one project that caught Steve's interest. An inveterate TV watcher, he thought the famous Israeli raid on Entebbe, about the freeing of hostages from a hijacked plane taken by Palestinians to Uganda, would make a great film, but he could not

---

[2] It was later cut to three days for Marlon Brando, who eventually played the part for a reported $3 million.

get it funded. It's unclear how hard he tried. The project eventually wound up as an Irvin Kershner TV movie in 1977 starring Peter Finch as Yitzhak Rabin, the role Steve had originally wanted to play.

In the spring of 1977, the *National Enquirer* ran an "exclusive" photo of Steve, claiming that he now weighed an unrecognizable 240 pounds (perhaps the real reason he couldn't get the Entebbe film made). He apparently didn't care. Steve's response to the photo was short and to the point: "I could go anywhere I wanted and not be recognized. It was great."

However, First Artists had something to say about that. Steve still had two pictures left on his three-picture deal with them. The company was not doing well and needed a big picture, and wanted Steve to deliver one. After consulting with his lawyers, he realized he could not get out of the contract; part of the original deal had included funding of *The Getaway*, which meant that if he broke the contract, he would have to turn over every cent he'd made from that movie, which was several million dollars and counting.

In 1977, Phil Feldman, the president of First Artists, met with Steve and Marvin Josephson, who had taken over control of CMA from Freddie Fields, and all three agreed Steve needed to get himself in shape and come in with a viable project he could make for the same $3 million budget he had agreed to ten years earlier, even though the budgets of nearly all films had quadrupled in the seventies.[3] It didn't

---

[3] Fields had decided to get out of the agent business and sold his company to Marvin Josephson's International Creative Management. Josephson agreed to take over the personal management and agenting of Steve's career. Steve went along with this, believing that it didn't matter who managed and repped him, because as far as he was concerned, he was retired from making movies. One of the first things Steve did was to remind Josephson of his "special" deal with Fields regarding commissions. No deal, Josephson told Steve; he had to pay the full 10 percent commission on all deals. Steve finally agreed, but continued to try to get Josephson to cut him special deals on commissions.

sit well with Steve that Barbra Streisand's third and final film for First Artists, *A Star Is Born*, had been given a $6 million budget because of the presumed commercial appeal of the project.

Not long afterward, while Steve was in Palm Springs with Barbara, Josephson personally delivered to him a script called *The Continuation of Gone with the Wind*. ICM held the rights to the Margaret Mitchell novel, and after resisting for several years, her estate had agreed to a sequel to the original film. ICM wanted Steve to play Rhett Butler.

Steve turned down the offer, went back to Feldman, and asked him for one $6 million payout, in return for which he would do two pictures that would complete his obligation to Feldman.

Feldman went for it, and the first film Steve chose to make was based on Arthur Miller's 1950 version of Henrik Ibsen's 1882 play, *An Enemy of the People*, a full-length political metaphor about a well that is the town's main attraction and primary source of income, and what happens when the well is discovered to be contaminated. Steve cast himself as Dr. Thomas Stockmann, who first discovers the well is no good. His brother, Peter (Charles Durning), who also happens to be the town mayor, tries to prevent Thomas from going public and ruining the town's financial golden calf.

Feldman was outraged by the selection of this film, but because Steve had the right to choose the project, he had to agree to it. Warner, wanting to have a piece of two new Steve McQueen films, came aboard *An Enemy of the People* as its distributor before it even knew what the project was, a deal it, too, couldn't get out of.

Steve managed to put together a great international cast, including Bibi Andersson (as Catherine Stockmann, Thomas's wife, after Julie Christie turned down the role), Durning (Nicol Williamson had agreed to play Peter but changed his mind and bowed out of the project), and Michael Cristofer (who would go on to become a noted playwright). To direct, Steve chose TV director George

Schaefer, who was a veteran of dozens of *Hallmark Hall of Fame* dramas during TV's golden age but had yet to direct a feature. Steve felt he was perfect for the job: competent and willing to take orders, someone who would make the film the way Steve wanted it made. He knew he couldn't get that with any name director, even if he could afford one. Over lunch, Steve convinced Schaefer to direct the picture. At the first production meeting, Steve showed up still grossly overweight, with a scraggly beard and round eyeglasses that all but hid his blue eyes.

The film that was meant to return Steve to the big screen after four years away took eighteen months to shoot, went way over budget (Steve paid for the cost overruns out of his own pocket), and never officially opened.[4]

No one could figure out why Steve had chosen a project that was so sure to self-destruct. Some saw it as his revenge against First Artists for holding him to his contract. Others saw it as Steve's desire to do some "real" acting. Still others thought he had finally and completely lost his mind. To Steve, the answer was simple: "At this stage in my life, I don't want to make ordinary movies anymore. If I can't make movies above average in quality, I'd rather take it easy. I wanted to do something I'd be proud of "—that also paid him millions of dollars.

Warner and First Artists made it no secret that they were furious. Steve, according to many who worked on the film and knew

---

[4] The film was "previewed" by Warner Bros. The strategy, according to Warren Cowan, McQueen's publicist at the time, was "At one location, *An Enemy of the People* opens at only one theater; at site number two, tickets went to group sales, in city three, the preview was preceded by advertising, including TV spots, and city four got a combination plate, at one theater with tickets for group sales and the general public." However, the film was pulled after one week of a four-week engagement in Minneapolis—a "group sales" site and not considered an official run. Two years later it was picked up by Joseph Papp's Public Theater, where it may have been publicly screened once or twice, but it never had any commercial release.

him personally, said he was crushed at their reaction to what he believed was his Method masterpiece.

In November 1977, while still making *An Enemy of the People*, Steve read something in the November issue of the *Ladies' Home Journal* that made him quite angry. Ali had told an interviewer, "If they put a freeze frame on my life right now, I'd say I'm leading exactly the sort of life I want. I don't know about Steve. You'd have to ask him."

Before the heat left his face, Steve signed the final divorce papers that officially ended his marriage to Ali, which she did not contest. He was determined now to start a new life with Barbara as far away from Hollywood as he could get. It meant cleaning house, in every way, and Steve was committed to doing it, even without having delivered his final film to First Artists.

At the same time, Tony Bill, then a producer at Warner as well as an up-and-coming movie actor, had found a script called *Nothing in Common* that he wanted Steve and Ali to do together; he was willing to let it be made under the banner of First Artists. Steve said no, and it never got as far as Ali.

Director Bob Rafelson, one of the hottest independent directors of the 1970s after his highly regarded 1970 film *Five Easy Pieces*, which helped cement Jack Nicholson's rise to stardom, wrote *Missouri Breaks* for Steve, but Steve turned that down too and it went instead to Nicholson and Marlon Brando, with Arthur Penn directing. Alexander and Ilya Salkind wanted him for the title role of *Superman*, in a film that would co-star Robert Redford, Dustin Hoffman, Barbra Streisand, Ned Beatty, Raquel Welch, Michael York, Telly Savalas, and Shelley Winters. Steve was interested in the project—for the right price, of course—but when the Salkinds saw him in person, they decided he was too old and fat to play Superman.

Steve was also offered the starring role in *The Betsy*, again with

Ali. It was a screen version of yet another Harold Robbins novel, this one about the car industry. He immediately turned it down, and Ali was never officially offered the film. Irwin Allen was set to do a sequel to *The Towering Inferno* but didn't even seek Steve out. *The Gauntlet* came Steve's way, via First Artists, after Brando bowed out of it, but Streisand, set as Brando's co-star, didn't want to work with Steve, and the two leads eventually went to Clint Eastwood and Sondra Locke, with Eastwood directing and producing. Sir Lew Grade ("Sir Low Grade," as he was often called, for the quality of his films) wanted Steve for *Raise the Titanic*, but Steve asked for too much money and Grade withdrew his offer. The same thing happened when Spielberg wanted him for *Close Encounters of the Third Kind*, but Columbia refused to meet his price and the role went instead to Richard Dreyfuss, after Gene Hackman, Al Pacino, Dustin Hoffman, and Jack Nicholson all passed.

In August 1979, Steve offered to film Harold Pinter's play *Old Times*. Both First Artists and Warner Bros. told him not to bother—there was no way they would ever distribute it.

Fed up with First Artists, Steve exercised the nonexclusive clause in his original deal and signed a $5 million contract to star in Richard Fleisher's film version of James Clavell's bestselling novel *Tai-Pan*.[5] To seal the deal, he demanded and got a $1 million nonrefundable payment upon signing, with another $1 million contractually guaranteed to be paid on a specific date. When the second check arrived late, Steve walked off the project, legally

---

[5] Reports vary as to how much Steve agreed to; $5 million is the price quoted most often, but there were reports of as little as $3 million and as much as $10 million. Steve's nonrefundable $1 million allowed the producers to sell the foreign rights prior to production. Steve was still a very strong attraction in Europe and the producers raised several million dollars off his signature. The film was eventually made in 1986, directed by Daryl Duke and with Bryan Brown in the starring role originally intended for Steve. It is unclear if Steve ever received the rest of his money. He threatened a lawsuit, but it never materialized.

free of it. According to Marvin Josephson, Steve's agent, "One large payment was made to McQueen when he signed the contract with [producer Georges-Alain Vuille and his Lausanne, Switzerland-based Beverly Films]. . . . [T]hey failed to meet one of the conditions in the contract, that of a major money payment. Therefore, Steve [did not] proceed with the film." What had really gotten Steve and Josephson angry was that Vuille had already made $18 million in foreign presales of the film using Steve's name, but was late making his second payment.

Steve and Josephson now set Steve's asking price at $5 million, with a $1 million nonrefundable advance upon signing. Amazingly—despite the fact he hadn't had a hit film in nearly five years, and was involved with the dismal failure of *An Enemy of the People*—because of the *Tai-Pan* contract and payouts, without shooting a single foot of film he had become 1979's highest-paid actor in Hollywood.

LATE THAT same year, First Artists stepped up the pressure to get the second movie Steve owed them. In response he sued them, claiming that their refusal to distribute *Old Times* had completed his obligation to them. Before the case went to trial, Steve and First Artists' Feldman reached an out-of-court agreement that stipulated Steve would star in *Tom Horn*, a film about the life of a man out of place and out of time. Horn was the man who captured Geronimo, became a folk hero, outlived his own legend, spent a brief time as a bounty hunter, and eventually was hanged for a murder he probably didn't commit. *Tom Horn*, both sides agreed, would satisfy all remaining obligations of the Steve McQueen/First Artists association.

However, even as the ink was drying on the deal, ABC Pictures announced it was making its own version of *Tom Horn*, directed by Sydney Pollack and starring Robert Redford, that would reunite

Redford with *Butch Cassidy and the Sundance Kid* screenwriter William Goldman. Pollack called Steve personally to discuss the situation and was told by him in no uncertain terms that his film was going ahead. Redford, not wanting to be involved in competing pictures with Steve (or anybody), dropped out of the film, and ABC put the project into turnaround. The much-coveted Goldman script was then picked up by CBS, with Lorimar Productions intending to turn it into a four-hour miniseries with David Carradine in the title role.

First Artists, eager to get their film made, decided that since the Goldman script was really all about the later years of Tom Horn and their film was about his early years (even though Steve was about to turn fifty), and since theirs had been written by Abe Polonsky based on *Life of Tom Horn, Government Scout and Interpreter*, they had the creative edge.

However, even before they went into production, Steve had Polonsky fired, claiming he didn't like his script. That spurred the immediate resignation of Don Siegel, who had signed on to direct only after First Artists assured him Steve would not give anybody any trouble on the project. Siegel was replaced by Elliott Silverstein, who also left before a single foot of film was in the can, and was replaced, at Steve's insistence, by James William Guercio, who had made a film in 1973 called *Electra Glide in Blue*, about motorcycles and solitude, two of Steve's favorite pastimes. Guercio was quickly fired by First Artists and replaced by William Wiard, and an entirely new script was ordered, to be written by Tom McGuane and Bud Shrake. With all of these changes, by the time the film was finally released, it looked as if it had come out of a blender, with the downbeat ending of Steve being hanged on camera not adding to its commercial prospects.

The night before he was set to do the stunt hanging, Barbara called Steve and told him she had had a bad dream, a premonition about the hanging, and begged him not to do it. He assured her he wouldn't—and then of course he did.

When the film finally wrapped early in March 1979, Steve and Barbara went up to Santa Paula, one of Steve's favorite getaways in California, a small agricultural town about as far removed from Hollywood and Beverly Hills as possible. Its terrain reminded Steve of his boyhood hometown, Slater.

Santa Paula is fifteen miles northwest of L.A. and fourteen miles inland from the Pacific Ocean within the Santa Clara River valley, filled with lush orange, lemon, walnut, and avocado trees. The main street of this community of twenty thousand, mostly farmers and other working-class non-show-business people, still had hitching posts for horses and a barnlike general store in business since the late 1880s.

Steve loved it there, especially because those people who recognized him made no fuss about his presence among them. He had been thinking for a while about permanently moving to Santa Paula with Barbara. Now, he decided he wanted to learn how to fly a plane. Santa Paula, he figured, was the perfect place to do it because it had a small, privately owned airport that would make the trip down the coast easier on those occasions when he still had to be in Hollywood.

Steve began taking lessons there late in March. By May 1, he was soloing in a 1940 Stearman biplane. Not long after, Steve heard about a 1931 Pitcairn Mailwing biplane that was for sale at the airport. Steve bought it for $65,000 cash. He also bought a private hangar for it that he turned into a little bachelor pad for himself, complete with potbelly stove, kitchen, bathroom, and bed. There he could eat, sleep, and work on the plane's engine.

What was this fascination with biplanes? Perhaps there is a clue in Andrew Sarris's whimsical observation that after the death of Steve's father, "Red McQueen remained a man in a mythological biplane flying, flying, flying through all eternity from his own baby who grew up to be Steve McQueen, King of Cool." Perhaps Steve was, after all, looking to find and reunite with his father's spirit, on Red's own sky-high turf.

At this point Steve and Barbara, who had been living in Trancas until now, decided they wanted to move to Santa Paula permanently. Together, they started looking for a house. After seeing several they liked, they settled on a fifteen-acre ranch, three miles from the airport, with a four-bedroom house built in 1896. It needed work, but it had all the requisite charm Steve was looking for. While he began the long process of fixing it up to meet his movie-star standards of rustic, he qualified to apply for his pilot's license, despite the fact that his hearing was less than perfect and he wore glasses most of the time offscreen.

On July 20, 1979, Steve received his radio communications license, the last step needed before taking his final flying test, which he passed. "He got up with the chickens [every morning]," Barbara would say with a smile, "and flew away."

All he needed to do now was to move the last of his belongings from the house at Trancas, and he and Barbara would be permanent residents of Santa Paula.

Back in February, while Ali was in L.A. on a break from filming Sidney Lumet's *Just Tell Me What You Want* in New York, she had received a call from Steve asking her if she would like to take a drive with him up to Santa Paula. He explained that he had bought a house up there for him and Barbara. Would she like to see it and meet Barbara?

Ali said okay, and when Steve showed up to get her wearing "one of those ghastly trucker hats," Ali later recalled, "and carrying a beer, and I had on my high heels and fingernails, both of which had disappeared during our marriage, the electricity was instant. I remembered exactly who it was that I had fallen head over heels in love with."

On the way, Steve told Ali that he intended to move to Santa Paula full-time and permanently, with Barbara, and that he was going to marry her. And then he pulled the truck over to the side of the road somewhere on the highway near Oxnard and suggested that he and Ali make love, right there and then. In her memoir, Ali wrote that she was upset and saddened that Steve had suggested such a thing. It was a glimpse back into who he really was, and what he had probably been like with other women when she had been married to him. She bowed out of the rest of the drive and somehow made her way back to Los Angeles.

It was the last time she ever saw him.

STEVE QUICKLY settled into his new life with Barbara in Santa Paula, perhaps the happiest and most peaceful time of his adult life. He even began going to church regularly. He wanted nothing more than to fly his plane, pray, and make love to his wife.

All of this was interrupted in late March 1979 by the arrival in Santa Paula of producer Mort Engelberg, a partner in Rastar Productions, headed by legendary producer Ray Stark. With script in hand, Engelberg found Steve at the hangar, where he personally delivered the screenplay for *The Hunter*, about the true-life exploits of a famed bounty hunter who had captured more than five thousand fugitives. Steve and Engelberg talked for a while and Steve said he would think about it. He liked the fact that in the film he would play a bounty hunter; he thought it was a neat end-of-career film that completed the circle all the way back to the beginning.

In truth, there was very little for him to mull over. Free from the horse-collar contract of First Artists, he had a chance to make a bundle (estimates for what he was offered range from $3 million to $10.5 million plus percentages). After talking it over with

Barbara, he agreed to do the film for Engelberg and Stark at Paramount.[6]

The five-week shoot, with an $8 million budget, was set to begin almost immediately. It would include a month on location in Chicago, a week in Kankakee, Illinois, and a brief postproduction stay in Los Angeles. Steve especially liked the timing of it all. Not only would it give the renovators a chance to finish all the work at the ranch, but it would also pay their fee. Barbara came with him for the duration, returning home occasionally to check on the progress of the construction.

Engelberg had reserved a luxurious suite for Steve and Barbara at the famed Drake Hotel in Chicago. When Steve arrived with Barbara, he looked the place over and then asked where Engelberg was staying. Engelberg said he would be at the Holiday Inn with the rest of the crew. Steve promptly checked himself and Barbara out of the Drake and moved into the smaller chain hotel. He had had his fill of star treatment, he explained, and just wanted to be among the crew while the film was being shot.

As it always seemed to on a Steve McQueen movie, trouble arrived even before the first foot of film was shot. At Steve's insistence, the original script by Richard Levinson and William Link, a well-known writing duo, was thrown out, along with their co-writer and the director of the film, Peter Hyams. Steve then said he wanted to direct the film himself, but ultimately couldn't, due to Directors Guild of America rules stating that no one previously involved in any way with the production of a film can take over as director if the original director leaves or is fired.

Steve reluctantly approved Buzz Kulik to direct (another director he had worked for back in the days of live TV on a couple of episodes of *Climax*). After months of haggling and time out for a new script to be written by Ted Leighton, adapted from the

---

[6] According to *Variety*, $3 million and 15 percent of the gross.

Ralph "Papa" Thorson biography by Christopher Keane (Hyams received sole screen credit), the film finally began shooting on September 10.

Steve showed up the first day slimmer than he had been (but not slim) and clean-shaven. His face looked lined and tired. One of the things Steve insisted upon was doing his own stunts, including riding atop a Chicago train at 40 mph in a tunnel with barely any headroom. His goal was to convince people he was at the top of his game. His attitude during the making was as affable as Steve was ever able to be. During one scene he laughingly instructed his makeup man to "make me look halfway between John Travolta and Robert Redford." At Steve's insistence, his son Chad was hired as a gofer so he could learn the business in case he ever wanted to be in it.

Kathryn Harrold played the love interest and soon discovered that she and Steve were graduates of the Neighborhood Playhouse. They had a good time together but no romance. Among other things, Harrold couldn't stand Steve's habit of chewing tobacco, one of the many tricks he tried in an effort to give up his twenty-five-year two-pack-a-day smoking habit.

The film wrapped in June 1979, early and $300,000 under budget, at which point Kulik and Engelberg, who had gotten along extremely well once everything had been sorted out, started talking about doing another film, one that Engelberg already had the rights to, called *Quigley Down Under.*

EVEN BEFORE *Quigley Down Under* was ready to go, and before *Tom Horn* was released, producers Herb Jaffee and Jerry Beck approached Steve about starring in a film version of Elmore Leonard's *Hang Tough.* Steve's career appeared to be on the upswing and about to return him to the A-list, but it was not to be. Through his agents, Steve abruptly turned the project down. The producers then upped their offer into the stratosphere, but Steve's answer was still no. They pleaded with him to reconsider. They insisted this was the best script Steve had been offered since *Bullitt*, perfectly tailored to the way he liked to make movies and sure to return him to superstardom.

But *The Hunter* was going to have to be Steve's last film.

He was dying of lung cancer.

I say to all my fans and all my friends, keep your fingers crossed and keep the good thoughts coming. All my love and God bless you all. This is Steve McQueen.

IN DECEMBER 1979, STEVE BEGAN TO THINK ABOUT MAKING another racing film, this one to chronicle a fictional cross-country bike race set back in the 1950s. It was his stuntman friend Charles Bail who first dared to tell Steve that, despite having shaved off his beard and trimmed a few pounds, he still looked terrible.

When Steve asked Barbara how he looked, she took the opportunity to ask him to get a complete physical before he thought about any more movies. Steve, who hadn't been feeling well for a while, took her advice and entered Cedars-Sinai Hospital in Beverly Hills the second week in December. He was examined and instructed to undergo exploratory surgery as soon as possible. The operation, performed on December 22, revealed a massive malignant tumor in his right lung. Steve was diagnosed with incurable mesothelioma, a rare cancer that grows between the chest wall and lungs of its victims and which is caused by excessive asbestos inhalation; it is usually detected thirty to forty years after initial exposure to asbestos fibers.[1] He remained in the hospital for three

---

[1] Although it is more common today, in 1979 mesothelioma was an extremely rarely diagnosed form of cancer. In a study by the National Cancer Institute that included 10 percent of the U.S. populaton for 1969–71, 120 cases of mesothelioma were diagnosed. By comparison, 24,000 cases of lung cancer showed up. Treatment is almost always limited to the alleviation of pain.

weeks on the eighth floor, famously known as the "VIP floor," under an assumed name. According to a staffer, describing what sounds like early postdiagnosis denial, "He was the hit of the ward. He threw several parties."

Steve had gotten the bad news from his doctor while still in the recovery room. He had at most a few months to live, and there was little in the way of conventional cancer treatment that would help. Steve made the doctors keep the worst of it from Barbara, agreeing to tell her he had easily four or five more years.

Not long after he was released from the hospital, he shocked Barbara by asking her to marry him. He professed that he was doing it out of love, but he also wanted to make sure she was not cut out of everything she deserved from his estate when the worst happened. And he knew that if she was his wife, she would not leave him, no matter how bad his condition became.

Minty recalled the moment of the actual proposal. It took place in Los Angeles, where they had gone so Steve could take care of some personal business. "It was barely a proposal. We were at the [Beverly] Wilshire when he dragged me to Tiffany's and said, 'Here, pick whatever ring you want.' Back at the suite he slipped the ring onto my finger and said, 'There, are you satisfied?' Not the most romantic of proposals, but it was classic Steve."

He spent his last Christmas with Barbara up at the newly redecorated ranch, driving into L.A. every day to undergo chemotherapy and radiation, mostly because there were no other treatments. He also volunteered to try a new, experimental drug, interferon. And he worked desperately to keep his illness out of the papers. He instructed everyone who knew that, if asked, they were to say he was suffering from a severe respiratory infection.

Steve and Barbara were married on a warm Wednesday afternoon, January 16, 1980. The ceremony was performed by Dr. Leslie Miller of the Ventura Missionary Church. The only witnesses were his flying instructor, Sammy Mason, and his wife. Steve dressed casually in jeans, sneakers, and a short-sleeved shirt. Barbara wore a white pants suit and a wreath of baby's breath. She carried a bouquet of daisies and looked dazzling. She was twenty-five years old; Steve was two months shy of fifty.

THREE DAYS later Neile remarried. Her second husband's name was Al Toffel. They had met a few months earlier at a luncheon for Princess Grace of Monaco. He was a former Air Force fighter pilot and an aeronautical engineer with NASA. As it happened, Steve was at the luncheon as well, and incredibly, later that night he called Neile and asked if she still loved him. Neile said sure, of course she did. He kept asking over and over again, and Neile kept on saying of course.

Neile remained married to Toffel until his death in 2005.

THE DOCTORS agreed that Steve's racing had probably caused his illness, as the interiors of race cars are swathed in asbestos, but Steve knew better. He remembered that six-week period in the marines when he had done little but clean the engine room. The pipes down there had been covered with layers of asbestos, which he was constantly having to pull out and replace; he'd hardly been able to breathe at night from all the particles of the stuff he'd inhaled. He was certain now those six weeks had been his death sentence.

He volunteered to have radioactive cobalt surgically implanted in his chest cavity for a month.

ON MARCH 18, 1980, the *National Enquirer* broke the story that Steve had terminal cancer. They published a front-page picture of him with a headline underneath that said, "Steve McQueen's

Heroic Battle Against Terminal Cancer." He vehemently denied it through his talent agency and threatened to sue the newspaper, insisting he was only battling an infection, but the *Enquirer* had the goods, apparently from a source deep inside the walls of Cedars-Sinai, and no lawsuit ever materialized.

TOM HORN began a week of previews on March 28, 1980, four days after Steve's fiftieth birthday. To deny the rumors that he was terminal, Steve, noticeably overweight and with a well-trimmed beard, attended one of the previews at Oxnard, California. While Barbara beamed for the cameras, Steve joked with the photographers and reporters: "Why don't you guys come in and see a good western!" His deep tan covered an unhealthy pallor. Afterward, as he left the theater, another barrage of photographers and reporters asked about the rumors of cancer. Steve only smiled and said, "Think you got enough pictures?" With that, he took Barbara by the arm, walked to his truck, got in, and drove away.

It was Steve's last live public appearance.

The film opened its regular run four months later, on July 28, 1980, dumped into release by Paramount in the last week of the month, when the fewest people go to the movies. There was little promotion (Steve was not available to do any) and little advertising.

The film received reviews that ranged from mixed to dismal. *Variety* wrote it off as "a sorry ending to the once high hopes of First Artists Productions. McQueen certainly looks like he's walking through the part and the picture as a whole is such a technical embarrassment the rest of the credits must have walked with him."

It was a sad ending indeed. During its ten-year tenure, First Artists produced a total of fifteen movies. However, the First Artists stars made poor choices of films in an effort to expand their images and do some "real" acting. Besides Steve's *The Hunter* and *An Enemy of the People*, Paul Newman made *Pocket Money* (Stuart

Rosenberg, 1972), Streisand made *Up the Sandbox* (Irvin Kershner, 1972), and *Yentl* (Streisand, 1983). As for the rest of the movies, the bad ones far outnumbered the good.[2]

Robert Osborne, the affable columnist for the *Hollywood Reporter* (who would go on to be the on-camera host for Turner Classic Movies), wrote a piece about the film that was probably the best and least hostile from the critics: "If McQueen doesn't appear to be acting, it's because—like Wayne and Cooper—he's learned to act this type of character so well, all theatrical trickery is virtually invisible. It's a genuinely fine piece of good filmmaking which does justice to any filmgoer's time. And it returns a genuine superstar to audiences after far too long an absence."

The film earned a mere $12 million in its initial domestic release, reflecting how little interest there was in it. Osborne's references to Wayne and Cooper were pointed—their style of film had long gone out of fashion. The big 1980 movies were George Lucas's *Star Wars Part V: The Empire Strikes Back*; Colin Higgins's *9 to 5*, with the triple-threat star power of Lily Tomlin, Dolly Parton, and Jane Fonda; Sidney Poitier's *Stir Crazy*, with Richard Pryor and Gene Wilder; Jim Abrahams and David Zucker's ensemble goofball comedy *Airplane*; and Buddy Van Horn's *Any Which Way You Can*, starring Clint Eastwood. The only two notable westerns that year were James Bridges's *Urban Cowboy*, a John Travolta vehicle that also starred Debra Winger and was not really a western at all in the traditional sense (a mechanical bull is the only animal that gets ridden in this contemporary love story, and cowboy hats are the only western thing about the picture), and Michael Cimino's

---

[2] After *Tom Horn*, First Artists unsuccessfully tried to diversify into a number of businesses, including shirt manufacturing and gambling, both of which were less than successful—it couldn't obtain a license to open a casino in London. It was the target of a successful takeover by Mascot Industries, an investment conglomerate, and shortly thereaafter was dissolved. The only valuable asset, its film library, remained with Mascot.

disastrous *Heaven's Gate*. By any measure, *Tom Horn* was hopelessly out of sync with the film tastes of the times.

Steve was increasingly desperate to find a cure for his cancer, even as he continued to deny that he was sick, although by now it was an open secret in Hollywood that he was seriously ill. In May, more surgery revealed not only that the cobalt implant had not done any good but also that the cancer was spreading rapidly through his body, killing him organ by organ. His doctors now gave him a month.

The first week of August, the *Los Angeles Herald-Examiner* reported that "McQueen spent several days last week at Cedars-Sinai Medical Center undergoing treatment for an unspecified disease."

Then through his PR spokesman, Warren Cowan, McQueen let it be known that he was indeed suffering from mesothelioma, but that his condition had dramatically improved during the last six weeks. Cowan's statement denied that Steve's illness was terminal.

But it was. The disease had metastasized to his neck, abdomen, and chest, ruling out any further conventional treatments such as chemotherapy or radiation. When his doctors told him he should start to put his affairs in order, he became even more desperate to find a cure.

On a friend's recommendation, he secretly traveled under an assumed name to Dr. William D. Kelley's four-month-old institute in Rosarita Beach, Mexico, about seventy-five miles south of San Diego. Dr. Kelley was a former dentist and metabolic researcher whose license had been suspended for five years by the Texas State Board of Dental Examiners for practicing medicine without a license. Kelley's team included Dr. Dwight McKee, medical director of the International Health Institute, and Dr. Rodrigo Rodriguez, medical director of his own unnamed center for degenerative diseases. They treated Steve with a daily regimen

of fifty vitamin and mineral pills and enzymes, with almonds substituting for meat, no protein allowed after one in the afternoon,
and a Japanese vaccine made from bacilli usually used in the treatment of tuberculosis.

Dr. Kelley's method of treatment had been on the American
Cancer Society's list of unproven methods of cancer management.[3]
At least one skeptical doctor dismissed Dr. Kelley's treatment as
nothing more than snake oil. "If doctors in Mexico tell McQueen
that he can be cured by vitamins, pits, enemas, exercise and sham-
poo, they're just kidding him," said Dr. David Plotkin, chief of
oncology at Brotman Medical Center in Culver City, California.
"In my opinion, that's snake-oil medicine. They can rub him down
with castor oil or olive oil from morning to night. That's not going
to cure his mesothelioma, if that's what he has."

As if in response, Steve released the following statement via Warren Cowan: "The reason I denied that I had cancer was to save my
family and friends from personal hurt and to retain my sense of dignity
as, for sure, I thought I was going to die. [Now I believe I am going to
recover and] hopefully, the cheap scandal sheets and curiosity seekers
will not try to seek me out so I can continue my treatment."

In August, Steve was placed under twenty-four-hour super-
vision and, in addition to his regular regimen, was given daily coffee and lemon juice enemas, shampoos, detoxification sweatings,
live cell injections from fetal pigs and cattle, and blood purifica-
tion treatments. He was also put on the controversial drug laetrile,

---

[3] Dr. Kelley was no stranger to controversy over his methods. In January 1970, a
Dallas judge issued an injunction against his practicing medicine in Texas after
the attorney general's office filed a suit accusing him of practicing medicine
without a license. Kelley, who claimed to have cured his own cancer eighteen
years earlier, called the case "a bunch of trumped-up charges." According to
Dr. Hans Weill, a professor of medicine at Tulane University Medical School
who specialized in occupational lung disease, "The survival rate [for this type
of cancer] is close to zero."

extracted from apricot pits. Miraculously, his condition started to improve, and he returned to Santa Paula. At that point, Dr. Kelley confidently predicted that Steve McQueen would completely recover and resume living a normal life.

But then, in October, his condition dramatically worsened. On October 9 he asked a reporter from *Televisa*, the Mexican national broadcast network, to come to the Santa Paula ranch, where outside the press had set up dozens of cameras, with reporters on hand twenty-four hours a day, to capture any message he wanted released to the public.

In his statement, Steve thanked the Mexican government for allowing him to pursue his choice of treatment there and noted that it had given him "an extraordinary improved quality of life. To all my fans and all my friends, keep your fingers crossed and keep the good thoughts coming. All my love and God bless you all. This is Steve McQueen." The tape was broadcast all over the world. The next day Steve returned to the Mexican clinic.

When Neile heard the broadcast, she rushed to the clinic to be by his side, to help care for him in any way she could. Ali also heard it but chose not to go.

Dr. Rodriguez then issued a statement that said, "Mr. McQueen has shown no new tumor growth, shows clear shrinkage of existing tumors and has a much better appetite."

On October 29, under a shroud of secrecy, Steve checked out of the clinic and, accompanied by his wife, returned once more to Santa Paula to put his affairs in order and to take one last look at the place he loved so much.

The hospital described it as a "holiday," made possible by Steve's improved condition. By now his stomach was grossly distended, and he had to walk with a cane. According to one doctor at the clinic, Steve "looked more pregnant than a fully pregnant woman, and weighed about 150 pounds." Other unsubstantiated reports placed Steve's weight at about 100 pounds.

On November 2, after Dr. Rodriguez ordered a CAT scan for Steve at the Eastwood Hospital Clinic in El Paso, he was returned to Mexico for an operation to remove a tumor on his neck (the tumor was officially described as "dead") before resuming cancer therapy.

On November 3 he was visited in the hospital by the Reverend Billy Graham.

On November 4 Steve was prepped for the surgery Dr. Kelley claimed was necessary to remove the tumor in his neck and an additional one in his abdominal cavity.

Early Friday morning, November 7, just before being wheeled into the operating room, according to Dr. Cesar Santos Vargas, a fifty-two-year-old heart and kidney specialist associated with the clinic who was actually going to perform the surgery, "Steve took my hand and made a signal with his thumb up, wishing me good luck."

Surgery revealed the cancer had spread to Steve's left lung and intestines, and while under anesthesia, he suffered a major heart attack. He lasted another sixteen hours, regaining consciousness once, asking no one in particular if his stomach was flat now. He then closed his eyes and slipped back under. At 2:00 on Saturday morning, November 8, 1980, he suffered a second heart attack, caused by an embolism, according to Dr. Vargas. At the age of fifty, Steve died in his sleep, with Neile, Barbara, and his two children, Terry, twenty-one, and Chad, twenty, at his bedside.

The body was removed from the hospital later that day and loaded onto a white Learjet that flew the plain brass-handled casket back to Santa Paula. The funeral was held four days later at the ranch. As per his instructions, his body was then cremated and his ashes scattered over the waters of the Pacific Ocean.

As THE world reacted with shock and sadness to the news, Barbara, acting on the instructions Steve left in his will, made arrangements to sell off all his tangible assets, which included nearly a hundred cars, two hundred motorcycles, and five planes. The auction would eventually bring in nearly $2 million. The Boys Republic in Chino received $200,000. The rest of his estate, valued at $12 million after taxes, was given over to his children and Barbara. As per his instructions, Neile and Ali got nothing.

Shortly before the auction took place, a memorial was held on November 9, 1980, attended by Steve's closest friends and all three wives. When it was her turn to speak, Neile summed up Steve's life with humor, brevity, and insight. "Steve liked to fuck blondes," she said, "but he married brunettes." After a moment's awkward silence, everyone threw back their heads and roared with laughter.

Filmography

FEATURE FILMS

1. *Somebody Up There Likes Me* (MGM) 1956. Director: Robert Wise. Producer: Charles Schnee. Screenplay: Ernest Lehman, based on the autobiography of Rocky Graziano that was written with Rowland Barber. With Paul Newman, Pier Angeli, Everett Sloane, Eileen Heckart, Sal Mineo, Harold J. Stone, Joseph Buloff. Steve McQueen appears in a bit part as Fidel.

2. *Never Love a Stranger* (Allied Artists) 1958. Director: Robert Stevens. Producer: Harold Robbins. Screenplay: Harold Robbins, Richard Day, based on a novel by Robbins. With John Drew Barrymore, Lita Milan, Robert Bray, Steve McQueen, Salem Ludwig.

3. *The Blob* (Paramount) 1958. Director: Irvin S. Yeaworth Jr. Producer: Jack H. Harris. Screenplay: Theodore Simonson, Kate Phillips. With Steve McQueen, Aneta Corsaut, Earl Rowe, Olin Howlin, Steven Chase, John Benson.

4. *The St. Louis Bank Robbery* (United Artists) 1958. Director: Charles Guggenheim and John Stix. Producer: Charles Guggenheim. Screenplay: Richard T. Heffron. With Steve McQueen, David Clarke, Crahan Denton, Molly McCarthy, James Dukas.

5. *Never So Few* (MGM) 1959. Director: John Sturges. Producer: Edmund Grainger. Screenplay by Millard Kaufman, based on a novel by Tom T. Chamales. With Frank Sinatra, Gina Lollobrigida, Peter Lawford, Steve McQueen, Richard Johnson, Paul Henreid, Brian Donlevy, Dean Jones, Charles Bronson.

6. *The Magnificent Seven* (United Artists) 1960. Director: John Sturges. Producer: Walter Mirisch. Screenplay: William Roberts, based on Akira Kurosawa's 1954 Japanese classic *The Seven Samurai*. With

Yul Brynner, Horst Buchholz, Steve McQueen, Eli Wallach, James Coburn, Charles Bronson, Robert Vaughn, Brad Dexter.

7. *The Honeymoon Machine* (MGM) 1961. Director: Richard Thorpe. Producer: Lawrence Weingarten. Screenplay: George Wells, based on the play *The Golden Fleecing*, by Lorenzo Semple. With Steve McQueen, Brigid Bazlen, Jim Hutton, Paula Prentiss, Dean Jagger, Jack Weston.

8. *Hell Is for Heroes* (Paramount) 1962. Director: Don Siegel. Producer: Henry Blanke. Screenplay: Robert Pirosh, Richard Carr, from an original story by Pirosh. With Steve McQueen, Bobby Darin, Fess Parker, Nick Adams, Bob Newhart, Harry Guardino, James Coburn, Mike Kellin.

9. *The War Lover* (Columbia) 1962. Director: Philip Leacock. Producer: Arthur Hornblow Jr. Screenplay: Howard Koch, based on a novel by John Hersey. With Steve McQueen, Robert Wagner, Shirley Anne Field, Gary Cockrell.

10. *The Great Escape* (United Artists) 1963. Director: John Sturges. Producer: John Sturges. Screenplay: James Clavell and W. R. Burnett, based on a book by Paul Brickhill. With Steve McQueen, James Garner, Richard Attenborough, James Donald, Charles Bronson, Donald Pleasence, James Coburn, John Leyton, David McCallum, Nigel Stock, William Russell.

11. *Soldier in the Rain* (Allied Artists) 1963. Director: Ralph Nelson. Producer: Martin Jurow. Screenplay: Maurice Richlin, Blake Edwards, from the novel by William Goldman. With Jackie Gleason, Steve McQueen, Tuesday Weld, Tony Bill, Tom Poston, Ed Nelson, Lew Gallo, Paul Hartman, Adam West.

12. *Love with the Proper Stranger* (Paramount) 1963. Director: Robert Mulligan. Producer: Alan J. Pakula. Screenplay: Arnold Schulman. With Natalie Wood, Steve McQueen, Edie Adams, Herschel Bernardi, Tom Bosley, Harvey Lembeck, Penny Santon, Arlene Golonka, Richard Dysart, Vic Tayback.

13. *Baby the Rain Must Fall* (Paramount) 1965. Director: Robert Mulligan. Producer: Alan J. Pakula. Screenplay: Horton Foote, based on his play *The Traveling Lady*. With Lee Remick, Steve McQueen, Don Murray, Paul Fix, Josephine Hutchinson, Ruth White.

14. *The Cincinnati Kid* (MGM) 1965. Director: Norman Jewison. Producer: Martin Ransohoff. Screenplay: Ring Lardner Jr., Terry Southern, based on the novel by Richard Jessup. With Steve McQueen, Edward G. Robinson, Ann-Margret, Karl Malden, Tuesday Weld, Joan Blondell, Rip Torn, Jack Weston, Cab Calloway, Jeff Corey, Theo Marcuse.

15. *Nevada Smith* (Paramount) 1966. Director: Henry Hathaway. Producer: Henry Hathaway. Screenplay: John Michael Hayes, based on a character in the novel *The Carpetbaggers*, by Harold Robbins. With Steve McQueen, Karl Malden, Brian Keith, Suzanne Pleshette, Arthur Kennedy, Janet Margolin, Howard Da Silva, Raf Vallone, Pat Hingle, Martin Landau, Paul Fix, Gene Evans.

16. *The Sand Pebbles* (20th Century Fox) 1966. Director: Robert Wise. Producer: Robert Wise. Screenplay: Robert Anderson, based on the novel by Richard McKenna. With Steve McQueen, Richard Attenborough, Richard Crenna, Candice Bergen, Marayat Andriane, Mako, Larry Gates, Charles Robinson, Simon Oakland, Gavin MacLeod.

17. *The Thomas Crown Affair* (United Artists) 1968. Director: Norman Jewison. Producer: Norman Jewison. Screenplay: Alan R. Trustman. With Steve McQueen, Faye Dunaway, Paul Burke, Jack Weston, Yaphet Kotto, Todd Martin, Sam Melville, Addison Powell.

18. *Bullitt* (Warner Bros.) 1968. Director: Peter Yates. Producer: Philip D'Antoni. Executive producer: Robert Relyea. Screenplay: Alan R. Trustman, Harry Kleiner, based on the novel *Mute Witness*, by Robert L. Pike. With Steve McQueen, Jacqueline Bisset, Robert Vaughn.

19. *The Reivers* (Cinema Center/National General) 1969. Director: Mark Rydell. Producer: Irving Ravetch. Executive producer: Robert Relyea. Screenplay: Irving Ravetch, Harriet Frank Jr., based on the novel by William Faulkner. With Steve McQueen, Sharon Farrell, Will Geer, Rupert Crosse, Mitch Vogel, Lonny Chapman, Burgess Meredith.

20. *Le Mans* (Cinema Center/National General) 1971. Director: Lee Katzin. Producer: Jack Reddish. Executive producer: Robert Relyea. Screenplay: Harry Kleiner. With Steve McQueen, Siegfried Rauch, Elga Andersen.

21. *On Any Sunday* (Cinema 5) 1971. Director: Bruce Brown. Producer:

Joe Wizan, in association with Solar Productions. Motorcycle racing documentary. McQueen appears in brief cameo as himself.

22. *Junior Bonner* (ABC-Cinerama) 1972. Director: Sam Peckinpah. Producer: Joe Wizan. Screenplay: Jeb Rosebrook. With Steve McQueen, Robert Preston, Ida Lupino, Joe Don Baker, Barbara Leigh, Mary Murphy, Ben Johnson.

23. *The Getaway* (National General) 1972. Director: Sam Peckinpah. Producer: David Foster, Mitchell Brower. Screenplay: Walter Hill, based on the novel by Jim Thompson. With Steve McQueen, Ali MacGraw, Ben Johnson, Sally Struthers, Al Lettieri, Slim Pickens.

24. *Papillon* (Allied Artists) 1973. Director: Franklin Schaffner. Producers: Robert Dorfman, Franklin Schaffner. Screenplay: Dalton Trumbo, Lorenzo Semple Jr., based on the book by Henri Charrière. With Steve McQueen, Dustin Hoffman, Victor Jory, Don Gordon, Anthony Zerbe.

25. *The Towering Inferno* (20th Century Fox and Warner Bros.) 1974. Director: John Guillermin. Producer: Irwin Allen. Screenplay: Stirling Silliphant, based on two novels—*The Tower* by Richard Martin Stern and *The Glass Inferno* by Frank M. Robinson and Thomas Scortia. With Steve McQueen, Paul Newman, William Holden, Faye Dunaway, Fred Astaire, Susan Blakely, Richard Chamberlain, Jennifer Jones, O. J. Simpson, Robert Vaughn, Robert Wagner, Susan Flannery, Don Gordon.

26. *An Enemy of the People* (Warner Bros.) 1978. Director: George Schaefer. Producer: George Schaefer. Executive producer: Steve McQueen. Screenplay by Alexander Jacobs, based on Arthur Miller's adaptation of the play by Henrik Ibsen. With Steve McQueen, Charles Durning, Bibi Andersson.

27. *Tom Horn* (Warner Bros.) 1980. Director: William Wiard. Producer: Fred Weintraub. Executive producer: Steve McQueen. Screenplay: Thomas McGuane, Bud Shrake, from *Life of Tom Horn, Government Scout and Interpreter, Written by Himself*. With Steve McQueen, Linda Evans, Richard Farnsworth, Billy Green Bush, Slim Pickens.

28. *The Hunter* (Paramount) 1980. Director: Buzz Kulik. Producer: Mort Engelberg. Screenplay: Ted Leighton, Peter Hyams, from the book by Christopher Keane, and the life of Ralph Thorson. With Steve McQueen, Eli Wallach, Kathryn Harrold, LeVar Burton, Ben Johnson.

THEATER

1. *Peg o' My Heart.* 1952. Produced by a local theater company in Fayetteville, New York.
2. *Member of the Wedding.* 1952. Rochester, New York.
3. *Time Out for Ginger.* 1952. National road company.
4. *The Fingers of Pride.* 1955. Summer stock, Ogunquit, Maine.
5. *A Hatful of Rain.* 1956. Broadway. Toured briefly, later that year, in the national road company.

TELEVISION

1. *Goodyear Playhouse,* "The Chivington Raid." NBC. Live telecast 3.27.55.
2. *U.S. Steel Hour,* "Bring Me a Dream." CBS. Live telecast 1.4.56.
3. *Studio One,* "The Defender." Live two-part telecast 2.23.57, 3.4.57.
4. *West Point,* "Ambush." CBS. Live telecast 3.8.57.
5. *Climax,* "Four Hours in White." CBS. Film. 2.6.58.
6. *Tales of Wells Fargo,* "Bill Longley." NBC. Film. 2.10.58.
7. *Trackdown,* "The Bounty Hunter." CBS. Film. 3.7.58.
8. *Wanted: Dead or Alive.* 94 episodes, three seasons. CBS. Premiere 9.6.58; final episode 3.29.61.
9. *Alfred Hitchcock Presents,* "Man from the South." CBS. Film. 1.3.60.
10. *Dick Powell's Zane Grey Theatre,* "Thunder in a Forgotten Town." NBC. Film. 3.5.63.

Various live appearances as himself on *The Perry Como Show, The Bob Hope Buick Hour, What's My Line?, The Tonight Show Starring Johnny Carson,* and *The Ed Sullivan Show.*

Sources and Notes

BOOKS

Aylesworth, Thomas G. *The Best of Warner Bros.* New York: Gallery Books, 1986.

Biskind, Peter. *Easy Riders, Raging Bulls.* New York: Simon & Schuster, 1998.

Bruccoli, Matthew, ed. *The Notebooks of F. Scott Fitzgerald.* New York: Harcourt, Brace, Jovanovich, 1978.

Douglas, Kirk. *The Ragman's Son.* New York: Simon & Schuster, 1988.

Eliot, Marc. *Reagan: The Hollywood Years.* New York: Random House, 2008.

Evans, Bob. *The Kid Stays in the Picture.* New York: Hyperion, 1994.

Finstad, Suzanne. *Natasha: The Biography of Natalie Wood.* New York: Harmony Books, 2001.

Gillett, Charlie. *The Sounds of the City.* New York: Pantheon Books, 1984.

Hadleigh, Boze. *Hollywood Babble On.* New York: Birch Lane Press, 1994.

Kelley, Kitty. *His Way: The Unauthorized Biography of Frank Sinatra.* New York: Bantam, 1986.

Levy, Shawn. *Paul Newman: A Life.* New York: Harmony Books, 2009.

MacGraw, Ali. *Moving Pictures.* New York: Bantam Books, 1991.

Meisner, Sanford. *Sanford Meisner on Acting.* New York: Vintage, 1987.

Newhart, Bob. *I Shouldn't Even Be Doing This and Other Things That Strike Me as Funny.* New York: Hyperion, 2006.

Nolan, William. *McQueen.* New York: Congdon and Weed, 1984.

Porter, Darwin, and Danforth Prince. *50 Years of Queer Cinema.* United States, Blood Moon Productions, Ltd., 2010.

Ragsdale, Grady. *Steve McQueen: The Final Chapter.* Ventura, CA: Vision House, 1983.

Relyea, Robert E., and Craig Relyea. *Not So Quiet on the Set.* Bloomington, IN: iUniverse, 2008.

Sarris, Andrew. *The American Cinema.* New York: Dutton, 1968.

Siegel, Don. *A Siegel Film: An Autobiography.* London: Faber and Faber, 1993.

Spiegel, Penina. *Steve McQueen.* London: William Collins and Sons, 1986.

St. Charnez, Casey. *The Films of Steve McQueen.* Secaucus, NJ: Citadel Press, 1984.

Terrill, Marshall. *Steve McQueen: Portrait of an American Rebel.* New York: Donald L. Fine, 1993.

Thomson, David. *A Biographical Dictionary of Film.* New York: Knopf, 2000.

Toffel, Neile McQueen. *My Husband, My Friend.* Bloomington, IN: Author-House, 2007.

Van Doren, Mamie. *Playing the Field.* New York: Putnam, 1987.

Vaughn, Robert. *A Fortunate Life.* New York: Thomas Dunne Books, 2008.

Wallach, Eli. *The Good, the Bad, and Me: In My Anecdotage.* New York: Harcourt, 2008.

Weddle, David. *If They Move . . . Kill 'Em!* New York: Grove Press, 2001.

Wiley, Mason, and Damien Bona. *Inside Oscar: The Unofficial History of the Academy Awards.* New York: Ballantine Books, 1986.

Wilson, Andrew. *Harold Robbins: The Man Who Invented Sex.* New York: Bloomsbury USA, 2007.

INTRODUCTION

3 **"that rarity of rarities"** Andrew Sarris, *Village Voice*, 11.12.80.

CHAPTER 1

11 **"I left home"** McQueen, quoted in *TV Life*, 4.59.

13 **"When I'd get lazy"** McQueen, quoted in Terrill. As a general note, Terrill rarely cites direct sources, offering instead a list of publications he used for each chapter.

13 **"When I was eight"** McQueen, quoted in Nolan, p. 8.

14 **"I was a dreamer"** McQueen, quoted in *TV World*, 4.59.

14 **"black hole"** From Rob Katz's 1998 documentary *Steve McQueen, King of Cool.* The entire sentence from Andrew Sarris, "King of Cool," *American Movie Classics*, 3.98.

16 **"win back the other kids' respect"** Toffel, p. 4.

16 **"You lay your"** Terrill, p. 8.

17 **"The place had a board of governors"** McQueen, quoted in Amy Lewis, "The Defiant One," *Silver Screen*, 6.60.

17 **Pantier's kind words** Recalled by McQueen in *Silver Screen*, 6.60.

CHAPTER 2

19 **"I'm from the Actors Studio"** McQueen, quoted in *TV Life*, 4.59.

20 **"Taking orders still bugged me"** McQueen, quoted in *TV World*, 6.59.

20 **"golden" pen points** Ibid.

21 **"The whole thing"** Ibid.

24 **"I was so broke"** McQueen, quoted in Erskine Johnson, NEA syndicated services, which distributed Johnson's column "Hollywood TV Closeup," 11.13.58.

24 **"Say, why don't you"** McQueen, quoted in *TV World*, 6.59.

25 **"That's when I became a man"** Johnson.

25 **"Until he got after me"** *TV World*, 6.59.

26 **"We did scenes together"** Casey St. Charnez, p. 15.

26 **"They put me on the stage"** Ibid., p. 40.

CHAPTER 3

30 **"I'm not a prodigy"** McQueen, quoted in *TV Life*, 4.59.

30 **"If I hadn't"** McQueen, quoted in *Silver Screen*, 6.60.

30 **"I spoke five languages"** Toffel, interviewed by Marjorie Farnsworth, *New York Journal-American*, 5.8.57.

31 **"I made the chorus"** Toffel, p. 26.

32 **"I was coming out of"** Toffel, during an interview at Lincoln Center following a screening of *Love with the Proper Stranger*, 3.22.09.

32 **Background on Midtown theatrical restaurants** "Old and Sold," *Antiques*, 1959.

33 **"As I sat down"** Toffel, speaking at Lincoln Center, following a screening of *Love with the Proper Stranger*, 3.22.09.

34 **Steve's salary of $20 a day for** *Somebody Up There Likes Me* Hollywood Reporter, 7.20.81.

34 **Steve's height** The subject of much early speculation, but after *TV Guide* (5.30.59) listed it as 5′11″, 178 lbs, it apparently settled into 5′8″ in most subsequent reports and profiles.

35 **"Sorry, buddy, but all's fair"** Toffel, pp. 34–35.

35 **"I wanted to marry Neile"** McQueen, quoted by Sidney Skolsky, "Hollywood Is My Beat," syndicated, 1.28.60.

36 **"Poor kid"** Ibid.

37 **McQueen trip to Cuba** Some of the background is from Toffel, pp. 44–47.

39 **"The phone bills"** Toffel, interviewed by Fred Dickenson, *Sunday Mirror Magazine*, 4.21.57.

40 **"She was doing very well"** Elkins, interview with author (henceforth AI). The middle part of the quote is from femalefirst.co.uk, 11.06.05.

41 **"One thing"** Sid Shalit, New York *Daily News*, 2.27.57.

41 **"had ever read"** Pat Knopf, quoted in Wikipedia.

43 **"That turkey"** McQueen, quoted in Terrill, p. 35. Original source attribution unclear.

43 **Steve and Lita "signaled"** Christopher Sandford, quoted in Wilson, p. 92.

43 **"Steve told me"** Toffel, pp. 67–68.

CHAPTER 4

45 **"I like John Wayne"** McQueen, quoted in *TV Life*, 4.59.

50 **Dick Powell telegram** The Herrick Academy of Motion Picture Arts and Sciences Library, Special Collections.

50 **"I'd done one or two"** McQueen, quoted in *TV Guide*, 5.30.59.

51 **Steve's gun considered a lethal weapon by LAPD** *TV Guide*, 5.30.59.

52 **"Steve McQueen, as Josh Randall"** From a full-page ad placed by the network in *TV and Movie Western*, 2.59.

52 **"Stanislavski . . . to the TV West"** Johnson, 11.13.58.

52 **"Brando on Horseback"** The title of an article ostensibly written by McQueen, "as told to Electra Yourke," *TV Picture Life*, 4.59.

52 **"When you're hot"** McQueen, quoted in Amy Lewis's magazine profile of him called "The Defiant One," *Silver Screen*, 6.60.

53 **Reviews for *Wanted: Dead or Alive*** From Toffel, but beyond their being quoted, no further source information is supplied, although they are all likely from the named publications that appeared shortly after the show went on the air, between September and November 1958.

53 **"a violent"** CBS/Four Star press release. Herrick, Special Collections.

54 **"He looked at me"** David Foster, AI.

55 **Clara Bow blurb** Various newspapers. The quip was syndicated nationally.

55 **McQueen driving incident** *Los Angeles Times*, 11.21.58.

55 **"one of the reasons I'm in successville"** The uses of hipster language are from plants by David Foster in two articles in which Steve is "quoted." They are "Hollywood TV Closeup," by Erskine Johnson, NEA services, 11.13.58, and "Confessions of an Ex-Beatnik," by John Quinlan, *TV Screen Life*, 6.57.

56 **"Of course!"** McQueen, quoted in *TV World*, 6.59.

56 **"I get up at 5:30"** McQueen, quoted by Sidney Skolsky, "Hollywood Is My Beat," syndicated, 1.28.60.

56 **"We can look down"** and **"And we can see coyotes"** McQueen and Toffel, quoted in "A Rebel Is Anchored," Louella Parsons, syndicated, 7.3.60.

57 **"ecstatic"** and **"barefoot and pregnant"** Toffel, p. 78.

57 **"one in the oven"** Toffel, p. 85.

CHAPTER 5

61 **"One of the main reasons"** McQueen, quoted in *TV World*, 6.59.

61 **"I may blow"** McQueen, quoted by Hal Humphrey, *Los Angeles Mirror-News*, 6.24.59.

61 **"I remember"** Ibid.

65 **"That was it for Sammy"** Peter Lawford, quoted in Kelley, p. 279.

65 **"Earlier that year"** Relyea, pp. 109–10.

66 **"honoring Miss Gina Lollobrigida"** Invitation for the reception. Herrick, Special Collections.

66 **"I kind of dig him"** McQueen, *Los Angeles Times*, 5.12.59.

67 **Hedda Hopper article** Original draft from the Academy Library Hedda Hopper collection. The article, "Steve McQueen: Storm Center," appeared nationally. It was, typically, a Sunday supplement front cover story.

68 **"Everybody was watching"** McQueen, quoted in "Steve McQueen: He Did It His Way," *Hollywood Then and Now*, October 1981.

68 **"Frank Sinatra kept saying"** McQueen, quoted in "Steve Always Wants to Win," by Erskine Johnson, *Los Angeles Mirror-News*, 9.29.59.

69 **"It's all yours, kid!"** Toffel, p. 87.

73 **"It was the beginning of the end"** Carpenter, accompanying DVD booklet *The Making of The Magnificent Seven*, p. 107.

75 **"a little accident"** Hilly Elkins, AI.

75 **"He promptly"** Elkins, quoted in femalefirst.co.uk, 11.06.05, p. 110.

76 **"Not only"** Ibid., p. 111.

77 **"mystified"** Eli Wallach, quoted in ibid.

77 **"In all the cowboy pictures"** Wallach, p. 201.

78 **"Eli became as attached"** Relyea, pp. 136–37.

78 **"After that"** Vaughn, quoted in Louis Heaton's *Guns for Hire: The Making of the Magnificent Seven*, MGM, 2001.

78 **"The film had to be cast"** James Coburn, quoted in ibid.

80 **"The film was important"** Elkins, AI.

80 **"We only had three"** Relyea, p. 139.

80 **"In one scene"** Vaughn, p. 221.

81 **"Brynner turned around"** Brad Dexter, quoted in Vaughn, p. 221.

81 **"No, we didn't get along"** McQueen, quoted in *Sunday Express* (London), 9.17.61, article by Roderick Mann.

81 **"When you work"** McQueen, quoted by Erskine Johnson in his syndicated column, *Los Angeles Mirror-News*, 4.26.61.

82 **"one of the finest"** Brad Dexter, quoted in Vaughn, p. 185.

82 **"I said to Steve"** Vaughn, p. 164.

83 **"I was in Spain"** Elmer Bernstein, interviewed by Roger Friedman on the red carpet at the 2003 Oscars.

84 **"from name to face to star"** Andrew Sarris, "King of Cool," *American Classics*, 3.98.

85 **"He races to get the garbage out"** Steve Ferry, quoted in *Look*, 10.11.60.

86 **"I'm going to be"** McQueen, quoted in Spiegel, p. 106. No further attribution or source given by Spiegel.

87 **"Hi, let's be friends"** Toffel, pp. 98–99.

88 **"I knew I wouldn't be"** Ibid.

CHAPTER 6

89 **"I've been through"** McQueen, quoted in *Los Angeles Herald-Examiner* by Harold Heffernan, 9.22.60.

89 **"Now I don't have to lean"** McQueen, quoted by Erskine Johnson in his syndicated column, *Los Angeles Mirror-News*, 4.26.61.

91 **"I take full credit"** Elkins, quoted in Terrill, p. 69.

91 **"go to the high desert"** and **"put the stuff"** Toffel, pp. 101–2.

93 **"What the hell's the matter with you?"** This and the dialogue that follows are from Siegel, pp. 229–30.

93 **The description and dialogue of the meeting** Siegel, pp. 230–31.

98 **"For one scene"** Siegel, p. 234.

100 **"Siegel's most successful films"** Sarris, p. 137.

100 **Kubrick telegram** On file at the Herrick Academy Library.

101 *"Hell Is for Heroes"* Elkins, AI.

102 **"Steve and his wife"** Moss, quoted in Terrill, pp. 74–75.

103 **"getting gassed and bounding"** and **"Balderdash . . . Somebody hollered fire"** are from Charles Denton's column, "TV," which appeared in the *Los Angeles Examiner*, 10.20.61.

103 **"The servants make me nervous"** McQueen, writing to Hedda Hopper, 10.17.61.

108 **"England's fun"** McQueen, letter to Hedda Hopper, 12.5.61.

108 **Skolsky Tintype** 12.23.61 The McQueen Tintype was revised and rerun several times after its initial appearance in 1959.

109 **"This production of John Hersey's novel"** *Variety*, 1.1.62 (based on the British release, which preceded by several months the American release).

109 *"The War Lover* **goes to remarkable trouble"** Richard Coe, *Washington Post*, date unknown.

110 **"It was a very tough decision"** McQueen, quoted in Nolan, p. 47.

112 **"It really twisted me up"** McQueen, quoted in Hedda Hopper, "Hedda Hopper's Hollywood," 6.10.62.

113 **"Everything went wrong"** McQueen, quoted by Bob Thomas, "Hands of a Mechanic," syndicated, 5.62.

114 **"I tried to make it"** Sturges, *The Great Escape* movie featurette, 12.5.07.

114 **"If I wanted"** Ibid.

114 **"After *The Magnificent Seven*"** Ibid.

116 **"He thought [adding Americans] would make"** Robert Relyea, *The Great Escape* movie featurette.

117 **"Besides the wire"** Ibid.

119 **"Steve's performance was perfect"** James Coburn, *The Great Escape* movie featurette.

120 **"We got to Germany"** Neile Adams, "Return to the Great Escape"

featurette, 1993. Directed by Steve Rubin, produced by Deborah Gordon, for Showtime Productions.

120 **"When Sturges . . . foolishly showed a rough-cut"** Donald Pleasence, "Return to the Great Escape."

120 **"Coburn and Steve"** James Garner, "Return to the Great Escape."

121 **"Steve was a little out-of-hand"** James Garner on *The Charlie Rose Show*, 6.25.02.

121 **Story of McQueen's driving to work every day** Hollywood Stories.com.

121 **"When you find somebody"** Sturges, quoted in Terrill, p. 91.

121 **"We're going to blend"** Sturges, quoted in Relyea, p. 184.

CHAPTER 7

124 **"The minute a picture is over"** McQueen, quoted in James Gregory, "Steve McQueen, Superstud," *Movie Digest*, 3.72.

124 **"fanatically"** Toffel, p. 109.

131 **Steve promises not to race for the duration of the film** Louella O. Parsons, "Escape from Delinquency," *Los Angeles Examiner*, 6.23.63.

132 **"She was able to use"** Tom Bosley, quoted in Finstad, p. 246.

132 **"she was vulnerable"** Edie Adams, quoted in Finstad, p. 246.

132 **"Making *Love with the Proper Stranger*"** Natalie Wood, interviewed by Bruce Bahrenburg for the *Newark Sunday News*, 6.15.69.

CHAPTER 8

141 **"It's very expensive to act"** McQueen, quoted in Rick Kraus, *Bruin Review*, 7.30.80.

142 **"Steve McQueen's splendid amalgam"** *Newsweek*, date unknown.

144 **"we devoted ourselves"** Toffel, p. 115.

144 **Background on Johnny Rivers and the Whiskey a Go-Go** Gillett, "The Rise of Rock and Roll," pp. 340–41.

145 **"a genius with hair"** Douglas, *The Ragman's Son*, p. 288.

147 **The details of the modification of Steve McQueen's motorcycle** *Cycle World*, "In McQueen's Service," 6.64. Article is unsigned.

148 **"He was good in that department"** Bruce Lee, from a rare TV

interview he gave on *The Pierre Berton Show*, originally broadcast in December 1971, now available on YouTube.

149 **pharmaceutical Sandoz** and **"I could feel the crinkle"** Van Doren, p. 122.

152 **"Next thing I know"** Dave Resnick, quoted in Spiegel, pp. 209–10. No attribution given by Spiegel.

152 **"we bought a lot of coke"** Ibid.

155 **Anthony Holden estimation of odds** Anthony Holden, *Big Deal: A Year as a Professional Poker Player* (New York: Viking, 1990).

157 **"produced heart-wrenching sobs"** Toffel, pp. 125–26.

157 **"[Steve] cried"** and **"He was a lost soul"** David Foster, IA.

CHAPTER 9

158 **"I've done pretty well"** McQueen, interview with Bob Thomas, syndicated, Associated Press, 7.25.66.

165 **"Look at the parallels"** From Tom Rothman's intro/outro bumpers for the uncut television screening of *The Sand Pebbles* on Fox Movie Channel. Continual airings.

168 **"At the time"** Ibid.

169 **"I've got apples"** McQueen, quoted by Abe Greenberg in his syndicated Hollywood column, "Steve McQueen Captures Taipei," *Citizen-News*, 4.22.66.

170 **"Taiwan was the pits"** Toffel, p. 128.

170 **"[t]he most difficult picture I ever made"** Robert Wise, quoted in St. Charnez, p. 124. No further attribution given.

171 **"For Chrissakes"** Wise, quoted in Spiegel, p. 243. No attribution.

172 **"Steve went wild"** Rupert Allan, quoted in Spiegel, p, 244. No attribution.

172 **"That gave Steve"** Spiegel, p. 206. The speaker is not identified and there is no further attribution.

173 *Day of the Champion* Relyea, pp. 252–54.

175 **"If Vietnam falls"** McQueen, interview with Sheilah Graham, *Citizen-News* (and syndicated), 5.25.66.

176 **"I don't mind telling you"** From an unpublished interview, date unknown.

177 **Details of McQueen's deal with Warner** Several sources, includ-

ing *Variety*, 9.27.66, and *Film Daily*, 9.27.66, which offer the best and most accurate details.

178 **"looking toward"** McQueen, quoted in "Just for Variety," Army Archerd, *Variety*, 10.27.66.

CHAPTER 10

180 **"Ten years from now?"** McQueen, quoted in *Los Angeles Herald-Examiner* by Toni Kosover for an interview to promote the upcoming release of *The Thomas Crown Affair*.

180 **modest bash** and **"Come as you are. Very casual"** Moe Greenberg, "The Voice of Hollywood," 12.12.66.

180 **"Set decorators"** Toffel, p. 153.

181 **Additional information about the party and descriptions of the outfits of Eva Gabor, Polly Bergen, and Elke Sommer** is from Joe Greenberg's column, "The Voice of Hollywood," *Citizen-News* and syndicated, 12.12.66.

181 **"If the bomb"** Quoted in both Toffel, p. 153, and Terrill, p. 140.

186 **Lyndon Johnson compared to John Wayne** Toffel, p. 160.

187 **"Right here"** Ibid.

188 **"If he'd won"** Wiley and Bona, p. 400.

189 **"Perhaps if I had announced"** McQueen, quoted by Sidney Skolsky in his column "Getting Intimate with—Steve McQueen," syndicated the first week of 4.73.

189 **"Lawyers sharpen up with law books"** McQueen, quoted in the *Citizen-News*, no interviewer identified, "Steve McQueen Believes in Keeping Physically Fit," 11.14.67.

189 **"high as kites"** Toffel, p. 164.

189 **"He can sit"** Neile McQueen, interviewed by Peer J. Oppenheimer, *Family Weekly*, 2.5.67, p. 282.

190 **Additional background information on *Butch Cassidy and the Sundance Kid*** David Foster, AI.

191 **"The original title"** Richard Zanuck, *Fox Legacy*, broadcast 5.20.11.

191 **"Paul was Steve's"** Tom Rothman, *Fox Legacy*, broadcast 5.20.11.

195 **"Faye Dunaway gave Steve a tough time"** Jewison, quoted in Terrill, p. 152. Attribution is not clear.

195 **The FBI memo** This document and others were found as part of the author's access to Steve McQueen's FBI file, obtained under the Freedom of Information Act.

197 **Steve and Jewison, the beach scene** A good, if unattributed, account of this appears in Spiegel, pp. 250–53.

199 **"I received his approval"** Relyea, p. 248.

199 **"With all due respect"** Relyea, p. 249.

200 **"Jack Warner, the guy"** Relyea, p. 248.

201 **"After finishing our location work"** Relyea, pp. 255–56.

203 **"a mélange"** Vaughn, p. 152.

203 **"I figured I would let"** Vaughn, p. 153.

206 **"The chase"** and **"Our goal"** Relyea, pp. 252–53.

207 **"Boy, I love this business!"** McQueen, quoted by Army Archerd, *Variety*, 4.23.68. Archerd later asked about the scene and inquired about using a dummy. He recorded McQueen's answer in his column.

209 **"this is gonna be a tough location, baby"** Toffel, pp. 167, 312.

209 **"Happy birthday, asshole!"** Toffel, p. 174.

CHAPTER 11

210 **"I feel very"** McQueen, quoted by Liz Smith, *Cosmopolitan*, 12.72.

211 **"gave me hope"** Toffel, p. 181.

212 **"I can't honestly say"** Jewison, quoted in Spiegel, p. 256. No further attribution given.

212 **"an upscale"** Source wishes to remain anonymous.

215 **"Steve didn't react"** Relyea, pp. 260–61.

215 **"This is career suicide"** McQueen, quoted by Relyea, p. 261.

217 **"He wanted to feel"** Mark Rydell, Bridget Byrne, "Golden Memories," *W*, 12.18–25.81.

CHAPTER 12

227 **"Marriage is really difficult,"** Nolan, pp. 141–42.

230 **Details of Solar's public sale** Most of the details are from *Variety*, "McQueen's Solar Prods. Going Public at $9 a Share," 3.30.70.

232 **Additional information on the Sebring race** Articles that appeared in *Los Angeles Herald-Examiner*, 3.22.70 and 3.31.70, discussing various aspects of the races.

233 **"The foot hurt"** McQueen, quoted in the *Los Angeles Herald-Examiner*, 3.23.70.

236 **"can't breathe"** and **"half my life is over"** Toffel, p. 208.

237 **"Look, ah"** Toffel, p. 219.

242 **"Why did you do it"** Toffel, p. 273.

245 **"Sam Peckinpah, boy . . . He and I"** McQueen, quoted by Joyce Haber in her syndicated column, *Los Angeles Times*, 6.29.71.

CHAPTER 13

246 **"Look, I'm an actor"** McQueen, quoted by Robert F. Jones, "On the Lam," *Sports Illustrated*, 8.23.71.

246 **"Brando's movie"** Ibid.

248 **"The role is a natural one"** and **"He's bad"** Both from Joyce Haber's syndicated column in the *Los Angeles Times*, 8.19.71.

252 **"Just before the actual filming"** MacGraw, pp. 15,16.

252 **"I had a great sex life"** Evans quoted in Biskind, p. 159.

253 **"Evans evinced a peculiar mixture"** Biskind, p. 146.

253 **"Peter Bogdanovich and I"** Walter Hill, quoted in Damien Love, "Blown Away: The Making of *The Getaway*," *Uncut*, 11.12.05.

254 **"get it"** and **"scrubbed away"** Peckinpah, quoted in Weddle, p. 434.

255 **"It was one"** MacGraw, pp. 87–88, 92.

256 **There was a ceiling** David Foster, AI.

256 **"If you ask me"** McQueen, quoted by Joyce Haber in her syndicated column, *Los Angeles Times*, 9.14.71.

257 **"I got a million dollars"** Quoted in Spiegel, p. 333. No further attribution given.

257 **"I was obsessed"** MacGraw, p. 95.

258 **"One night"** MacGraw, p. 96.

259 **"Steve and Sam"** Hill, quoted in Damien Love, "The Making of *The Getaway*," *Uncut DVD*, 11.12.05.

259 **"McQueen's playing it safe"** Peckinpah, quoted in Damien Love, "The Making of *The Getaway*," *Uncut DVD*, 11.12.05.

259 **"He had to know"** Foster, IA.

260 **"Evans pushed them together"** Frank Yablans, quoted in Biskind, p. 160.

260 **"My wife was fucking another guy"** Evans, quoted in Biskind, p. 162.

261 **"Fuck you, Sam"** Evans, quoted in Damien Love, "The Making of *The Getaway*," *Uncut DVD*, 11.12.05.

261 **"McQueen is fucking me"** Evans, from *The Kid Stays in the Picture*, audio recording, New Millennium Audio, 2001.

262 **"Ali was a saint"** Sue Mengers, quoted in Sheila Weller, "Once in Love with Ali," *Vanity Fair*, 3.20.10.

262 **"She was the biggest"** Weller, quoted by Frank Swertlow, *Los Angeles Herald-Examiner*, 1.3.84.

262 **"It was very, very passionate"** MacGraw, pp. 32–33. The quote has been slightly condensed without changing its meaning.

CHAPTER 14

263 **"Me a legend?"** McQueen, quoted by Liz Smith, "Steve McQueen, An Embarrassment of Paradoxes," *Cosmopolitan*, 12.72.

264 **"Give it to me straight"** McQueen quoted in Spiegel, p. 346. Confirmed by David Foster, AI.

264 **Polyp operation** There are literally dozens of sources for this story; among the most detailed are Spiegel, p. 346, and Toffel, pp. 283–84.

265 **"I made a film"** Peckinpah, quoted in Weddle, p. 434.

265 **"There's a rare quality"** McQueen, interviewed by Grover Lewis, *Rolling Stone*, 10.12.72.

265 **"If you really want to learn"** Peckinpah, interviewed by Grover Lewis, *Rolling Stone*, 10.12.72.

266 **"I may be doing the film"** McQueen, interviewed by Liz Smith, *Cosmopolitan*, 12.72.

269 **Additional background regarding their life in Trancas** Spiegel, p. 361.

270 **"[Ali] works only with *me*"** William Nolan, a biographer of Steve McQueen, quoted by Frank Swertlow, *Los Angeles Herald-Examiner*, 1.3.84.

270 **Steve . . . threw the mailbox . . . into the Pacific** *Los Angeles Times*, 2.10.76.

271 **"I tried to raise him"** McQueen, quoted by Robert F. Jones, "On the Lam," *Sports Illustrated*, 8.23.71.

271 **"He never wanted Ali to work"** David Foster, AI.

271 **"They lived a simple life"** Foster, quoted in Sheila Weller, "Once in Love with Ali," *Vanity Fair*, 3.20.10.

272 **"we had a terrific fight"** MacGraw, pp. 104–5.

272 **"very cowboy-romantic,"** Ali quoting Steve, "Love Lives," *Marie Claire*, 7.77.

272 **"Steve and Chad"** Ali, quoted in Sheila Weller, "Once in Love with Ali," *Vanity Fair*, 3.20.10.

273 **"blocks and blocks"** MacGraw, p. 111.

273 **"In spite of the fact"** MacGraw, p. 112.

279 **"It didn't make"** Paul Newman, quoted in *Variety*, "Bit Player of 1956 Now Co-Equal with Paul Newman," 3.20.74.

CHAPTER 15

285 **"Ali MacGraw is a good wife"** McQueen, quoted in Hadleigh, p. 126.

285 **"much-needed office"** McQueen, quoted in the *Los Angeles Times*, 9.14.76.

285 **top ten most popular movie stars** Poll conducted by Quigley Publications, reported by the *Los Angeles Times*, 12.8.75.

286 **"I never even knew"** MacGraw, p. 112–13.

288 **"The early warning"** MacGraw, p. 106.

288 **Steve wanted dinner at six** *Los Angeles Herald-Examiner*, 11.9.77.

288 **"a pathetic attempt to be civilized"** Ali, quoted in "Love Lives," *Marie Claire*, 7.77.

288 **"somewhat stoned every day"** Ibid.

288 **"Baby . . . you have a great ass"** Ali, quoting Steve, "Love Lives," *Marie Claire*, 7.77.

289 **"I did the sullen holdback"** Ali, quoted in Sheila Weller, "Once in Love with Ali," 3.20.10.

289 **"He resisted"** Ibid.

290 **"he was sitting"** MacGraw, p. 113.

290 **Details of Steve's conversation with Billy Friedkin** Biskind, pp. 308–9.

291 **Details of Terry's eighteenth-birthday party** *Variety*, 6.9.77.

291 **"a study in"** MacGraw, p. 115.

291 **"Steve McQueen and Ali MacGraw"** Liz Smith's syndicated column, *Los Angeles Herald-Examiner*, 11.4.77.

292 **"I had no idea"** Barbara Minty, quoted by Ian Woodward, *Hello!* (London), 6.12.07.

292 **"I called Steve"** MacGraw, p. 118.

293 **Some of the background information on Steve's rejection of film offers** Several sources, including *New York*, 2.9.76.

294 **"I could go anywhere"** McQueen, quoted in the *Los Angeles Times*, reflecting on his overweight, bearded period, 3.9.78.

295 **Streisand received $6 million for** *A Star Is Born* *Hollywood Reporter,* 12.17.76.

296 **"At this stage"** McQueen, quoted in *Us,* 10.3.78.

296 **Steve was crushed** The actor who expressed this opinion, one of the stars of *An Enemy of the People,* did not want to be directly quoted.

297 **"If they put a freeze"** MacGraw, quoted in *Ladies' Home Journal,* and Steve's reaction, *Newsweek,* 11.21.77.

297 **Steve considering co-starring in** *The Betsy Los Angeles Herald-Examiner,* 12.29.76.

299 **"One large payment"** Marvin Josephson, quoted in *Variety,* 8.8.79.

299 **Details of the lawsuit** *Variety,* 12.16.76.

300 **Sydney Pollack's call to McQueen** *Los Angeles Herald-Examiner,* 5.20.77.

301 **Descriptions of Santa Paula and Steve's attraction to it** Ragsdale, pp. 14–15; Spiegel, p. 394.

301 **"Red McQueen"** Andrew Sarris, "King of Cool," *American Movie Classics,* 3.98.

302 **"He got up"** Barbara Minty, quoted in Ragsdale, p. 26.

302 **"one of those ghastly"** MacGraw, p. 121.

305 **Steve doing his own stunts and instructions to makeup man** Army Archerd, *Variety,* 10.8.79.

CHAPTER 16

307 **"I say to all my fans"** McQueen's radio broadcast on *Televisa,* 10.9.80.

308 **"He was the hit of the ward"** Unidentified staffer, quoted by the *Los Angeles Herald-Examiner,* 10.3.80.

308 **"It was barely"** Barbara Minty, quoted by Ian Woodward, *Hello!* (London), 6.12.07.

308 **Some of the details of the wedding** Ragsdale, p. 67.

310 **McQueen appearance and comments at the preview for** *Tom Horn* Yani Begakis, "Steve McQueen: Today's Superstar," Hollywood GreekReporter.com, 6.80.

310 **Details about the demise of First Artists** Pamela G. Hollie, *New York Times,* 12.23.79.

312 **"McQueen spent several days"** *Los Angeles Herald-Examiner,* 8.6.80.

312 **Denial cancer is terminal** Warren Cowan, in a statement he gave to the *Los Angeles Herald-Examiner,* 10.02.80.

313 **the American Cancer Society's list of unproven methods of cancer management** Ibid.

313 **"If doctors in Mexico tell"** Dr. David Plotkin, *Los Angeles Times,* 10.14.80.

313 **"The reason I denied"** McQueen, quoted in Richard West and Paul Jacobs, "Steve McQueen Has Rare Form of Lung Cancer," *Los Angeles Times,* 10.3.80.

314 **"Mr. McQueen"** Dr. Rodrigo Rodriguez, quoted in *People,* 10.20.80.

314 **"looked more pregnant"** Dr. Cesar Santos Vargas, quoted in the *Los Angeles Times,* 11.08.80.

315 **"Steve took my hand"** Ibid.

316 **a hundred cars, two hundred motorcycles, and five planes** Sean Macaulay, "The Lost Action Hero," *Times* (London), 3.24.2005.

316 **"Steve liked to"** Several sources, including MacGraw, p. 92.

Author's Note and Acknowledgments

THE YEAR Steve McQueen died, 1980, was also the year Alfred Hitchcock slipped the surly bonds. Although they never made a movie together, their deaths are nonetheless linked by the high placement of these two iconic figures of Hollywood in my revisionist auteurist pantheon. Classically, auteurism reevaluates the films and directors of the golden era of film, the studio-dominated years from the earliest days of filmmaking through the mid-1960s, to identify talented directors and in some cases restore their devalued reputations for making films that "transcend their technical problems with a personal vision of the world."[1]

In the post–World War II era, when the centralized studio factory system began to come apart, independent producers, screenwriters, cinematographers, and even actors were also legitimate auteurists, rather than mere hired hands. Marlon Brando remains the greatest of the actor auteurists on the basis of his collective body of work because his personality, or personal vision, not just dominated but defined the style of most of the films he appeared in. Elia Kazan's 1954 *On the Waterfront* is now widely recognized as a seminal film in the great director's body of working-class realism. But it should be equally acknowledged

---

[1] Andrew Sarris, *The American Cinema: Directors and Directions* 1929–1968, rev. ed. (New York: Da Capo, 1996).

as Marlon Brando's greatest performance, a virtuoso display of acting that marked him in some circles as the greatest film actor of his time. Today, without compromising auteurist values, we think of *On the Waterfront* as Marlon Brando's movie as much as, if not more than, Kazan's.

Steve McQueen is one of those actors who, along with Eastwood and Newman, became a seminal force in the wake of the post-war Brando cinematic tsunami, and he remained so from the early 1960s through the mid-1970s. Their individual rising stars coincided with the general film industry shift from studio-originated creativity to the big business of marketing, finance, and distribution. Steve's career, although cut tragically short, nonetheless left enough of a legacy to allow for several of his films to be auteuristically redefined as "a Steve McQueen" movie. In that sense, *Bullitt*, one may effectively argue, is really more Steve McQueen's film than director Peter Yates's.

Steve and the others were essentially transitional figures just as auteurism was entering the American mainstream consciousness. Andrew Sarris's essential revisionism of American films has guided this biographer to a deeper insight not only into the movies Steve McQueen made but into the nature of his individual creative input.

Because of the incessantly personal nature of the films he chose, the characters he played, and the era in which he made films, I trust this revisionist biography of Steve McQueen reveals how this artist lived through his work as much as his work lived through him.

As must always be the case, many people helped with this book. Those who granted interviews or pointed me in the right direction are noted in the "Sources and Notes" section. Here I especially want to thank David Foster for his wonderful generosity of time and his belief in the process, even when those closest to Steve asked him and many others not to talk to me (most of those I approached, in the end, granted some degree of audience).

I also wish to thank the late Hilly Elkins for his cooperation and earnest recollections.

I want to highlight Robert E. Relyea's book *Not So Quiet on the Set*, one of the more perceptive Hollywood memoirs.

I am indebted to the Margaret Herrick Library of the Academy of Motion Picture Arts and Sciences, Beverly Hills, California. Their Special Collections is one of the most formidable sources of film history available. Thanks to Neile McQueen Toffel for generously placing her dozens of scrapbooks in the Special Collections, where I was able to view them and glean an incredibl amount of information. Special thanks to Barbara Hall and Jen Romero for their invaluable research assistance at the library.

I thank the authors of earlier biographies of Steve McQu many of which had something of value that helped guide a place I wanted to get to. I must confess, some were bette others, some to my taste not very good at all, and some wo none were definitive. But I understand and appreciate th raphy is a cumulative effort that depends upon those v before and paves the way for those still to come. If r phy differs from the others, I think it is mostly becaus previously ventured into the foreground of Steve M did not have enough knowledge or experience of l the backdrop against which it needs to be placed. B am talking about a place beyond physical borders ambiguous industry of dreams. I have spent a life living in, working in, and trying to understa geographic realm of America's dream factory b culture in which it thrives.

I also wish to thank the New York Pub York Public Library for the Performing Institute, the Cinemathèque in Paris, anc *Angeles Times*.

I thank Mary Steifvater for her great research assistance. She deserves special recognition.

I thank Beatrice Winner for her tireless fact-checking.

At Crown Archetype, I thank Tina Constable, Julia Pastore, Annie Chagnot, and the entire marketing, publicity, production, and publishing team.

Thank you to Shaye Areheart for all her wonderful support through the years.

Thanks to my agent, Alan Nevins at Endeavor. And to you, faithful readers, I am forever grateful and assure you we will meet again soon, a little further up the road.

Index

About the Author

MARC ELIOT is the *New York Times* bestselling author of more than a dozen books on popular culture, among them the highly acclaimed biographies of Clint Eastwood, Cary Grant, and Jimmy Stewart; the award-winning *Walt Disney: Hollywood's Dark Prince*; *Down 42nd Street*; what many consider the best book about the sixties, his Phil Ochs biography, *Death of a Rebel*; *Take It From Me* (with Erin Brockovich); *Down Thunder Road: The Making of Bruce Springsteen*; *To the Limit: The Untold Story of the Eagles*; and *Reagan: The Hollywood Years*. He has written on the media and pop culture for numerous publications, including *Penthouse*, *L.A. Weekly*, and *California* magazine. He divides his time among New York City; Woodstock, New York; Los Angeles; and the Far East.

www.marceliot.net